Burns and Other Poets

Burns and Other Poets

Edited by David Sergeant and Fiona Stafford

Edinburgh University Press

© in this edition Edinburgh University Press, 2012, 2013
© in the individual contributions is retained by the authors

Edinburgh University Press Ltd
22 George Square, Edinburgh EH8 9LF

First published in hardback by Edinburgh University Press 2012

www.euppublishing.com

Typeset in 10.5/12 Ehrhardt
by Servis Filmsetting Ltd, Stockport, Cheshire, and
printed and bound in Great Britain by
CPI Group (UK) Ltd, Croydon, CR0 4YY

A CIP record for this book is available from the British Library

ISBN 978 0 7486 4357 8 (hardback)
ISBN 978 0 7486 6488 7 (paperback)
ISBN 978 0 7486 4358 5 (webready PDF)
ISBN 978 0 7486 5086 6 (epub)

Contents

Acknowledgements

We would like to thank members of Somerville College and the Faculty of English at the University of Oxford for their support. This publication arises from research funded by the John Fell Oxford University Press (OUP) research fund.

Abbreviations

Unless stated otherwise, all quotations from Burns's poems are taken from *The Poems and Songs of Robert Burns*, edited by James Kinsley, 3 volumes (Oxford: Clarendon Press, 1968), and are abbreviated as follows: K poem number, volume number, page number(s), line number(s), for example, K 57, I, 87, 61–72. The poem numbers are useful for locating the poems cited in the one-volume edition of Kinsley's work published by Oxford University Press in 1969 and frequently reprinted.

The Devil's Elbow

Andrew McNeillie

I could show you where it used to be,
the left one anyway, where the road
home hairpinned in among the trees.
And winter and its wild night-weather
drowned the beat of Tammy's hooves
above the swollen Bladnoch.
What shade was there but yours,
what story but your own enacted there?
Unspoken because no need to say
when raising an elbow what was afoot
in that world still in living memory.

CHAPTER I

Introduction: Burns and the Performance of Form

David Sergeant

From the beginning Robert Burns was a poet among poets. The collection that launched his career, *Poems, Chiefly in the Scottish Dialect* – that astonishing success of 1786 – presented him as an heir to his great Scottish predecessors, Allan Ramsay and Robert Fergusson, and summoned up the image of an enabling band of local brother bards. It turned to the Irish poet, Goldsmith, and the English poets, Milton and Gray, for epigraphs, but alluded to and engaged with a wide range of poets beyond these, as the following chapters show. His poems use Scottish verse forms as well as the forms of eighteenth-century English poetry; they switch between Scots and English, sometimes in the course of a single poem. And as well as acting as a condenser for a range of literary currents – formal and otherwise – which were running through the British Isles in his lifetime, Burns's poetry itself became a powerful current, feeding into the work and thought of poets who came after, in Scotland, Ireland and England, and in every period. If the poetry of these islands can be envisaged as a network, with the poets as a series of points through which connecting lines stream, converge and part, then Burns is a central conduit.

Appropriate recognition of this, however, has occurred only fitfully. From the start Burns was discussed as much for who he was – or seemed to be or could appear to be – as he was for the poetry he'd composed. After being greeted with universal acclaim in his local Ayrshire, he transferred to Edinburgh and a more qualified reception: excitement at his appearance, a Scottish genius fresh from the plough, mingling with regret that he should have chosen to write in Scots. The move from Ayrshire seems to have triggered a corresponding self-consciousness in Burns, and many critics have traced a decline in his poetry to this period. More recently, a renewed appreciation has attached to his work as a writer, collector and adapter of songs, the task he set himself in what turned out to be the final portion of his life. He died in 1796 at the age of thirty-seven, and since then his importance as everything but a poet seems only to have increased. A socio-cultural phenomenon, cult figure and national emblem – Burns has become them all. Radical politics and Masonic rites, antiquarianism and Arminianism, sexuality and smuggling, slavery, songs and satire – all are discussed under the aegis of his name.

But fundamental to any discussion of Burns must be his poetic craft, and it is to this idea that the following chapters hold close. They emphasise the highly innovative and technically accomplished nature of Burns's verse and its remarkable place in the complicated literary history of Scotland, England and Ireland since the eighteenth century – a place that has too often been denied him by those assuming he belongs only north of the Scottish border. While appreciations of Burns's seriousness and influence as a literary artist have never been entirely absent, the combined effect of the essays in this book is to give that appreciation a new heft and three-dimensionality. Douglas Dunn starts us off with a meditation on some familiar Burnsian concerns – nationality, influence, performance – underwritten by an appreciation of 'the consummate artistry' of the verse. The negotiations and navigations entailed by Burns's artistry come into sharper focus in the essays that follow, as Rhona Brown provides a freshly nuanced reading of how Burns both inherits from his Scottish forebears, Allan Ramsay and Robert Fergusson, and adapts that inheritance to his own ends; while Gerard Carruthers provides an unexpected and fascinating account of a Burns who as much dreamt his circle of Ayrshire poets into being as found them waiting for him. Freya Johnston traces the history and meanings of 'dominion' in Burns's poetry and his creative engagement with sources ranging from the Bible to Milton, Addison to Pope, Johnson to Sterne; while Mina Gorji returns attention to a poem largely neglected by modern critics, 'To a Mountain-Daisy', and so reveals a similar allusive fluency at work, informed by the contemporary culture of sentimental reading. Burns's poetry entailed complex dialogues at every level of composition, and while Claire Lamont shows the deftness with which he could explore and amplify a particular theme, feeding ideas of power through images of house and home, Murray Pittock returns attention to Burns's linguistic choices, arguing for his use of Scots as being more complex and particular than has previously been thought. Patrick Crotty and Michael Griffin then open a furrow which will run throughout this volume: Burns's influence on, and parallels with, Irish poets, an aspect of his literary existence that has often gone underrated. Burns is revealed as an important creative figure to the entire British archipelago, and not just to the land extending either side of the Scottish-English border. Griffin explores the influence of Burns's life and work on the troubled young Ennis-born poet Thomas Dermody, while Crotty's discussion of 'Tam o' Shanter' alongside Brian Merriman's *Cúirt an Mheán Oíche* is exemplary not only for its perforation of 'the watertight partitions' which have separated these two literary cultures but also for the influx of readerly vitality which buoys them up together, allowing for fresh insights into both.

Griffin's chapter also opens up the hugely important theme of Burns's relationship to the Romantics, and the essays of Meiko O'Halloran, Brean Hammond and Stephen Gill show – contrary to some recent critical assumptions – how central was the example and idea of Burns to the

Scottish poet, James Hogg, the English poet, William Wordsworth, and the Anglo-Scot, Lord Byron. Their relationships to Burns prompt questions about the Romantic cult of personality and the poetic prodigy, the projection and denial of self in poetry and the ethical dimension of literature and critical analysis: a cluster of concerns which carries into the essays exploring Burns's creative legacy in the twentieth century. Robert Crawford touches on potential futures for Burns in Scotland through his analysis of how the poetic development of Christopher Murray Grieve (Hugh MacDiarmid) engaged with contemporary Burnsians' arguments about modern literature, while Bernard O'Donoghue recalls the importance of Burns's songs to the rural Ireland in which he grew up. Fiona Stafford then closes the volume by keeping us in Ireland, with Seamus Heaney's response to the 1996 Bicentenary of Burns, but in so doing also takes us far beyond this starting point, demonstrating how Heaney's response to Burns is exemplary for moving creatively beyond him, to other poets and other worlds, while also never leaving him behind. There is, of course, no question of this (or any other) volume providing a definitive account of Burns's poetic reach; and neither are the chapters that follow homogenous in their approach, instead choosing to come at his work via a range of methodologies. But what they hold in common is an appreciation of the poetic skill which underpins Burns's achievement, and a sense of how this feeds into and out of the creative endeavour of other poets through the centuries, across borders both local and national.

And in so doing they also take us to the present day – and not only encourage but also bolster a questioning of what the poets of today might make of Burns. One of the foremost poets writing in English, Douglas Dunn, gives us a sense of his perspective on the question at the start of this volume, while Robert Crawford, another practising poet, touches on it as well. And, of course, the two poems written specially for this book, by Andrew McNeillie and Bernard O'Donoghue, provide concrete examples of how Burns's legacy can inform contemporary poetry. But I want now to (ab)use my position as writer of this introduction, and first reacting reader to the chapters that follow, to go on to consider at greater length, and from a slightly different perspective, this question of what a contemporary poet might take from Burns. Although McNeillie's and O'Donoghue's poems are very different, both respond to a Burns that has been filtered out from the forms he used, from his acoustical arrangements – not inappropriately, given that this can be part of any act of poetic inheritance, and was a process that started almost as soon as Burns was published. But as Stafford notes Heaney noting of Burns via Brodsky, the 'real data' of poets is 'in the way they sound. A poet's biography is in his vowels and sibilants, in his metres, rhymes, metaphors'.

But what might be taken from Burns's 'sound'? Perhaps the most obvious answer, because most easily transfused into our time and tastes, is his hybridisation of registers and languages. His facility with rhyme and metre is trickier to consider, because it is inseparably bound up with stanza forms of a complexity rarely seen in current or recent poetry. In a 1997 essay Douglas Dunn, briefly surveying how Burns's typical verse forms have been used since his death, noted: 'it is difficult to see how these stanzas, or Burns's metric and resonance, can inform contemporary and future Scottish poetry'.[1] Yet if these stanza forms are such an integral part of Burns's poetic being, his 'real' biography, can they really be left behind so easily – by Scots or anyone else? Can Burns offer more to the working present of poetry than an example, a series of lessons abstracted from the formal being of his work – however deep those lessons, however salutary that example? The difference, when conceived like this, is between practical and principled instruction: the apprentice poet watching Burns in action, out on the pitch of poetry, or sitting inside the dressing room while Burns – tracksuit, towel round his shoulders – gives a rousing team talk. *Draw on a range of registers, speak high and speak low, be funny and serious, simple and subtle, go out and give 'em hell!*

To reconsider what use – if any – Burns's 'real data' might be to contemporary poetry, I want to look again at how he used the stanza form that became so closely associated with him it now bears his name: the Standard Habbie, or Burns Stanza. Like many of the verse structures he used, the Habbie foregrounds rhyme, and not simply because there are so many of them – the short tetrameter and dimeter lines also play their part. The Standard Habbie is a delicate beast, and one of the many ways to kill it is to lengthen its lines, as Liz Lochhead's deliberately kamikaze effort demonstrates:

> Arguably I am a poem wha, prescient, did presage
> Your Twentyfirst Century Global Distress Age.
> I'm a female *mouse* though, he didna give a sausage
> For ma sparkling een!
> As for Mother Nature? Whether yez get the message
> Remains to be seen. (55–60)[2]

Enjambment is equally problematic. In Standard Habbie the rhymes are king, and the short, regularly rhythmic lines must deliver all sense to them as tribute. Although Burns might sometimes appear to run lines over, the enjambment will be matched to a natural break in the sentence: so he will generally avoid, for instance, the kind of line breaks employed by Les Murray in his deliberately unstable version of the Burns stanza:

> When January is home to visit her folks
> and official work is a public hoax,
> soy sprouts dotting the serpentine strokes
> ploughs combed in the lacquered

hill soil that each afternoon's rainstorm soaks
weave a green jacquard (1–6)[3]

Reading Murray's poem is like walking over Burns territory during an earthquake, everything shifting beneath your feet. Here the anapaest-like skip and the enjambment both distract from the rhyme sequence. Burns's short, discrete lines and accumulative rhyme sequences have the concomitant effect of making conjunctions unusually important. Glance down the left margin of most Burns Standard Habbie poems and you'll come away with a list dominated by *while, an', aboon, this, on, to, at, or* and so on. This is an almost inevitable consequence of beginning each line with an unstressed syllable and not running over. To bring out the possibilities of the Standard Habbie Burns needed not only a mind like a rhyme rolodex but also the agility to keep the body of the stanza twisting round the trellis of rhetorical progress, levering off a variety of syntactic constructions. So many of his poems are dramas because the Standard Habbie naturally inclines to a syntactical structure in which each line accumulates and co-ordinates narrative action: *an', while, as, then, when.* So many are contentious because it harbours a similar predisposition towards an accumulating rhetorical argument: *so, but, whether, let, tho'.* Burns's historical biography and a critical history drawing heavily upon it have given us a man of many guises, an actor of himself. His biography of sound comes up with a not dissimilar figure, though for rather different reasons. As Douglas Dunn put it in his brilliant 1997 essay on Burns's verse forms, concurring with Heaney and Brodsky: 'they guided him, and they refused to let him go. They controlled him as much as he controlled them.'[4]

By running over between lines four and five, the Les Murray variation demonstrates how the creation of expectation, and then its fulfilment, is one of the pleasures of Burns's use of rhyme in the Standard Habbie. The stanza's emotional schemata might be paraphrased as: lines one–three: *this must go wrong*; four: *it's stopped, and changed, has it gone wrong?*; five–six: *ah, it's come right.* Or, one–three: *it's going*; four: *it's stopped, but it must go on again, how will it?*; five–six: *ah, that's how, and now it's stopped properly.* One consequence of this is that we are always aware of the poet as the one who takes the responsibility for continuing the stanza, or for putting it right, upon himself: it is thus highly performative.[5] This is the case even when the poet is envisaging the poem being conveyed on paper rather than performed aloud. The verse forms favoured by Burns relied on others seeing him as different from everyone else. In the Standard Habbie one of the constant, immutable differences is that the poet is the one who can bring the world to order, even while he risks exposing it to overthrow: as Dunn has noted, he gains 'the prestige of a commemorating master-of-ceremonies, the poet as lord of misrule'.[6] Anything and everything can be thrown at him and the omnivorous maw of the Standard Habbie will chomp it into rhyme and chew it down: different languages, parts of speech, registers, proper names, sounds ('*quaick, quaick*');[7] rhymes masculine or feminine. Burns's frequent depiction of himself as a rhymer rather than a 'poet' was as much a covertly aggressive celebration of rhyming as concept and practice as it was a self-deprecatory defence of his own rights to poetry; and, however comic their effect, Burns's rhymes are never less than an act of authority. Indeed, to gloss the Standard Habbie as a comic form is to sell it a little short. Although it obviously possesses great comic potential this need not be its defining quality, and its structure can be turned to other ends.

Reuven Tsur has drawn on Gestalt psychology and cognitive research in suggesting some reasons why this might be so. He notes that compared to an *aabb* stanza form an *abab* arrangement requires 'longer and more complex processing before a complete, closed whole can be achieved. That is why it is perceived as slower, less witty, perhaps more emotional.'[8] This is suggestive for a form like the Standard Habbie, which starts as a triplet before seeming to change its mind halfway through. Indeed, one might say that the stanza manages to wring both an *abab* quatrain and a triplet *aaa* from only six lines, with the overlap and transition between the two possessing all sorts of potential for 'more complex processing'.

To Burns rhyme was a kind of proof, perhaps because its ability to make different things the same in a way that also strengthens their individuality matched something in his own protean nature and heterogeneous sympathies: his relish for difference rhyming with a recognition of what people hold in common. When each stanza of 'Epistle to Davie, a Brother Poet' ends with a crush of rhymes, it as if their density must guarantee the concluding sentiments:

> It lightens, it brightens,
>   The tenebrific scene,
> To meet with, and greet with,
>   My Davie or my Jean! (K 51, I, 69, 137–40)

'Tam o' Shanter' is in couplets, but starts by colliding two of them together using half-rhyme (street/meet/late/gate), as though to generate sufficient energy to take off. 'Address to the Unco Guid' recruits some extra, internal rhymes in its penultimate stanza to brace the brilliant change in register:

> Then gently scan your brother Man,
>   Still gentler sister Woman;
> Tho' they may gang a kennin wrang,
>   To step aside is human: (K 39, I, 53, 49–52)

Conversely, in some of his songs Burns well knew that a displacement of rhyme could jolt even the simplest of arrangements into something more challenging, as when the last four lines of the second and final stanza of 'John Anderson My Jo' call its mortal subject back into completion, where the last four lines of the first stanza had let it run away, released, from the rhymes before it:

> But now your brow is beld, John,
>   Your locks are like the snaw;
> But blessings on your frosty pow,
>   John Anderson my Jo.
>
> Now we maun totter down, John,
>   But hand in hand we'll go;
> And sleep the gither at the foot,
>   John Anderson my Jo. (K 302, II, 529, 5-8, 13–16)

Or the way the internal rhyme in 'Ca' the yowes to the knowes' seems both to delight in itself for being the means by which the stanza will approach its 'bonie dearie', while at the same time rushing forwards to meet that end:

> Ca' the yowes to the knowes,
>   Ca' them whare the heather grows,
> Ca' them whare the burnie rowes,
>   My bonie Dearie. (K 456, II, 738, 1–4)

Or the way 'for ever' in 'Ae Fond Kiss' is used in the second line to refer to the finality of parting ('Ae fond kiss, and then we sever! / Ae farewell, and then for ever!'), but later slips back, in the third stanza, to trouble the rhyme scheme and give what is generally read as a straightforward love lyric a potentially sceptical edge:

> I'll ne'er blame my partial fancy,
> Naething could resist my Nancy:
> But to see her, was to love her;
> Love but her, and love for ever.— (K 337, II, 592, 9–12)

All the rhymes in the poem are of two syllables ('fancy' / 'Nancy') which makes 'love her' and 'for ever' a break, oddly compensated for by the sudden preponderance of 'her'. This could be taken as a kind of tragic irony: their end was foreshadowed in their beginning. It might, however, be read as the words of a speaker whose mind was always on 'for ever' as parting rather than constancy, with this sudden flurry of *her, her, her* an overcompensation for this flightiness. Such a reading would also focus on the question to whom the poem is addressed, and therefore who it is for (the performer seems to lapse into thinking of the kiss's recipient as already absent in the lines above); whether there might be other reasons in the lover's psychology for 'blame' making an appearance; whether the way it turns 'first and fairest' into 'best and dearest' might not suggest another, rather belated, exculpatory correction ('first' implying 'second, third, fourth . . . '?); whether the wishing of 'Love and Pleasure!' for the beloved might imply a performer who foresees the same things in his own post-separation 'for ever'; and finally, whether the repeated lines 'Deep in heart-wrung tears I'll pledge thee, / Warring sighs and groans I'll wage thee' aren't a little too smoothly conclusive, as well as evoking the idea of paying someone off. In this reading, prompted by a single slippage of rhyme, the performer of 'Ae Fond Kiss' becomes someone assuming the convenient role of stricken lover to ease the *fait accompli* of a separation he is already looking beyond.

The authority Burns gains through his mastery of a foregrounded rhyme scheme in the Standard Habbie is only increased by the constant performative risk the stanza entails in its breach between the first four and the last two lines – not too dissimilar to a juggler who nearly drops every fourth ball, or a tightrope walker who wobbles on every fourth step.[9] A crude glossing of this structure's logic might run: *he can do it therefore it must be right*. Or: *what he says fits the form therefore it must be true*. Of course, this doesn't make the resultant poem an infallible instrument of conversion, but it does mean the auditor is more likely to go along with the poet's train of thought. While the rhyme is the most obvious determinant of this two-partedness, the rhythm also guarantees it. The first syllable of the fifth line will often carry slightly more stress than the other first syllables in the stanza, and the second syllable will often carry the most pronounced stress (excepting the rhyme words, which it rivals, or matches). This is caused by the curtailed momentum of the stanza being released again, redoubled; but its effect is to reinforce the sense of the wobble being corrected, of what was risked in the first four lines, and cut short, commencing its completion. Robert Frost compared poetic form to a tennis net and, adopting that analogy, Burns strings his net in the Standard Habbie between the first four and the last two lines.

To take an example: in 'To a Mouse, On turning her up in her Nest, with the Plough, November, 1785' – a poem important to several of the chapters that follow – the fourth–fifth line transition becomes crucial for developing and then confirming the link between observed (mousie) and observer ('I'). In the first stanza the 'tim'rous beastie' is observed and addressed in lines one to four, before the speaker's attention diverts to himself and what he might do in lines five to six. In the second stanza Burns pulls off something of a surprise:

> I'm truly sorry Man's dominion
> Has broken Nature's social union,
> An' justifies that ill opinion,
>   Which makes thee startle,
> At me, thy poor, earth-born companion,
>   An' *fellow mortal*! (K 69, I, 127, 7–12)

It is rare for the Standard Habbie to run over between lines four and five, and given this we might expect it to be used as a climactic dramatic device – and yet here it is, in only the second stanza. And yet, here it isn't. Even if we'd never encountered the Standard Habbie before, the first stanza establishes its pattern firmly enough for us to pause after the fourth line's 'startle', and the comma – which will soon seem rather out of place – also prompts us to stop. This pause makes the continuation of sense into line five immensely powerful. The first four lines are complete and our sense of this completion cannot be destroyed by what comes next – it's too late, we've already experienced it. By having the line of thought continue in the fifth – 'At me' – the completion of the first four lines is not destroyed but extended. This is a perfect example of how Burns can manipulate the Standard Habbie to boost us out of the expectations he has mapped to it (the mouse is not us, the poet is a simple ploughman, the doctor is against death, the devil has the poet). The almost-enjambment in this stanza levers Burns's perspective out of a safe ensconcing in 'Man's dominion'. We glimpse Burns as the mouse sees him, and it is as if this triggers, in turn, his realisation of himself as a 'poor, earth-born companion'.

The rhymes in this stanza do much of the narrative and dramatic work. *Dominion – union – opinion* have a show-off's flourish, half serious and half audacious, as the poet yokes together the language of philosophy and governance using the Latinate *-nion* suffix. We might be expecting a familiar comic mode here: the 'non-high' form being matched with a 'high' conceptual approach. There are intimations, however, that the speaker isn't quite as in control as he thinks he is: *un*ion in the second line fails to completely unify the *-in*ion of *dominion* and *opinion*. 'Startle' then startles us: not only for coming in the short dimeter line, but for being a verb rather than a noun, for breaking from the tri-syllabic Latinate into the colloquial, and for reprising the *s* and *t* sounds which were associated with the beastie (brea*st*ie, ha*st*y). 'Companion' then completes but also modifies the first unit of rhyme for being a word of human relations rather than abstractions, and for possessing an *a* (ə) which breaks from the pinched vowels of *i* (ɪ) and *u* (u), while also reaching back to connect with and modify the earlier rhymes that had conjectured a murderous connection between mouse and man: br*a*ttle, p*a*ttle. 'Mortal' is then heartbreakingly frank – thus the philosophising creature[10] – and also, heartbreakingly, not a complete rhyme with 'startle'. There can be no easy connection between the two, even after the poet's astonished extension of his sympathy. This is the kind of complex drama Burns can wring from the basic dramatic scaffold that is the Standard Habbie – and, like any drama, it seems to demand performance. An adept reader might start with a faintly showy knowingness in the first three lines; pause after the fourth; a dawning, wounded amazement at the start of the fifth, shifting into a mixture of heartfelt conviction and increasingly distraught realisation ('I'm mortal too!'). As every student knows, the Victorians invented the dramatic monologue – except they didn't, except Burns got there first.

Shakespeare's *King Lear* suggests itself just as strongly for a point of comparison. Perhaps no poet before or since Burns has come as close to matching the wrenching emotional effect of that play, and, for all that drama and poetry are awkward things to compare, a reading of Burns's poetry can benefit from the comparison. The various components of the poem – rhyme, line break, rhythm, stanza unit – might be imagined as analogous to a drama's characters, with the analogy for the entire play being the poet's character or voice, which alters through the stanzas as a play alters through its scenes. To adapt Dickens: he do himself in different voices. In terms of thematic similarities, 'To a Mouse' has the theorising man reduced to the poor, earth-born mortal, just as *King Lear* has Edgar reduced to Poor Tom, Lear's companion and philosopher in the storm; and as Lear himself becomes shockingly exposed to his own and others' mortality. Just as the mouse is turned out from its housie into bleak December's winds and blasts, so Lear is turned out into the storm's blasts and led to reflect on all those who suffer their 'unhoused heads' in the storm. As Claire Lamont notes in this book, this passage from *Lear* was used by Burns as an epigraph for his polemical 'A Winter Night', which appeared after 'To a Mouse' in the Edinburgh edition.[11]

Lamont also shows how troubled Burns's imagination could be by images of homelessness, and as 'To a Mouse' goes on Burns insinuates, with increasing urgency, a connection between the mouse's homelessness and human eviction. Although stanzas one to four shuffle us neatly from scene to scene, in the fifth and sixth stanzas it stalls over the destruction of the mouse's home: a brilliantly polemic lingering. In the fifth stanza the destruction is replayed, in the poem's first foray into a time outside the present, anticipating the poet's own ejection from the present moment in the final stanzas. The sixth stanza redevelops the negative that is the mouse's experience to expose its human form, and so begins to truly realise the connection between frightened mouse and mortal which had been bruited – but, crucially, not *earned* – in the second stanza. To be 'turned out' is the language of eviction (poetry is 'turned out of doors' in an inscription Burns wrote for James Elphinstone;[12] many were threatened with the loss of their homes by enclosure and lowland clearances); people, more than mice, live in houses and halds, and have to 'thole' the elements; and, as everyone knows, more than ploughs can be cruel ('th' Oppressor's cruel smile' in 'Lines written on a Bank-note').[13] We might recall that it was perhaps slightly odd for Burns to have proceeded straight from an electrifying identification with the mouse in the second stanza ('an' *fellow mortal*!') to naming it as a thief at the start of the third. Burns's humanity, his identification with the poor, the underdog, the outsider, is such a commonplace that it has become almost easy to miss the full force of it, as we no longer hear the meaning of words we know too well; or, conversely, its biographical veracity might be challenged with reference to Burns's life and times. Properly realised through the medium of his poetry, however, it is a force that comes from us having to share, via a self-dramatising manoeuvring through a fore-grounded poetic form, the process of earning the right, as well as the right way, to express it. Anyone could have said: *the best laid schemes o' Mice an' Men gang aft agley*. But Burns said it differently, and allows us to say it differently, for having fought it clear from its origins: the diamond carries the shape of its mine, the statue the sweat of its quarrying.

This quality in Burns, his ability to torque the plain statement of every-day truths in poetic structures till they take on a power disproportionate to their paraphrased sentiment, was perhaps one of the things that appealed most in him to Wordsworth – and which can bridge the productive dia-logue opened up in this volume between the essays of Murray Pittock and Stephen Gill. Gill shows beyond doubt the central place Burns held in Wordsworth's affectionate imagination; Pittock's analysis forces us to ask why, if Burns was so important to Wordsworth, they differed so radically in their use of dialect. We are back to the question of how poets might inherit from other poets. Wordsworth shows that they can assimilate some-thing of the underlying dynamic while also finding their own, radically different 'sound': picture a cathedral and a mosque extrapolating very dif-ferently from the underlying principle of the pointed arch. In this sense Wordsworth was perhaps the profoundest learner from Burns – unsurpris-ingly, given his depth of feeling for the man. In this sense Heaney, too, found encouragement in Burns, as Fiona Stafford shows in the final chapter of this book, with Burns's 'art speech' a confirmation of his own attempts to keep the complexities of poetry close to communal plain speaking, in such a way that neither one is required to condescend to the other.

But what about those who have learnt from Burns's sounds, his use of forms, rhymes, rhythms and structures, and how might poets of the future do so? The Standard Habbie demonstrates how key the skilled perform-ance of form, of structured rhyme, is to Burns's poetry: and this applies equally to those poems of his in other forms, particularly the horrendously difficult 'Montgomerie stanza', as deployed with effortless grace in 'Epistle to Davie', 'To Ruin' and 'Despondency'.[14] Of course, questions of poetic influence can be difficult to assess, given how poets will blend a multitude of voices into their own, but there are a number of poets who not only make for a useful comparison with this aspect of Burns but also demon-strably knew his work. Byron's journal description of Burns's antithetical qualities, for instance, 'all mixed up in one compound of inspired clay', might draw upon the protean biography but is equally suggestive in the light of both poets' use of highly performable rhyming stanzas, in which antitheses are inspiredly mixed – one might equally say buoyed – up.[15] Swinburne, a rhyming virtuoso sometimes criticised for his mellifluous inconsequentiality,[16] seems to have intuited something of his situation when he wrote, sighingly: 'I could wish I had more in me of Burns and less of Shelley, that I might write something that should do good.'[17] Twenty or so years later finds Kipling twice comparing himself not to Burns but Robert Fergusson, albeit in rather uncharacteristically Burnsian imagery: 'I don't believe very much in my own genius, my own notion being rather that I am set to do Ferguson [sic] for some yet-to-come-along Burns whose little finger will be thicker than my loins.'[18] It is, nevertheless, a very Kiplingesque train of thought, both in the tribal assumptions which condition it (Burns as definitively Scottish and Kipling's thick-fingered progeny as definitively Commonwealth) and in its self-sacrificing efface-ment: sapper Kipling clears the way for the poetic stormtrooper to come. Notwithstanding Kipling's modesty, however, his parallels with Burns are obvious, from their shared use of strongly rhymed and rhythmed stanza forms to an affinity for musical composition (Kipling would compose to contemporary tunes) and huge popularity. Ten or so years later finds Ezra Pound setting W. B Yeats to

> read a little Burns aloud, telling him he cd. read no cadence but his own, or some verse like Sturge Moore's that had not any real characteristics strong enough to prohibit W.B.Y. reading it to his own rhythm. I had a half hour of unmitigated glee in hearing "Say ye bonnie Alexander" and "The Birks o Averfeldy" *keened*, wailed with infinite difficulty and many pauses and restarts to *The Wind Among the Reeds*. [Pound's italics][19]

Although there is no real question of direct, conscious influence here – Yeats's mention of Burns in his essay 'What is "Popular Poetry"?' buries him even as it praises[20] – it is at least enlightening to overlay the two poets. Think of the direct tone, insistent rhymes and tight rhythms Yeats devel-oped in poems such as 'September 1913', 'To a Friend whose Work has come to Nothing' or 'The Fascination of What's Difficult' – a far cry (or wail) from the cadences of some of his earlier volumes.

Perhaps the strongest performer of poetic form in the twentieth century is W. H. Auden – who, of course, employed a rhyming stanza of Byronic deft-ness in his 'Letter to Byron', as well as Yeats's pressingly trochaic tetram-eter in 'In Memory of W. B. Yeats'.[21] However, it was Burns who popped into Auden's head as a point of comparison when reviewing John Skelton in 1932, just as he was beginning to consider the need for a poetry of direct language and 'public service';[22] and only a few months later, as Edward Mendelson notes, he was composing poems in variants of the Standard Habbie.[23] Indeed, the lover of 'As I Walked Out One Evening', who sings of how ' "I will love you, dear, I'll love you" ' till ' "the ocean / Is folded and hung up to dry" ', is clearly the Burns of 'A Red, Red Rose', who sings of how his love will last 'till a the seas gang dry' (K 453, II, 735). Auden natu-ralises an overtness of poetic form to an age largely unsympathetic to it by making strange everything the form unfolds. The base weirdness of rhyme, its ability to make things alike which are not alike, is used by Burns to bring

together different registers, worlds, perspectives; it is pushed to the point
of breaking by Auden, who brings together things which are perceptively
difficult, if not outright impossible:

> When the green field comes off like a lid,
> Revealing what was much better hid –
>   Unpleasant:
> And look, behind you without a sound
> The woods have come up and are standing round
>   In deadly crescent.   ('The Witnesses', 31–6)[24]

> That later we, though parted then,
> May still recall these evenings when
>   Fear gave his watch to look;
> The lion griefs loped from the shade
> And on our knees their muzzles laid,
>   And Death put down his book.   ('A Summer Night', 19–24)[25]

To apply the lessons about performance learnt from Burns to these kinds of
Auden poem, one might say that he creates a poetic voice in possession of
strongly foregrounded stanza forms as well as being possessed of contents
that struggle against this form's anticipatory dynamic. We know a rhyme
will be coming and when, but we can never be sure we will recognise or
understand it, in the way that we can recognise a Burns line on first hearing,
even if it contains depths which only further consideration will reveal.[26]
This mismatch helps account for the eerie, nightmarish quality of much of
Auden's Thirties' work. As Europe became possessed by horrors, so Auden
let the most guilelessly reader-oriented of poetic modes become possessed
by something darker, stranger. To read much of his poetry of this period is
like having a familiar face turn to you, before glimpsing black holes where
the eyes should be.

In the present day, when the performance of poetry – that is, poetry being
read aloud to an audience, rather than consumed silently by a reader – seems
to be an increasingly important aspect of its being, the example of Burns's
performance of form becomes correspondingly resonant. Recordings of
poets reading aloud are archived online; poetry readings and slams are
common and well-attended, and make their way to wider audiences via the
internet; the shortlisted poets for the T. S. Eliot Prize read their poems
on a daily radio programme which attracts over six million listeners. Yet
the use of overtly performative forms of the kind Burns excelled in is rare,
and it is hard to escape the conclusion that this is, in part, because they are
extremely difficult to write well in; or perhaps, to put it another way, they
make ineptitude and inconsequence more unambiguously detectable. But as
Don Paterson put it, in his controversial 2004 T. S. Eliot lecture, 'The Dark
Art of Poetry':

Only plumbers can plumb, roofers roof and drummers drum; only poets can write poetry. Restoring the science of verse-making would restore our self-certainty in this matter, and naturally resurrect a guild that, I believe, would soon find it had some secrets worth preserving.[27]

Burns shows us how the poet can – if good enough – step out as necessarily different, taking on the role of Promethean darer on his audience's behalf: he risks form as we, beyond the experiencing of the poem, risk the life he describes. This sounds grandiose but it is no different from an audience empathising with the step-by-step adjustments of a tightrope walker, and such empathetic engagement is a fundamental part of being human.[28] Of course, there is no guarantee that demanding verse structures will result in great poetry, but at its best, in the hands of someone like Burns (and why not aim high?), poetry's transformative potential can be boosted by the use of verse structures which recruit the empathetic, moment-by-moment engagement of the audience.

It is sobering to contemplate the sheer number of qualifications required when broaching this topic. There is, of course, no question of declaring this to be the direction in which poetry should go: there are few things more fatuous than poetic proscription, more tiresome than an artistic manifesto. It is a case, rather, of letting Burns remind us of the potential of a mode of poetry which has slipped into the shadows – indeed, which seems to be regarded by many as definitively dead – at a moment when the ways in which poetry is consumed seem increasingly suited to it. It is common to regard the way Burns had to earn the right to call himself a poet as a bad thing, and no doubt it was, in many ways: all that self-deprecation, that deferential manoeuvring. But perhaps, in one sense at least, it is a salutary model to keep in mind in an age when poetry is definitively marginal, if not outright foreign, to most people's experience. Are we all ploughmen now? James Fenton has described seeing an African poet at a literary festival, who sang and accompanied himself with instruments and extemporised, responding to an American poet who criticised him for making things difficult for the poets who came after:

> The African replied in terms which surprised me at first. You American poets, he said, and you European poets, you think that because you are poets you are very important, whereas I am an African, and I don't think I am important at all. When I go into a village and begin to tell a story, the first thing the audience will do is interrupt me. They will ask questions about the story I am telling, and if I do not work hard they will take over the story and tell it among themselves. I have to work to get the story back from them.[29]

What are you going to do for me? Are you going to entertain me? Why should I keep listening? Foregrounded form, form that requires the negotiation of its own structure, evolved in the satisfaction of these demands:

a mental space in which – even when composing on and for paper – the poet and his audience are foregathered to 'hae a swap o' *rhyming-ware*' ('Epistle to J. L[aprai]k', K 57, I, 88, 107), in which a sense of fellowship turns the handling of difficult stanzas into an act of courtesy, a tribute to the envisaged audience. This celebration of what Liam McIlvanney has called the 'non-material values – good-fellowship, fraternity, sympathy – against the corrupt self-seeking of the governing class' might resonate with our political situation today, particularly given the non-hierarchical, non-corporate nature of live readings and the internet.[30] Of course, the adoption of particular stanza forms will never be enough on its own, but to bear them in mind, and in mouth, might expand the resources and reach of poetry at a time when new channels of communication are opening before it. I'm sure that anyone who's been to a sampling of poetry readings has come away, at one time or another, having been bored to tears by poetry they might even have found effective on the page. Fenton describes meeting some aspiring American poets who are interested only in 'open form', which is to say, no form at all:

> And there was another notable thing about these aspiring poets, when seen in action in front of an audience – it was quite clear that they would have liked to *perform* for the pleasure of the audience, but that they were hampered by the fact that what they were reading out had been written for the page . . . But these poets also would be happier, it occurred to me, if they – even without going so far as to change their basic poetic practice – did themselves a favour and wrote *something*, a single poem even, which they could perform. So that, after the agony of standing in front of an audience reading words which were *specifically designed not to be read out loud*, they could, before leaving the podium, cheer everyone up with something worth listening to. (Fenton's italics)[31]

This might simplify the far from simple divisions between poetry read aloud and what Eric Griffith's has called 'the printed voice' of poetry,[32] but as a rough-and-ready observation it does its job. Of course (again, *of course*) this is not to argue that poetry needs to be strongly rhymed and complexly structured to be performable – though it is notable that forms like the Habbie and the sonnet seem to have originated with the troubadours[33] – or that all poems should shape themselves to this kind of consumption. It is, however, to address in a practical manner – as Burns did – the particular demands of one kind of poet-audience relationship, and to bring out again, and polish up, one of the most powerful weapons in a poet's armoury. Close attention to the intricate brilliancies of Burns's poetry make it clear that there's more to it than performance, drama, entertainment, imme-diacy. But that 'more than' arises through those things, as leaves arise through trees. Burns's 'spavet *Pegasus*' ('Epistle to Davie', K 51, I, 69, 147) is both dray-horse bearer of local loads and prancing Lipizzaner, a high utility art form – as relevant now, in practice as well as principle, as it has ever been.

Notes

1. Douglas Dunn, '"A very Scottish kind of dash": Burns's native metric', in Robert Crawford (ed.), *Robert Burns and Cultural Authority* (Edinburgh: Edinburgh University Press, 1997), pp. 58–85, 83.
2. Lochhead notes that she was deliberately trying to write 'a very imperfect form of "Burns Stanza"' (Liz Lochhead, 'From a Mouse', in Douglas Gifford (ed.), *Addressing the Bard: Twelve Contemporary Poets Respond to Robert Burns* (Edinburgh: Scottish Poetry Library, 2009), pp. 9–12).
3. Les Murray, 'Variations on a Measure of Burns', in Les Murray, *Collected Poems* (Manchester: Carcanet, 1994), pp. 299–300.
4. Dunn, '"A very Scottish kind of dash"', p. 76.
5. I use 'performative' in its plainer sense of 'of or relating to performance', and am not concerned with the theoretical dimensions the word has accrued.
6. Dunn, '"A very Scottish kind of dash"', p. 65.
7. Robert Burns, 'Address to the Deil' (K 76, I, 170, 45).
8. Reuven Tsur, 'Rhyme and cognitive poetics', *Poetics Today*, Spring 1996, pp. 55–87, 66.
9. Compare Reuven Tsur contrasting the 'genuine security' aroused by Pope's couplets with the 'false sense of security' created by Coleridge's unpredictable rhyming patterns in 'Kubla Khan': Burns might come somewhere between the two (Tsur, 'Rhyme and cognitive poetics', p. 70).
10. Murray Pittock has described the voice of the second stanza as that of 'the benevolent bystander of Enlightenment theory' (Murray Pittock, 'Nibbling at Adam Smith', in Johnny Rodgers and Gerard Carruthers (eds), *Fickle Man: Robert Burns in the 21st Century* (Dingwall, Ross-shire: Sandstone Press, 2009), pp. 161–73, 162).
11. For an extended consideration of Burns's relationship to *King Lear* see Fiona Stafford, *Starting Lines in Scottish, Irish, and English Poetry: From Burns to Heaney* (Oxford: Oxford University Press), pp. 66–89. Seamus Heaney also compares 'To a Mouse' to the play (Seamus Heaney, 'Burns's art speech', in Crawford (ed.), *Robert Burns and Cultural Authority*, pp. 216–33, 220).
12. Robert Burns, 'To Mr E —— on his translation of and commentaries on Martial' (K 146, I, 324, 2).
13. Robert Burns, 'Lines written on a Bank-note' (K 106, I, 251, 7).
14. The stanza was first used by Alexander Montgomerie in *The Cherrie and the Slae* (1597).
15. George Gordon Byron, Lord Byron, *Selected Letters and Journals*, ed. Leslie A. Marchand (London: Pimlico, 1993), p. 346.
16. See for example Jerome McGann, *Swinburne, an Experiment in Criticism* (Chicago: University of Chicago Press, 1972), pp. 132–3.
17. Algernon Charles Swinburne, Letter to Edwin Harrison, 4 June 1873, in Algernon Charles Swinburne, *The Swinburne Letters*, 6 vols, ed. Cecil Y. Lang (New Haven: Yale University Press, 1959), vol. II, p. 251.
18. Rudyard Kipling to Charles Eliot Norton, 31 December 1896, in Rudyard Kipling,

Letters of Rudyard Kipling, ed. Thomas Pinney, 6 vols (London: Macmillan, 1994–2004), vol. II, p. 279. See also a remark in a letter to John St Loe Strachey, 2 January 1899: 'I am roughing out the work for that man – as Ferguson [sic] did for Burns: and I think if he hasn't appeared when I die I shall leave him a private letter of suggestions' (*Letters of Kipling*, vol. II, p. 358).

19. Ezra Pound, Letter to Felix E. Schelling, 8 July 1922, in Ezra Pound, *The Letters of Ezra Pound 1907–1941*, ed. D. D. Paige (London: Faber and Faber, 1951), p. 247.

20. 'Despite his expressive speech which sets him above all other popular poets, he has the triviality of emotion, the poverty of ideas, the imperfect sense of beauty of a poetry whose most typical expression is in Longfellow' (W. B. Yeats, 'What is "popular poetry?"', in W. B. Yeats, *Essays and Introductions* (London: Macmillan, 1961), p. 6.

21. Compare Dunn's description of Auden as 'the most interestingly stanzaic of all modern poets' (Dunn, '"A very Scottish kind of dash"', p. 83).

22. W. H. Auden, 'A Review of *The Complete Poems of John Skelton*', *The Criterion*, January 1932; reprinted in W. H. Auden, *Prose*, ed. Edward Mendelson, 3 vols (London: Faber and Faber, 1996), I, p. 11).

23. Edward Mendelson, *Early Auden* (London: Faber & Faber, 1981), p. 119.

24. W. H. Auden, *Collected Poems*, ed. Edward Mendelson (London: Faber & Faber, 1976), p. 77.

25. Ibid., p. 117.

26. Seamus Heaney makes a nice distinction, calling Auden 'a civic poet' where Yeats, for example, is a 'public poet' (Henry Cole, 'Seamus Heaney, the art of poetry no. 75', *Paris Review* 144, Fall 1997, p. 104.

27. <http://www.poetrylibrary.org.uk/news/poetryscene/?id=20> (accessed: 8 March 2011).

28. See, for example, Paul R. Ehrlich and Robert E. Ornstein (eds), *Humanity on a Tightrope: Thoughts on Empathy, Family and Big Changes for a Viable Future* (Plymouth: Rowman & Littlefield Publishers, 2010).

29. James Fenton, *An Introduction to English Poetry* (London: Penguin, 2003), p. 14.

30. Liam McIlvanney, *Burns the Radical: Poetry and Politics in Late Eighteenth-Century Scotland* (East Linton: Tuckwell, 2002), p. 119.

31. Fenton, *Introduction to English Poetry*, pp. 12–13.

32. Eric Griffiths, *The Printed Voice of Victorian Poetry* (Oxford: Clarendon Press, 1989).

33. Dunn, '"A very Scottish kind of dash"', pp. 61–2.

CHAPTER 2

Burns and Loyalty

Douglas Dunn

In a review written in 1954 Graham Greene wrote:

> It is a sad thing about small nationalities that like a possessive woman they trap
> their great men: Walter Scott, Stevenson, Burns, Livingstone – all have to
> some extent been made over by their countrymen, they have not been allowed
> to grow or to diminish with time. How can they even shift in the grave under
> the weight of their national memorials? A whole industry of trinkets and
> souvenirs and statuettes depends on the conformity of the dead.[1]

Scotland may be a relatively small nation and Scots a relatively small nationality; but the literature of Scotland is not small, and certainly not insignificant. As the historian Renan said, a nation or a nationality might best be
defined as 'a large-scale solidarity', although such a robust phenomenon
can be shattered by the commonplace divisions of politics. Observations on
a country's literature, coming from, as it were, outside, while often welcome
and interesting, are not always crucial, although they can sometimes budge
aboriginal complacency. Many of the important studies of Burns, Scott,
Stevenson and MacDiarmid have been undertaken by critics and scholars
who were not, or are not, Scots.

Graham Greene's glance at Scottish posterities, at habits of memorialising that can be epic on one hand and tawdry on the other, neglects the
international impact of Burns, Scott and Stevenson, and their importance
within the larger context of literature. Many indigenous readers of Burns
preen themselves on their poet's international celebrity while preferring
their own intimate relish of his language, attitudes and beliefs.

Edwin Muir considered it almost impossible for a Scotsman to see Burns
simply as a poet. 'Burns is so deeply embedded in Scottish life that he
cannot be detached from it, from what is best and what is worst in it, and
regarded as we regard Dunbar or James Hogg or Walter Scott.' And I'll
continue with more from Muir's essay, 'Burns and Popular Poetry':

> He [Burns] is more a personage to us than a poet, more a figurehead than a
> poet, more a figurehead than a personage, and more a myth than a figurehead.
> To those who have heard of Dunbar he is a figure, of course, comparable to
> Dunbar, but he is also a figure comparable to Prince Charlie, about whom

everyone has heard. He is a myth evolved by the popular imagination, a communal poetic creation, a Protean figure; we can all shape him to our own likeness, for a myth is endlessly adaptable; so that to the respectable this secondary Burns is a decent man; to the Rabelaisian, bawdy; to the sentimentalist, sentimental; to the Socialist, a revolutionary; to the Nationalist, a patriot; to the religious, pious; to the self-made man, self-made; to the drinker, a drinker.[2]

And, we could add, to the amorist, an amorist.

A contemporary Scottish poet seeking to understand and learn from Burns is therefore faced with kaleidoscopic or Protean personalities, both actual and poetic, in the best-known figure of his or her traditions. Or is it an entirely male exercise? The problem is increased when you consider that 'national poet of Scotland' is too conventional a term for Burns, as Edwin Muir claimed, suggesting that 'the poet of the Scottish people' is a better description. Burns, said Muir, 'is an object-lesson in what poetic popularity really means – the prime object-lesson in the poetry of the world, perhaps the unique instance'. And that lesson is to be learned from the ways in which Burns has been constantly refashioned according to the special pleadings of whoever adopts him as 'their' poet, resulting at times in what Muir termed a 'vulgarised' reputation or posterity.[3]

To seek Burns's influence, or that of any major poet, is probably unwise in any case. It's better just to let these things happen, because there are many poets. Burns occupies so much space in the Scottish poetic consciousness that to compete with his prestige – as Hugh MacDiarmid attempted – is a loser's wager as much as ignoring it, while to try to replicate his techniques and habits of mind would condemn a poet to the avoidance of any hope of originality. While this is understood by poets, critics, scholars and readers with a literary awareness, it tends not to be by many of those who have embraced his poetry with affection and enthusiasm. When I published my first book back in 1969 I gave a copy to an uncle of mine whom I knew loved Burns. He took a look at it and said, 'Why do you bother? You'll never be as great as the immortal Robert Burns.' Well, thanks; but I think I knew that then even if I'm rather more certain of it more than forty years later.

Extending Edwin Muir's inventory even further, would be to add 'to a poet, a poet'. (We can still leave room for Burns being more than that.) He was one of the great virtuosi of verse. Burns's poetry is so quick, so direct and forthright, so 'A' to the life', that a reader can almost be pardoned for being convinced by it without giving much thought to the skill with which it's been put together. Standard Habbie's not the easiest stanza to write while keeping up the audible sensation of a speaking voice, a voice that – whoever the reader is – the reader believes he or she can trust, because he's obviously 'one of us'. You can't be 'popular' in poetry, you can't be a 'poet of the people', if the ordinary person perceives you as being his or her adversary. Hence Burns's playfully reductive revelations of his allegedly amateur status in 'Epistle to John Lapraik', where his tongue is so much in his cheek that you can imagine it poking out first one ear and then the other.

> I am nae *Poet*, in a sense,
> But just a *Rhymer* like by chance,
> An' hae to Learning nae pretence,
>> Yet, what the matter?
> Whene'er my Muse does on me glance,
>> I jingle at her.
>
> Your Critic-folk may cock their nose,
> And say, 'How can you e'er propose,
> 'You wha ken hardly *verse* frae *prose*,
>> 'To mak a *sang?*'
> But by your leaves, my learned foes,
>> Ye're maybe wrang.
>
> What's a' the jargon o' your Schools,
> Your Latin names for horns an' stools;
> If honest Nature made you *fools*,
>> What sairs your Grammars?
> Ye'd better taen up *spades* and *shools*,
>> Or *knappin-hammers*.
>
> A set o' dull, conceited Hashes,
> Confuse their brains in *Colledge-classes*!
> They *gang in* Stirks, and *come out* Asses,
>> Plain truth to speak;
> An' syne they think to climb Parnassus
>> By dint o' Greek!
>
> Gie me ae spark o' Nature's fire,
> That's a' the learning I desire;
> Then tho' I drudge thro' dub an' mire
>> At pleugh or cart,
> My Muse, tho' hamely in attire,
>> May touch the heart. (K 57, I, 86–7, 49–78)

Or think of his agile and confident skill in the very difficult stanza of 'Epistle to Davie, a Brother Poet', a stanza devised by Alexander Montgomerie for his late sixteenth-century masterpiece *The Cherrie and the Slae*:

> While winds frae off BEN-LOMOND blaw,
> And bar the doors wi' driving snaw,
>> And hing us owre the ingle,
> I set me down, to pass the time,

And spin a verse or twa o' rhyme,
  In hamely, *westlin* jingle.
While frosty winds blaw in the drift,
  Ben to the chimla lug,
I grudge a wee the *Great-folk*'s gift,
  That live sae bien an' snug:
    I tent less, and want less
      Their roomy fire-side:
    But hanker, and canker,
      To see their cursed pride. (K 51, I, 65, 1–14)

That's the Burns I fastened myself to when I was younger – the Burns whose work said to me that if you're going to write then make your poems as well as a good carpenter makes tables and chairs, as a baker bakes, or a farmer ploughs a field, or at least aim for that; and leave room for the chance of humour, for good nature, a reasonable hedonism; take yourself and your work seriously, but don't overdo it; and don't forget your loyalties – loyalties above royalties. Burns took no remuneration for his devoted labours on Scottish song, which is salutary to remember at a time when more than a few poets these days refuse to cross the door for less than £500.

Much of Burns's genius stems from his loyalty, by which I don't mean patriotism, although that is implicated, but a pervasive allegiance to the people he came from. A ground bass of political principle and conviction runs through his work. At times he was obliged to subtract from it by episodes of what Burke would have called 'expediency'. But it's the robustness of his principled and passionate loyalty that survives, his need to appear 'loyal' to orthodox expectations being an understandable tactic in dangerous times. He kept his promises, and lived with his compromises.

The bedrock of his fidelity is the consummate artistry of his verse. As with all the great Scots poets, from Henryson, Dunbar, Douglas, Lindsay, Montgomerie, through Ramsay and Fergusson, Scott, Stevenson, Davidson, the earlier MacDiarmid, Muir, MacCaig, Garioch and Morgan, Burns's genius rises above technical accomplishment. For a poet from a working-class background, Burns's gestures, particularly his loyalty to people and place, are still meaningful and valid.

It's instructive, too, that Burns is a poet of both the microcosm and the macrocosm, of lice, mice and liberty, of wee beasties and transcendental declarations, as well as the lively and wicked exploder of hypocrisy and sanctimonious beliefs and behaviour. He is a love poet, a poet of the many moods of love, from the song of the old married lovers 'John Anderson', of lost love in 'Mary Morison', and the simple, exultant farewell song 'A Red, Red Rose'. Opinions vary, as opinions by their nature must, on which poems are his masterworks. Many would opt for 'Tam o' Shanter', 'Holy Willie's Prayer', 'To a Mouse' and 'A Man's a Man'. I love these poems too, but my attachment to 'Epistle to John Lapraik' is strong, if only that it's good to know a poet wrote my personal manifesto and not Karl Marx. *The Jolly Beggars*, sometimes known as *Love and Liberty*, is the performance I'd choose. Anarchic, tender and angry by turns, it took an inventive twentieth-century musical score by Cedric Thorpe Davie to bring it to life. I saw it performed in St Andrews, just a couple of weeks prior to writing this.

I chose the term 'performance' deliberately. If ever there was a poet whose work lives best between tongue and teeth, whether spoken or sung, it's Robert Burns's. His work is decisively social and sociable. It presupposes not an audience so much as a community, whether or not it's interested. Identifying national 'characteristics' in poetry can very often turn out to be an exercise in the lowering of horizons, or in precluding change and innovation. It can be conservative or reactionary. But I think it undeniable that a continuing feature of poetry written by Scots is its engagement with vernacular, demotic languages and forms. Or with a contest between demotic address and the imaginative and softer lyrical reaches of poetry, between the forthright and matter-of-fact, and the dream-like, or visionary, spiritual and mystical.

Notes

1. Graham Greene, 'Books in general', *New Statesman and Nation* 48, 2 October 1954 (3 July 1954–25 December 1954), p. 411.
2. Edwin Muir, 'Burns and popular poetry', in Edwin Muir, *Essays on Literature and Society* (London: Hogarth Press, 1949), p. 57.
3. Ibid., p. 60.

CHAPTER 3

Allan Ramsay, Robert Fergusson and Robert Burns

Rhona Brown

Eighteenth-century Scots vernacular poetry, and indeed the criticism which surrounds it, has traditionally been dominated by the triumvirate of so-called 'Vernacular Revivalists', Allan Ramsay (?1684–1758), Robert Fergusson (1750–74) and Robert Burns (1759–96). While the sheer enormity of their stature has sometimes overshadowed other Scots vernacular writers in their century-long period of prominence, Ramsay, Fergusson and Burns nevertheless share a powerful literary relationship, just as they set potent literary standards. They have been portrayed, on the one hand, as the Scots vernacular tradition's board of rulers, as its true triumvirate. On the other, they have been affectionately depicted as the literary pseudo-family which enabled the eighteenth-century linguistic and formal 'Revival'. Each paved the poetic way for his descendant, and while Ramsay and Fergusson have sometimes been derogated as mere precursors of Scotland's bard, Burns self-consciously saw himself as entering a hallowed literary succession when he began as a Scots poet.

Despite never meeting, Ramsay, Fergusson and Burns's lifetimes overlapped in small but commanding ways. Fergusson's biographer, A. B. Grosart, outlines their generational relationship:

> Robert [Fergusson] is found in 1756 at a private or adventure school. His first teacher therein was a Mr. Philp, who had . . . opened an English school in Niddry's Wynd. This was nearly opposite Allan Ramsay's old book-shop and circulating library. This locality reminds us that, in the better than pseudo-apostolic succession of the poets, 'honest Allan's' predestined successor might have seen and been seen by the little dapper cheery old gentleman . . . Memorable, too, that contemporaneous in distant Ayrshire little Robert Burns – born 1759 – was soon to arrive to succeed *his* predecessor.[1]

Grosart, a Church of Scotland minister, offers a characteristically sentimental account of the poets' alliance. Their 'succession' is dubiously termed 'pseudo-apostolic', implying a continuous transmission of literary authority which mirrors the diffusion of spiritual right from Christ's disciples through succeeding popes and bishops. Alongside this view of Scotland's literary apostolate is a familiar Presbyterian emphasis: for Grosart, Ramsay, Fergusson and Burns are Scotland's literary Elect. They are genius artists, but also arbitrarily controlled objects of fate, 'predestined' to their poetic places.

Grosart's portrayal of the 'little dapper cheery old gentleman' smiling benevolently on the youthful Fergusson and Burns is not only reminiscent of Grosart's Victorian literary context but also illustrative of insistent bio-graphical and critical focus on the extremes of sentiment and tragedy in the poets' lives and the attendant emasculation of their literary personalities. According to Susan Manning, accounts such as Grosart's encourage a limit-ing 'linguistic nationalism' which 'implicitly consigned Fergusson's work to a prophetic and proleptic position in a teleological story following the hints thrown out by Allan Ramsay and leading to the glorious flowering of Burns, where each 'is the saviour . . . of a moribund linguistic tradition which their genius resuscitated for a new generation'.[2]

Although Burns was aware of his immediate predecessor's tragic exist-ence, his portrayal of Fergusson is dissimilar to Grosart's. His under-standing of Fergusson's death at the age of twenty-four in Edinburgh's asylum for pauper lunatics prompts him to bemoan Fergusson's neglect by 'ungrateful man' and to curse the 'whunstane hearts' of the 'Enbrugh gentry' who, in his view, refused to ease the 'iron grasp of Want and Woe' of Fergusson's final days.[3] When he turns to Fergusson's poetry, this tone of infuriated sentiment dissipates. In the 'Epistle to J. Lapraik, an Old Scotch Bard' (K 57, I, 86–7), Burns's concise description of Fergusson as 'the bauld an' slee' exposes literary admiration for his predecessor's work, encapsulating with two simple but loaded vernacular terms, its audacity, humour, shrewdness, verve and vigour. That Fergusson's work is an inspi-ration is indubitable; as Burns asserts in his autobiographical letter to John Moore, he had 'given up' poetry until 'meeting with Fergusson's Scotch poems', which ensured that he 'strung anew my wildly-sounding, rustic lyre with emulating vigour'.[4]

While depicting Fergusson as a literary port in a storm and poetic cat-alyst, Burns's identification with his predecessor is also biographical; as Robert Crawford states, Fergusson's was an 'example' which 'both terrified and inspired him'.[5] His depiction of Ramsay, however, is one of pure liter-ary esteem. In the Preface to *Poems, Chiefly in the Scottish Dialect* (1786), Burns deals with his Scots vernacular predecessors directly, and presents himself, by means of a shrewd utilisation of *sprezzatura*, as one of their line:

It is an observation of that celebrated Poet, whose divine Elegies do honour to our language, our nation, and our species, that 'Humility has depressed many a genius to a hermit, but never raised one to fame.' If any Critic catches at the word *genius*, the Author tells him, once for all, that he certainly looks upon himself as possest of some poetic abilities, otherwise his publishing in the manner he has done, would be a manoeuvre below the worst character, which, he hopes, his worst enemy will ever give him: but to the genius of a Ramsay, or

the glorious dawnings of the poor, unfortunate Ferguson, he, with equal unaffected sincerity, declares, that, even in his highest pulse of vanity, he has not
the most distant pretensions. These two justly admired Scotch Poets he has
often had in his eye in the following pieces, but rather with a view to kindle at
their flame, than for servile imitation.[6]

In this elaborate statement of artistic 'humility' – the modesty topos itself
being an enduring feature of the Scottish literary tradition since medieval
times – Burns belies his pretended intellectual meekness by demonstrating
knowledge not only of William Shenstone's Elegies, much admired in the
1780s, but also of the work of Ramsay and Fergusson. And again Burns
offers projections of his predecessors' lives and works. Thanks to his long
life, Ramsay is succinctly described as 'genius', while Fergusson's works
are 'glorious dawnings' despite a wretchedly 'unfortunate' existence. While
seemingly rejecting association with his forefathers, Burns simultaneously
informs his reader that he is of their lineage.

Burns's self-effacing yet knowledgeable persona finds echo in the works
of Ramsay and Fergusson, demonstrating his complex rapport with their
literary legacies. In particular, all three writers indulged in epistolary relations which are revealing of their approach to their craft. Ramsay is a master
of the verse epistle in vernacular Scots and neoclassical English, engaging in
literary relationships with prominent figures including William Hamilton
of Gilbertfield, Josiah Burchet, William Aikman and James Arbuckle.
Fergusson's case is dissimilar but comparable. In his position as laureate of
Walter Ruddiman's *Weekly Magazine, or Edinburgh Amusement*, Fergusson
was a poet of the Scottish public sphere and, as such, was often the subject
of poetic commentary by magazine correspondents. Perhaps attempting, as
Fiona Stafford has argued, to imitate the literary relationships of his predecessors, Burns was productive in the verse epistle mode, addressing pieces
to, among others, John Lapraik, William Simson, Francis Grose and Robert
Graham of Fintry.[7]

Arguably replicating the conviviality of the social organisations of which
each was a member – Ramsay of the Easy Club, Fergusson of the Cape Club
and Robinhood Debating Society and Burns of the Tarbolton Bachelors'
Club – the poets' verse epistles give insight into the social life and dialogue
of eighteenth-century clubs.[8] More importantly, in these epistles, Ramsay,
Fergusson and Burns analyse themselves while responding to constructions of their personae by others, giving a privileged glimpse of their poetic
methods.

An illustration of Ramsay's approach is found in 'An Epistle to Mr.
James Arbuckle, Describing the Author'.[9] Depicting himself – much as
Burns would in 1786 – as untutored, he describes his poetry as emanating
from 'my blyth auld-fashion'd whistle' (19), while his work is 'Without
rule, compasses, or charcoal, / Or serious study in a dark hole' (21–2).

Immediately, Ramsay presents himself as an autodidact, while portraying
the moment of inspiration in an astutely self-deprecating manner:

> Three times I ga'e the muse a rug,
> Then bit my nails, and claw'd my lug;
> Still heavy – at the last my nose
> I prim'd with an inspiring dose,
> Then did ideas dance (dear safe us!)
> As they'd been daft. – Here ends the preface. (23–8)

Despite presenting himself as lacking 'serious study', Ramsay nonetheless
depicts poetic inspiration as originating with the classical muse: although
humorously reluctant to give assistance, she is nevertheless his guide. Just
as Burns denies knowledge of Theocritan originals in his Preface to the
Kilmarnock edition, and just as Fergusson will reject comparisons of his
work with Ramsay's, the epistle's *sprezzatura* works in shrewd literary and
political ways. As Murray Pittock argues, Ramsay's utilisation of classical
originals in a Scots framework was 'designed to protect and promote a distinctive national voice by transforming predominantly English uses of literary kinds, not surrendering to them'.[10] Here, after describing the mechanics
of concentration and stimulation – the chewing of fingernails, scratching of
ears and taking of snuff – Ramsay's narrator is ready to begin. Poetic 'ideas'
are, like the muse, humanised: they 'dance, / As they'd been daft'.

A comparable account of the creative process is found in Burns's letter to
George Thomson of September 1793. Although describing song-writing,
Burns's depiction echoes Ramsay's concoction of personal compulsion and
classical literary duty:

> My way is: I consider the poetic Sentiment, correspondent to my idea of the
> musical expression; then chuse my theme; begin one Stanza; when that is
> composed, which is generally the most difficult part of the business, I walk
> out, sit down now & then, look out for objects in Nature around me that are in
> unison or harmony with the cogitations of my fancy & workings of my bosom;
> humming every now & then the air with the verses I have framed: when I feel
> my Muse beginning to jade, I retire to the solitary fireside of my study, &
> there commit my effusions to paper; swinging, at intervals, on the hind-legs
> of my elbow-chair, by way of calling forth my own critical strictures, as my
> pen goes on.[11]

Both accounts emphasise the physicality of composition, while demonstrating simultaneous cerebral attachment to the concept of the classical muse.
Just as Fergusson's muse in 'The King's Birth-Day in Edinburgh'[12] is a
'limmer' who is 'fairly flung' (5), Burns's begins to 'jade'; just as Fergusson's
muse of 'Leith Races'[13] is nicknamed 'Mirth' (32) and 'loup[s] like HEBE
o'er the grass' (25), Ramsay's familiarised muse requires a 'rug' from the
impatient poet. The muse retains classical associations but is recognisably

human. It is also the case that, in an ironic role reversal, each poet must protect or revitalise his muse. Ramsay 'rugs', or tears, at his muse's garments to reanimate her, while Burns sits down to write as his muse begins to tire. In 'The King's Birth-Day', Fergusson informs his muse that she has 'drunk your fill' (19): to have another glass would 'ding you doitet; / Troth, 'twould be sair agains my will / To hae the wyte o't' (22–4), while in 'Auld Reikie', his narrator shields her eyes from Edinburgh's unpalatable excesses:

> To sing yet meikle does remain,
> Undecent for a modest strain;
> And since the poet's daily bread is
> The favour of the Muse or ladies,
> He downa like to gie offence
> To delicacy's bonny sense;
> Therefore the stews remain unsung,
> And bawds in silence keep their tongue. (351–8)[14]

This complex relationship between poet and muse is revealing: although familiarised and not always reliable, the muse, and therefore English neo-classical tradition, is ever present and, particularly in Fergusson's construction, worth protecting. In examples such as this, as Pittock argues, Ramsay initiates a process which would 'justify a continuity of kinds and forms in a distinctively Scottish literature, for which he was in reality largely personally responsible'.[15] He would simultaneously sow the seeds of contemporary Scottish Augustanism and future Scottish Romanticism.

While Ramsay presents a carefully crafted persona in the epistle to Arbuckle, poetic tributes addressed to him by fellow authors provide alternative perspectives of his reception. Ramsay's 1720 edition opens with 'To Allan Ramsay, on his Poetical Works', by Josiah Burchet, in which Ramsay is compared to Horace and Virgil while being hailed as 'Northern Bard', as 'Fav'rite of the Nine' (1).[16] As well as commending the poet's original productions, Burchet also extols Ramsay's antiquarian work, being particularly grateful for his uncovering of the 'bonny lines call'd *Christ's-kirk on the Green*' (77) and 'Royal JAMES the Bays' (79). Significantly, Burchet's closing lines recommend Ramsay as poet, not of Scotland, but of Britain:

> Go on, fam'd Bard, thou wonder of our Days,
> And crown thy Head with never-fading Bays,
> While gratefull *Britons* do thy lines revere,
> And value, as they ought, their *Virgil* here. (99–102)

Ramsay is, for Burchet, a local Virgil; he is chronicler not only of official and unofficial life in contemporary Edinburgh but also of collective human nature. Although he is congratulated for unearthing older Scots poetry and song, Burchet argues that Ramsay's rightful tradition is at once Scottish, British, classical and, arguably, universal.

Burchet's sentiments are echoed in the correspondence between Ramsay and Hamilton of Gilbertfield. Hamilton begins his first epistle, dated 26 June 1719, with an address to 'fam'd and celebrated Allan! / Renownéd Ramsay, canty callan', a poet unmatched by 'nowther Highlandman or Lawlan' (1–3).[17] It is clear from Burchet's and Hamilton's accounts that Ramsay enjoyed happy personal fame; indeed, Hamilton would 'create / Thee upo' sight the Laureat / Of this our age' (26–8). While Hamilton asserts that Ramsay is superior to all moderns, Ramsay's response indicates the poetic credo to which he adheres:

> The chiels of London, Cam, and Ox,
> Ha'e raised up great poetick stocks
> Of Rapes, of Buckets, Sarks and Locks,
>   While we neglect
> To shaw their betters. This provokes
>   Me to reflect
>
> On the lear'd days of Gawn Dunkell,
> Our country then a tale cou'd tell,
> Europe had nane mair snack and snell
>   At verse or prose,
> Our kings were poets too themsell,
>   Bauld and jocose. (49–60)[18]

While alluding to the productivity of Pope and Dryden, Ramsay opines that Scots must look to history to find an 'authentic' poetic self. That identity is to be found in 'Gawn Dunkell' or Gavin Douglas, Bishop of Dunkeld, poet and translator of Virgil's *Aeneid* whose name Ramsay chose as pseudonym (after abandoning the Augustan English moniker of 'Isaac Bickerstaff') in his membership of the Easy Club.[19]

While Ramsay finds nationalistic and literary pride in Douglas, he also eulogises Scotland's past and significantly – particularly for a Jacobite reading of Ramsay's corpus – his ideal Scotland is pre-1603. Furthermore, Douglas was the first thinker to extol the poetic possibilities of the Scots vernacular, *Scottis*. To Douglas and his followers, it was a language of range and sophistication while, in his 'Proloug' to his *Aeneis*, according to F. W. Freeman, Douglas 'purposes to give Scottis the status of other heroic languages'.[20]

Ramsay's implicit comparison of himself to Douglas – in both epistle and Club pseudonym – demonstrates that Douglas was enjoying new regard in early eighteenth-century Scotland. His *Aeneis* had recently been reprinted by Ramsay's editor, Thomas Ruddiman, himself a Latinist, keen to brand certain Scottish works, both ancient and modern, as, according to Freeman, 'classic; on a par with that of Chaucer and Gower', while positing vernacular Scots as 'equal to Greek and Latin'.[21] Ramsay's identification with Douglas is, therefore, philosophical and practical. United in their scholarly conception and utilisation of vernacular Scots, both are patronised by Ruddiman, who was, according to Pittock, one of many 'Jacobite notables'[22] who subscribed to Ramsay's 1721 edition. Through Ruddiman, pre- and post-Union literary Scotlands are linked.

While Ramsay's poetic admirers present their subject as a Scottish spokesman without peer, Fergusson and Burns receive contrasting treatment. Fergusson established his poetic persona in Edinburgh's *Weekly Magazine*, edited by another Ruddiman: Thomas's nephew, Walter. Patronised by the same publishing dynasty and part of a comparable literary, linguistic and political circle to that of Ramsay, Fergusson served a valuable apprenticeship in the magazine's poetry section. The first tribute to Fergusson appears in the *Magazine* dated 3 September 1772. 'To Mr. Robert Fergusson' by 'J.S.' begins in questioning tone:

> Is Allan risen frae the deid,
> Wha aft has tun'd the aiten reed,
> And by the muses was decreed
>   To grace the thistle?
> Na; Fergusson's cum in his stead
>   To blaw the whistle. (1–6)[23]

For 'J.S', Fergusson is the literary 'grace' of Scotland, of 'the thistle'. But he is appreciated in an existing context and according to an existing template, that of Ramsay: 'Is Allan risen frae the deid?' However, whereas Ramsay was commended in a British and even classical literary context, 'J.S.'s' terms are distinctly Scottish. Praised for his 'sonsy, canty strain' (8) and for his 'easy stile and plain' (9), Fergusson is placed in the vacuum left by Ramsay: just as Burns 'kindles at the flame' of his predecessors, Fergusson is to fill Ramsay's 'stead'. And in terms which foreshadow Grosart's portrayal of the 'pseudo–apostolic succession' of the Scots triumvirate, 'J.S.' sees Fergusson's literary place as having been 'decreed'. The literary independence experienced by Ramsay is compromised for his poetic offspring.

Fergusson's response is self-effacing, foreshadowing Burns's modest respect for his antecedents. Describing his muse in familiar terms, his 'Answer to Mr. J.S.'s Epistle' anticipates Burns's Preface to the Kilmarnock edition:

> But she maun e'en be glad to jook,
> And play *teet-bo* frae nook to nook,
> Or blush as gin she had the yook
>   Upon her skin,

> Whan *Ramsay* or whan *Pennicuik*
> Their lilts begin. (25–30)[24]

With a tone of knowledgeable embarrassment, Fergusson asserts that his muse can only 'blush' at comparisons with Ramsay and Clerk of Penicuik, while his *sprezzatura* demonstrates, as does Burns's, that he is capable of filling Ramsay's vacant seat. However, Fergusson does not, unlike Ramsay and Burns, present himself as – or more accurately, collaborate with constructions of himself as – an autodidact; his engagement with 'J.S.' is self-consciously literary. Utilising the Standard Habbie in decorous response to 'J.S.', Fergusson also revives the form of Ramsay's poetic correspondence with Hamilton. While apparently rejecting comparisons with his predecessor, Fergusson encourages them.

Burns, in turn, had two Scots predecessors from whom to learn, and it is clear that his admirers saw him as of their extraction. The little-known Scots poet, William Taylor, whose *Scots Poems* were printed in 1787, constructs Burns, who by this point had been lionised in Scotland's capital, as Fergusson's successor in 'On Reading Mr. Burns's Poems':

> Whan Scotia, clad in wae, bemoan'd
> 　Her *Fergusson* laid i' the yird;
> The God o' Verse, heegh, heegh enthron'd,
> 　Confess'd he was a hopefu' bird.
>
> Than this his Peers o' State address'd:
> 　"*Peers! wha shall wawk the Scottish lyre?*"
> Than his braw Peers, wi' grief oppress'd,
> 　Into the rows o' fate enquire:
>
> Whare written was, "Tho *Rob* be dead,
> 　"Scots need na greet, nor mak a bustle,
> "An Ayrshire Blade shall beet their need,
> 　"For *Robie Burns* shall blaw the whistle." (1–12)[25]

Just as Fergusson was urged to fill the 'chair of state' left vacant by Ramsay, so too is Burns implored to 'wawk the Scottish lyre' following Fergusson's death. Furthermore, as with portrayals by 'J.S.' and Grosart, Taylor depicts Burns's role as having been 'written' in the 'rows o' fate'. This familiar concept of 'apostolic' literary succession is, however, one from which Burns would recoil.

Although Burns went to considerable expense in erecting a physical monument to Fergusson's memory, he is also concerned with memorialising the epistolary relationships of both predecessors. Even if his endeavours to generate a verse exchange with Lapraik proved abortive, his self-conscious appropriation of the Standard Habbie form demonstrates a compulsion to follow the leads of Ramsay and Fergusson. In 'To William Simson', Burns makes this point:

> My senses wad be in a creel,
> Should I but dare a *hope* to speel,
> Wi' *Allan*, or wi' *Gilbertfield*,
>   The braes o' fame;
> Or *Ferguson*, the writer-chiel,
>   A deathless name. (K 59, I, 93, 13–18)

Although diffidently hoping for comparable fame, Burns's mention of Ramsay and Hamilton demonstrates a wish to emulate their literary relationship. Having said this, Burns also emphasises difference from his ancestors:

> *Ramsay* an' famous *Ferguson*
> Gied *Forth* an' *Tay* a lift aboon;
> *Yarrow* an' *Tweed*, to monie a tune,
>   Owre Scotland rings,
> While *Irwin, Lugar, Aire* an' *Doon*,
>   Naebody sings. (43–8)

As with Fergusson, Burns will admire but not imitate, giving poetic expression to the convictions of his Preface: he will 'kindle at their flame'. Burns's uniqueness is geographical: while his predecessors 'sang' of the Forth, Tay, Yarrow and Tweed, Burns bemoans the fact that 'Naebody sings' of Ayrshire's rivers. This distinction is illustrative of the development of the literary personae of the three eighteenth-century Scots vernacular 'bards'. Ramsay is poetic spokesman for Scotland and perhaps humankind, while Fergusson is regarded, by *Weekly Magazine* correspondent Frederick Guion, for his role as 'laureat' of Edinburgh although he is, of course, much more than this.[26] Burns, by contrast, presents himself as Ayrshire's poet, signalling a movement towards Scottish Romanticism. While all three poets do indeed address fellow 'Britons', Burns's pre-Wordsworthian concern is with the regional as well as the national; as Stafford argues, the work of Burns and Wordsworth was 'not "local" in the sense of having meaning only for those living in the areas where they were set, but represented a kind of art whose truthfulness was universally recognizable'.[27]

Burns's geographical point is not without basis: as badges of national identity, Scottish waters provide powerful imagery for Ramsay, Fergusson and Burns. However, as Burns confirms, each utilises the image for dissimilar poetic and political ends. Ramsay's 'Prospect of Plenty: A Poem on the North-Sea Fishery' is practical and political, presenting Scotland as an economically viable entity.[28] A plea to Scottish rulers to exploit the country's marine riches, 'The Prospect of Plenty' echoes the terms of William Drummond of Hawthornden's 'Forth Feasting', a poem which urges James VI to return to Scotland after the Union of Crowns, asking 'why should *Isis* only see Thee shine' (383), when Forth 'doth love Thee more' (386).[29]

While Drummond admits that English waters 'hath more Wealth in store'
(385), Ramsay emphasises Scotland's unlimited resources:

> Thalia anes again in Blythesome Lays;
> In Lays immortal chant the NORTH-SEA's Praise.
> Tent how the CALEDONIANS lang supine,
> Begin, mair wise, to open baith their een.
> And, as they ought, t'employ that Store which Heaven,
> In sic Abundance to their Hands has given. (1–6)

Scotland's waters are given classical and Christian endorsement. Indeed,
Ramsay implies that it is blasphemous that the North Sea remains
untapped; Caledonians have been, he asserts, too 'lang supine'. If the
North Sea is cultivated, attendant financial potency will allow Scots to
stand proudly:

> Nae Nation in the Warld can parallel
> The plenteous Product of this happy Isle;
> But Past'ral Heights, and sweet prolific Plains,
> That can at Will commant the saftest Strains.
> Stand yont; for *Amphratite* claims our Sang,
> Wha round fair *Thule* drives her finny Thrang,
> O'er Shaws of Corral, and the Pearly Sands,
> To SCOTIA's smoothest Lochs and Chrystal Strands. (15–22)

Poets have, according to Ramsay, long been content to immortalise
Scotland's landscapes; Scottish waters also merit commemoration. Pastoral
poets are to stand aside; Amphratite, the wife of sea god Neptune, 'claims
our sang' as Ramsay's periphrastic, James Thomson-esque 'finny Thrang'
floats past coral and 'Pearly Sands'. Ramsay creates, with 'The Prospect
of Plenty', a new pastoral: one which does not rely on plains and oak trees
but rivers and seas. But this water pastoral is, like his more conventional
Scots pastorals, aligned with national pride. The exploitation of the North
Sea's resources will, Ramsay implies, encourage Scotland's self-sufficiency.
Fishers are to utilise 'artfu' Nets' (33) to harvest abundant pike, trout,
salmon, herring and ling: 'Thus may our FISHERY throu' a' the Year /
Be still imploy'd, t'increase the publick Gear' (39–40). In this poem, which is
aware of the latest developments in European politics but unafraid to utilise
Scots proverb, Ramsay is politically optimistic: he is the assured Scottish
literary spokesman. The North Sea is an economic opportunity; if properly
exploited, it could be Scotland's saviour.

Perhaps taking cue from Drummond and Ramsay, Fergusson's 'The
Rivers of Scotland: An Ode', set to music by John Collett, was as M. P.
McDiarmid asserts, 'fairly popular', having been reprinted throughout the
1770s in song collections.[30] Fergusson's piece classicises 'Fortha's' journey to the sea, and while Ramsay bemoans the fact that Scotland stands

back 'While a' the rest of *Europe* milk her mines' (51), Fergusson asserts that '*Caledon* to foreign foes / Should ne'er be known to bow' (97–8). For Fergusson, Scottish waters have political significance:

> Let England's sons extoll their gardens fair,
> Scotland may freely boast her gen'rous streams,
> Their soil more fertile and their milder air,
> Her fishes sporting in the solar beams,
> *Thames, Humber, Severn*, all must yield the bay
> To the pure streams of Forth, of Tweed, and Tay. (120–5)

Fergusson's narrator, like Ramsay's, speaks with supreme national confidence. He allows that England has strengths, but all must 'yield the bay' to Scotland's might.

Fergusson also celebrates Scotland's marine wares. In 'Caller Oysters',[31] a catalyst for Burns's gastronomic nationalism in 'To a Haggis' and 'Scotch Drink', Fergusson echoes the preoccupations of 'The Prospect of Plenty'. Both Ramsay and Fergusson reject representations of Scotland as poverty stricken; both emphasise its significant individual wealth. 'Caller Oysters' begins with the assertion that no water can 'reward the fishers trouble' and that 'There's nane sae spacious and sae noble' as 'Firth o' *Forth*' (3, 5–6). Chief of its treats, however, is the oyster, a 'rare cathartick' (26): 'Whether you hae the head or heart-ake, / It ay prevails' (29–30). That Burns's poems of culinary patriotism find basis in these Fergussonian originals demonstrates their political import. Scotland is, in 'The Prospect of Plenty', 'The Rivers of Scotland' and 'Caller Oysters', a wealthy land of abundance which is no poor relation of England.

Burns takes this inheritance and, as he asserts in his epistle to Simson, adapts it to his own regional ends. In 'The Banks and Braes o' Bonny Doon', 'Flow Gently, Sweet Afton', 'Behind yon Hills where Lugar Flows' and 'The Banks of Nith', Burns commemorates the landscapes of Ayrshire and later, Dumfriesshire. While Ramsay's water pastoral conveys practical descriptions of fishing opportunities, Fergusson's nationalistic pride is in Scottish waters' beauty and plenty. Burns's rivers are, by contrast, often the setting for human romance: Doon is the backdrop to heartbreak; Afton provides the landscape for 'Mary's' slumbers; while Lugar offers refuge to the speaker and his 'Nanie'. 'The Banks of Nith' is, however, closer in substance to the river poetry of Burns's predecessors. Just as Ramsay and Fergusson depicted Scottish rivers as equalling, if not surpassing, those of its neighbour, so too does Burns extol the beauties of the Nith:

> The Thames flows proudly to the sea,
> Where royal cities stately stand;
> But sweeter flows the Nith, to me,
> Where Cummins ance had high command:

> When shall I see that honor'd Land,
> That winding stream I love so dear! (K 229, I, 424, 1–6)

Exceeding the 'stately' beauties of the Thames, the 'Nith' is not only 'sweeter': it is 'honor'd' and 'loved'. Just as Fergusson emphasised the nobility of Scottish waters, Burns highlights the Nith's 'fruitfulness': it is a source of political and aesthetic pride.

With his utilisation of the river image, previously exploited by Ramsay and Fergusson, Burns reveals the eighteenth-century Scots vernacular tradition's continuity and evolution as he moves towards a Scottish Romanticism. But Ramsay, Fergusson and Burns are united in their portrayal of Scotland as a financially viable entity; they are cohesive in their rejection of a depiction of Scotland as a poor, unworthy partner in Union. The Scotland of the vernacular 'revivalists' is abundant and vigorous; it is no artificial construction illustrating a nostalgic yearning for a lost time of political potency.

While river imagery allows Ramsay, Fergusson and Burns to make specific points about the potential future of their own Scotlands, imagery of gold allows them to make arguments about its past. Ramsay's first published poem, 'A Poem to the memory of the famous Archbald Pitcairn, M.D. By a Member of the Easy Club', elegises the Scots Humanist, Latinist and Jacobite icon, Archibald Pitcairne, by dramatising his Virgilian journey to the afterlife, while the physician and author is characterised as a 'Noble *Scot* of Antient Race' (5), whose death demonstrates his 'Disdaining further stay, / 'Mongst *English* slaves' (12–13).[32] As Pitcairne meets those who 'sold' Scotland in 1707's Union of Parliaments, Ramsay utilises the multilayered image of gold:

> There he Observ'd a Pool of Boyling Gold,
> On which did float, those who their Country Sold.
> They Howl'd and Yell'd, and often Curs'd the Gods,
> Who had not made them Vipers, Asps, or Toads,
> Here he the Faces of some Traitours knew,
> Who at the U— did their hands embrew,
> In the heart Blood of Antient Caledon,
> Which Mortal wound makes her dear Children Groan,
> They're so well known, it's vain their Names to tell,
> But be assur'd they're firmly Chain'd in Hell. (33–42)

Ramsay's narrator assures his listeners that justice, and arguably Jacobite justice, prevails in hell: those 'traitours' 'who their Country Sold' are tortured by the very gold they received for facilitating Union.

Fergusson also utilises gold imagery in a poem which revives dead figures of Scottish history. 'The Ghaists: A Kirkyard Eclogue' revitalises George Herriott and George Watson in order to challenge the Mortmain Bill, which proposed that charitable monies in Britain be pooled at an interest rate of 3 per cent.[33] Herriott and Watson are apposite opposers: both had bequeathed funds to run hospital schools in Edinburgh; schools which, had the Mortmain Bill become law, would have been at risk of closure. Herriott – aptly chosen, too, as James V's goldsmith – remembers Scotland's golden past in Fergusson's first concatenated image:

> Ah, CALEDON! the land I yence held dear,
> Sair mane mak I for thy destruction near;
> And thou, EDINA! anes my dear abode,
> Whan royal JAMIE sway'd the sovereign rod,
> In thae blest days, weel did I think bestow'd,
> To blaw thy poortith by wi' heaps o' gowd;
> To mak thee sonsy seem wi' mony a gift,
> And gar thy stately turrets speel the lift; (28–35)

Here, 'gowd' is a positive image, which encapsulates the peaceful, benevolent reign of the Stuart ruler. Herriott's memory of 'thae blest days' is in direct contrast to the 'Black' day when 'to England's ground / Scotland was eikit by the UNION's bond' (57–8). Positive connotations of gold are lost when the image is reprised in Herriott's depiction of 1770s Scotland:

> There's einow on the earth a set o' men,
> Wha, if they get their private pouches lin'd,
> Gie nae a winnelstrae for a' mankind;
> They'll sell their country, flae their conscience bare,
> To gar the weigh-bauk turn a single hair.
> The government need only bait the line
> Wi' the prevailing flee, the gowden coin,
> Then our executors, and wise trustees,
> Will sell them fishes in forbidden seas,
> Upo' their dwining country girn in sport,
> Laugh in their sleeve, and get a place at court. (104–14)

Gold, as indicative of an arguably Jacobite golden age, is benevolent and good. Gold 'einow' is mere lucre; the 'prevailing flee' which allows 'a set o' men' to 'sell their country' as they line their 'private pouches' and gain a stake in its future. Fergusson's gold image is multifaceted: symbolising the wrongs committed in Scotland at the Union, as in Ramsay's work, Fergusson's gold also represents Scotland's golden age of rightful monarchy.

Gold imagery reaches political climax in Burns's work. 'Such a parcel of rogues in a nation', according to Thomas Crawford, 'shows Burns working in the spirit of his source material to produce an imaginative reconstruction of the patriot's feelings in 1707'.[34] This 'source material' surely includes the work of Ramsay and Fergusson, as Burns denounces the 'parcel o' rogues'

(7) responsible for the loss of 'Scotish fame' (1). According to Burns's narrator, 'English gold has been our bane' (15), while historical figures are again revivified to remind Scotland of its 'ancient glory' (2):

> O would, or I had seen the day
>> That treason thus could sell us,
> My auld grey head had lain in clay,
>> Wi' BRUCE and loyal WALLACE!
> But pith and power, till my last hour,
>> I'll mak this declaration;
> We're bought and sold for English gold,
>> Such a parcel of rogues in a nation! (17–24)

Just as Ramsay communicates Pitcairne's afterlife conversations with Bruce and Wallace, and as Fergusson reanimates Herriott and Watson, here Burns resurrects Bruce and Wallace to demonstrate Scotland's descent from former glory. In all three poets' work, gold represents both past contentment and present dissatisfaction; it is a concatenative symbol which looks simultaneously backwards and forwards in time, allowing Ramsay, Fergusson and Burns to analyse the present using the examples of the past.

Ramsay opened a literary passageway through which Fergusson and Burns would pass, while his reanimation of older Scottish verse forms and linguistic traditions allowed Fergusson and Burns to capitalise on his cultural enterprise. An exploration of all three poets' responses to constructions of their personae by other artists illustrates something of their creative methodology. However, Fergusson's and Burns's self-conscious response to comparisons with their respective predecessors demonstrates Ramsay's role as cultural initiator, while their shared use of specific images and literary devices is evidence of a cultural and literary dialogue which was immensely influential. Although the pigeonholing of Scottish vernacular literature's 'triumvirate' has, at times, obscured their individual contributions, their relationship allowed them to harvest from the past, capitalise on the present and project the future. If, for Carol McGuirk, 'Burns follows Fergusson in often dramatising Scotland as a heated argument between "then" and "now"', he also follows Ramsay.[35] While Ramsay reclaimed a Scots vernacular golden age, he and Fergusson contributed to it, stoking the 'flame' at which Burns would 'kindle'. Burns is more than the sum of his influences. Although the examples of Ramsay and Fergusson would prompt Burns to present himself, in 'To W. Simson, Ochiltree', as the bard of 'Coila's haughs an' woods' (67), his striving to 'gar our streams an' burnies shine / Up wi' the best' (53–4) allowed him to achieve an unrivalled regionality and yet universality. If Burns's narrator asserts that, in 'Love and Liberty', he 'never drank the Muses' Stank, / Castalia's burn an' a' that', Ramsay's and Fergusson's poetic tributaries allowed his literary 'stream' to 'richly ream' (K 84, I, 206, 216–18).

Notes

1. A. B. Grosart, *Robert Fergusson* (Edinburgh: Oliphant, Anderson and Ferrier, 1898), pp. 32–3.

2. Susan Manning, 'Robert Fergusson and eighteenth-century poetry', in Robert Crawford (ed.), *'Heaven-Taught Fergusson': Robert Burns's Favourite Scottish Poet* (East Linton: Tuckwell, 2003), pp. 87–112, 91.

3. Robert Burns, 'On Fergusson' (K 143, I, 323, 1–2); 'To W. S****n, Ochiltree' (K 59, I, 94, 21–2); 'On Fergusson II' (K 144, I, 323, 6).

4. Robert Burns, To John Moore, 2 August 1787, in Robert Burns, *The Letters of Robert Burns*, ed. J. De Lancey Ferguson and G. Ross Roy, 2nd edn, 2 vols (Oxford: Clarendon Press, 1985), vol. I, p. 143.

5. Robert Crawford, 'Introduction', in Crawford (ed.), *'Heaven-Taught Fergusson'*, pp. 1–18, 1.

6. Robert Burns, *Poems, Chiefly in the Scottish Dialect* (Kilmarnock, 1786), pp. iv–v.

7. Fiona Stafford, 'Scottish poetry and regional literary expression', in John Richetti (ed.), *The Cambridge History of English Literature 1660–1780* (Cambridge: Cambridge University Press), pp. 340–62, 342.

8. See Corey Andrews, *Literary Nationalism in Eighteenth-Century Scottish Club Poetry* (Lewiston, NY: Edwin Mellen Press, 2004); and Robert Crawford, 'Robert Fergusson's Robert Burns', in Robert Crawford (ed.), *Robert Burns and Cultural Authority* (Edinburgh: Edinburgh University Press, 1997), pp. 1–23.

9. Allan Ramsay, *The Works of Allan Ramsay*, ed. Burns Martin and John W. Oliver, 2 vols (Edinburgh: Blackwood, 1951–7), vol. I, pp. 212–17.

10. Murray Pittock, *Scottish and Irish Romanticism* (Oxford: Oxford University Press, 2008), p. 32.

11. Robert Burns to George Thomson, September 1793, in Burns, *Letters*, vol. II, p. 242.

12. Robert Fergusson, *Poems of Robert Fergusson*, ed. M. P. McDiarmid, 2 vols (Edinburgh: Blackwood, 1954–6), vol. II, pp. 52–5.

13. Fergusson, *Poems*, vol. II, pp. 160–7.

14. Ibid., pp. 109–20.

15. Pittock, *Scottish and Irish Romanticism*, p. 32.

16. See Allan Ramsay, *Poems* (Edinburgh, 1720), pp. iii–viii.

17. Ramsay, *Works*, vol. I, pp. 115–18.

18. Ibid., pp. 118–21.

19. See Stafford, 'Scottish poetry and regional literary expression', pp. 344–5; and Murray G. H. Pittock, *Poetry and Jacobite Politics in Eighteenth-Century Britain and Ireland* (1994; rpt. Cambridge: Cambridge University Press, 2006), pp. 154–5.

20. F. W. Freeman, *Robert Fergusson and the Scots Humanist Compromise* (Aberdeen: Aberdeen University Press, 1986), p. 2.

21. Ibid., p. 4.

22. Pittock, *Scottish and Irish Romanticism*, p. 48.

23. Fergusson, *Poems*, vol. II, pp. 69–71.

24. Ibid., pp. 71–4.

25. William Taylor, *Scots Poems by William Taylor* (Edinburgh, 1787), pp. 30–1.

26. Frederick Guion, 'The Muses Choice', *Weekly Magazine*, 22 October 1772.

27. Fiona Stafford, *Local Attachments: The Province of Poetry* (Oxford: Oxford University Press, 2010), p. 21.
28. Ramsay, *Works*, vol. I, pp. 157–67.
29. L. E. Kastner (ed.), *The Political Works of William Drummond of Hawthornden*, 2 vols (Edinburgh: Blackwood, 1913), vol. I, pp. 140–53.
30. Fergusson, *Poems*, vol. II, pp. 40–6, 258.
31. Ibid., pp. 66–9.
32. F. W. Freeman and Alexander Law, 'Allan Ramsay's first published poem: the Poem to the Memory of Dr Archibald Pitcairne', in *The Bibliotheck*, 9.7, 1979, pp. 153–60.
33. Fergusson, *Poems*, vol. II, pp. 141–5.
34. K 375, II, 643–4; Thomas Crawford, *Burns: A Study of the Poems and Songs* (Stanford: Stanford University Press, 1960), p. 239.
35. Carol McGuirk, '"The rhyming trade": Fergusson, Burns, and the marketplace', in Crawford (ed.), *'Heaven-Taught Fergusson'*, pp. 135–60, 144.

CHAPTER 4

Robert Burns's Scots Poetry Contemporaries

Gerard Carruthers

In 'Poor Mailie's Elegy', probably Robert Burns's first poem in the Habbie Simson stanza and written in fully fledged form in 1784, the narrator hails 'a' ye *Bards* on Bonie DOON' (K 25, I, 36, 43), the river which flows through a long tract of scenic Ayrshire including Burns's own birthplace of Alloway.[1] From 1784 to 1786 Burns produces a series of verse epistles to his fellow Ayrshire poets, John Lapraik, David Sillar and William Simpson. On the face of it, then, there would seem to be a ready-made poetic community in the geographical area around him within which Burns is locating himself. As is sometimes the case with Burns, however, it might be suggested that it is his fictional projection, to some extent, that creates a later reality.

John Lapraik (1727–1807) becomes popularly known at some undetermined point as 'the bard of Muirkirk', most widely, however, after Burns's first flush of published success. Muirkirk is a place near Cumnock, over twenty miles from Alloway, and Lapraik is the recipient of three poetic epistles from Burns. It has sometimes been assumed that Lapraik co-operated with Burns in a sequence of poetic exchange prior to the publication of the latter, though curiously none of the former's verse renderings for Burns from that time survive (if, indeed, these ever existed). Weighing against the existence of such early Lapraik poetic epistles to Burns, perhaps, is the fact that the latter in his second and third epistles speaks merely of 'letters' received in response to his first and second verse epistles; and, much more tellingly, the fact that in Lapraik's collected works, *Poems on Several Occasions* (1788), only one verse epistle to Burns appears, clearly post-dating Burns's published success. Lapraik's poetry, generally, is in a much lighter Scots idiom than that of Burns. His most substantial work is a piece in the Habbie Simson stanza on the failure of the Ayr bank in 1773 (perhaps written around that time, though the dating is highly uncertain) which ruined him financially and which Burns may not have known before the publication of the piece in Lapraik's *Poems* of 1788. Burns's own first encounter with this stanza form occurs around 1774 or 1775 when he first reads the works of Robert Fergusson. What specifically inspired Burns to write his first 'Epistle to J. L*****k, An Old Scotch Bard' in that stanza-form on 1 April 1785 was Lapraik's song, 'When I upon thy bosom lean', a standard-English folk song written by Lapraik for his wife, whom he

depicts with some convincing passion as the crucial support through a life
that was, clearly, not without its troubles. Burns had heard the song at
a country 'rockin'' (K 57, I, 85, 7) and admired it, but a second version,
superior in scansion and in Scots, was to appear in James Johnson's *Scots
Musical Museum*, most likely altered for the better by Burns.

David Sillar (1760–1830), hailing like Lapraik from Irvine, publishes
his collected verse in the wake of the success of Burns's first book, *Poems,
Chiefly in the Scottish Dialect* of 1786. *Poems, by David Sillar* (1789) is a
volume spotlighting sometimes a prudish, contemporary bourgeois sensibility (as one of its texts in the Habbie stanza warns of the dangers of alcohol, especially to the morals of young men and women) and, at other points,
a rather voyeuristic interest in femininity (across these seemingly different
moods one might argue for a unifying prurience, implicit on the one hand
and explicit on the other). Sillar was not much of a poet, either in quality
or quantity, and Burns berates him for laziness, jokingly, but probably with
an underlying serious edge, in the second of his two epistles to Sillar. What
was it Burns valued of Sillar's creativity? Author of some surviving verse
commending to women consideration of the size of a man's penis and a
quantity of other bawdry seemingly no longer extant, Sillar may well have
been Burns's 'partner in crime' in exchanging appreciation and perhaps also
composition of salacious material during 1785.[2] A propos the argument I am
advancing here, Burns, looking for fellow-poets around him in a not very
promising field, had perhaps to take whomsoever he could find. There was,
at least, one (and probably only one) verse epistle by Sillar to Burns written,
as with the case of Lapraik, by the time Burns was a successful poet. Sillar's
verse epistle refers to Burns's published fame by which time Burns had
no need to reply (which he did not). Having so consummately achieved a
reading community with his fully subscribed and sold-out Kilmarnock edition of 1786, it might be suggested, his fellow Ayrshire 'bards' had largely
outlived their usefulness.[3]

The least seemingly impressive of the three fellow poets immortalised
by Burns's verse epistles is William Simpson of Ochiltree (1758–1815).
Simpson left behind a manuscript volume of a couple of dozen poems, but
was never properly published in his lifetime. His most significant poetic
intervention, if the following version of the story is true, was when he
signed one of his texts 'Robert Burns' and sent this to Thomas Walker (d.
c.1812) who had previously posted to Burns his 'Epistle from a Tailor to
Robert Burns'. Half admiring of, and half appalled by, the Alloway poet,
Walker in his poem warned that Burns risked going to hell for treating
Presbyterianism with such impiety. Receiving no response from Burns,
Walker complained long and loud about this, with the result that Simpson
(possibly with the connivance of Burns) wrote his impersonating text. It
begins, 'What ails ye now, ye lousie bitch, / To thresh my back at sic a
pitch' (K 119b, I, 278, 1–2) and goes on to shovel on even more impiety

against the kirk as well as boasting of its supposed author's sexual prowess. Bizarrely, Walker was not offended when he viewed the text but rather delighted at last to have been noticed, rushing to meet his acquaintance, William Simpson, to show him what 'Burns' had sent him. This poem's caricaturing of some of Burns's key themes and attitudes played a part in the poet's over-determined reputation for scurrility for its own sake, and was included in some early editions of Burns until Robert Cromek in 1810 became the first of a line of critics to view it as not being a text by Burns.[4]

Taken in the round, what do these three key Burns-referenced Ayrshire contemporaries tell us about Burns's local Scots poetry 'scene' of the mid-1780s? Generally, that there was not much of any such thing, and that the conclusion sometimes reached *a propos* the verse epistles to Lapraik, Sillar and Simpson that Burns was readily slotting himself into a vibrant Ayrshire Scots poetry writing community is far from the exact truth. We might note, of course, the realisation of Lapraik and Sillar that there was a strong market possibility for their work as that of Ayrshire 'bards', following the overwhelming success from 1786 of Burns's Kilmarnock edition (much of their work probably tidied and even specially written for their post-Burns volumes). More directly telling, the poor return of probably only two verse epistles to Burns, and these after his poetry was beginning to operate well beyond the local Ayrshire context, shows him coming nowhere close to achieving (as he probably desired, at least in a dreaming sense) an emulation of the verse epistle exchanges that his great Scots poetry predecessor, Allan Ramsay, had enjoyed with individuals of some writing skill. Notable here would be Ramsay's poetic correspondence with William Hamilton of Gilbertfield and the English poet, William Somerville, where Ramsay had marked out strong cultural space for himself as a Scots writer with the help of these other poets. I am suggesting, then, that the idea of the 'Bards on Bonie Doon' was largely a creative fantasy (not unhelpful, however, even in its one-sidedness) when Burns conceived it in 1784, and remained so until his own published success largely spawned a shoal of imitators who did not do much for the reputation of poetry in Scots.[5] The long reach and concentrated effect of the Burns imitative phenomenon is well described by Colin Affleck:

> following the publication and success of his *Poems, Chiefly in the Scottish Dialect* . . . many Scottish versifiers paid tribute to the poet and his book – or perhaps hoped for similar success by association – by publishing books with exactly the same title. These included David Morison (1790), David Crawford (1798), the Reverend James Nichol (1805), Thomas Donaldson, "weaver at Glasgow" (1809), Peter Forbes, "merchant of Dalkieth" (1812), David Anderson, "mechanic" (1826), etc. etc.[6]

To these generally derivative authors must be added Lapraik and Sillar, with Simpson rather exempt (ironically enough since he actually impersonates Burns). There is a bigger irony in the title of James Paterson's, *The*

Contemporaries of Burns, and more recent poets of Ayrshire with Selections from their Writings (1840), given the tenor of its contents. Paterson's very useful book provides much information, including some of that drawn upon above, which serves to highlight that Burns actually had no Ayrshire contemporaries to any substantial degree. To a great extent, the idea of the late eighteenth-century Ayrshire poet writing in Scots is created by Burns, in a sense and obviously enough in relation to himself, and simultaneously with regard to those other 'bards' to whom he writes verse epistles, though none of them have anything like a cogent body of work until galvanised to frame what they have as such for publication purposes post-1786.

Paterson's *The Contemporaries of Burns*, as well as dealing with those Ayrshire poets personally addressed by Burns in his verse epistles, also includes Gavin Turnbull (1758–1801), who completes the incestuous post-publication poetic effect engendered by Burns in writing in the wake of the Kilmarnock edition a verse epistle of his own to David Sillar (much lighter in Scots than Burns's own). In a familiar pattern, when Burns and Turnbull's paths crossed in Dumfries from 1793, the former admired, at least, the latter's songwriting, sending three of these to his songeditor, Thomson (though all three texts, it might be said, are rather insipid English texts). Paterson includes, too, the aforementioned, semi-antagonistic Thomas Walker and the completely hostile Alexander Tait (no dates) of Tarbolton, sometime town Baillie, tailor and possibly also, at one point, a pedlar. Tait's words comprise the chief documentary evidence of Burns and Sillar's profane poetic partnership, as he addresses the latter:

> Search Scotland all around by Lorn,
> Next round by Leith and Abercorn,
> Through a' Ayrshire, by the Sorn,
>   Tak merry turns,
> There's nane can soun the *bawdy* horn
>   Like you and Burns.[7]

Tait writes several scurrilous satirical pieces on Burns, helping to initiate a line of anti-Burnsian poetry. Most of the prominent texts in the anti-Burnsian mode, interestingly, are in English. The Paisley poet, James Maxwell (1720–1800) produces his book, *Animadversions on Some Poets and Poetasters of the Present Age Especially R—T B—S, and J—N L—K* (1788) and in his attempt to obtain the moral high ground over the irreligious Burns and Lapraik writes in English couplets, not without some elegance.[8] This English language, Presbyterian tradition with an innate hostility to the Scots language continues, it might be suggested, with some vigour in Scotland down to the Reverend William Peebles's *Burnomania: The Celebrity of Robert Burns considered in a discourse addressed to all real Christians of every denomination*, published in Edinburgh in 1811, which finds not only the work of Burns but also his posthumous celebration in

Burns Clubs to be hugely distasteful.[9] Sceptical of Burns in a different way was the Edinburgh printer, James Macaulay (about whom very little is known), who published his 'Rhyming Epistle to Mr. R-B-, Ayrshire' in the *Edinburgh Evening Courant* for 23 June 1787. This was not ideologically hostile to Burns but did (quite rightly) misdoubt the genesis of Burns's poetic sensibility in untutored, natural inspiration:

> The prints—newspapers an' reviews,
> Frae time to time may aft you rouse,
> An' say you're *Heaven-taught*—your views
> > Are clear an' fair,
> An' a' your ain, gi'en by THE MUSE
> > O'er the Banks o' Ayr.
>
> But, waesuck, that'll no gae down
> Wi' ilka chiel about this town
> That struts in black, an' eke a gown;
> > Na, na, they canna
> Believe that poets fa' aroun'
> > Like flakes o' manna![10]

This Scots language/Habbie Simson stanza text demonstrates the home of Ramsay and Fergusson writing back to Burns with rightful disbelief. True influence and tradition cannot be denied in Edinburgh, at any rate, even if it can in credulous Ayrshire.

Taken together and on the whole, Burns's admirers and detractors in Scots poetry during his lifetime and in the couple of decades that follow make for a not very distinguished corpus of work in artistic terms. His true Ayrshire artistic contemporaries, where he finds positive fruitfulness for himself, are not poets as such but rather songwriters, as in the case of Jeanie Glover (1758–*c*.1801). Glover was author of 'O'er the Moor Amang the Heather', which Burns sent Johnson for inclusion in the *Scots Musical Museum*. Likewise, there is Isobel Pagan (*c*.1740–1821) probably the author of an even more famous song, 'Ca' the Yowes to the Knowes', again sent by Burns to the *Museum* and later also revised by the poet for his other great songeditor, George Thomson. A third woman writer, from the southwest although Dumfriesshire originally, is Janet Little (1759–1813), styled 'The Scottish Milkmaid'. Little is an infatuated follower of Burns, acting as something akin to his stalker, making a nuisance of herself in her attempts to secure Burns's patronage as well as a face-to-face meeting. As Little in her 'Epistle to Mr Robert Burns' hails the messianic primitivism of Burns, she produces an effect little more palatable than the severest anti-Burnsian poetry of the period:

> Did Addison or Pope but hear,
> Or Sam, that critic most severe,

A ploughboy sing with throat sae clear,
They in a rage
Their words would a' in pieces tear
And curse your page.[11]

The Poetical Works of Janet Little (1792) made its author the tidy sum of fifty pounds, as she enjoyed for a time a little popularity and fame – ironically enough, considerably in advance of the Burns-approved Lapraik, Sillar or Turnbull.[12] Including Little in his 1840 volume, James Paterson confirms the virulence of the idea of verse epistles routinely whizzing between the poets of Ayrshire. At the same time, he approaches revelation of the actual truth – of the insubstantiality – of the situation with which he is dealing. Paterson writes:

> Janet is said to have carried on a correspondence with a Jean Murray, another rustic Poetess, who resided at a place near Mauchline, called the Muir. This appears to have been subsequent to the publication of her poems, as none of their epistles appear in the volume. Jean Murray was a person of little note. It is remembered about Loudon, that, a short time previous to her death, Janet was visited by the daughter of Burns, the 'image' of his 'bonnie Betty'.[13]

Poetic exchange between writers in Ayrshire was, while clearly not unknown, more imagined than real and, essentially, a post-Burnsian phenomenon. A larger exchange, not completely one way either, went on between Burns and his great Scots poetry predecessors, Allan Ramsay and Robert Fergusson. For, as well as deriving models, themes and attitudes from Ramsay and Fergusson, Burns gave back something to both in return. He renewed and widened the appeal of the two as the eighteenth century drew to a close and set in train a process by which during the nineteenth and twentieth centuries a holy trinity in Scots poetry of 'Ramsay, Fergusson and Burns' would be established. However, this latter aspect, as I shall argue, was not an entirely healthy development. As well as name-checking Robert Fergusson in his writings, Burns's memorialising of the Edinburgh poet went further as he commissioned the erection of a headstone at Fergusson's unmarked grave in the Canongate kirkyard. Fergusson's readership during his lifetime had been by no means confined to Edinburgh, but had been largely dependent on the readership of the Edinburgh periodical, the *Weekly Magazine,* edited by Walter Ruddiman. Fergusson's partially collected works saw the light of day in 1773 with reprints through the later 1770s and early 1780s. Following 1786, however, editions of Fergusson accelerate noticeably in frequency, a situation that pertains into the early 1800s. Prior to the 1780s, Allan Ramsay was probably better known than Fergusson, though primarily as a songwriter, including those songs which featured in his popular pastoral drama, *The Gentle Shepherd* (1725). It was largely as a result of Burns's late 1780s success, both in his textual homage to his two predecessors and his reinvigoration of Scots poetry generally, that a contest conducted via newly composed poetry was mounted to decide on the primacy of Ramsay and Fergusson relative to one another. This took place in public in the Pantheon, at Edinburgh, on Thursday, 14 April, 1791, with the brief, 'Whether have the exertions of Allan Ramsay or Robert Fergusson done more honour to Scotch poetry?'[14] The competition was won by Alexander Wilson (1766–1813) with his 'The Laurel Disputed' (1791), in which he decided that, good though Ramsay was, Fergusson was superior. The reasons given in the poem for this conclusion are not all that important for our discussion here. More interesting is Wilson's account of the essence of Scots poetry in the eighteenth century, from Ramsay to Burns. Wilson identified an honest realism based on country life, especially, which had brought about a refreshed eighteenth-century poetry in Scots. Part of this picture in Wilson's poem is an anti-classicism, extending even towards an anti-intellectualism:

> Learn'd fouk, that lang in colleges an' schools,
> Hae sooket learning to the vera hools,
> An' think that naething charms the heart sae weel's
> Lang cracks o' gods, Greeks, Paradise, and deils;
> Their pows are cram't sae fu' o' lear an' art,
> Plain simple nature canna reach their heart;
> But whare's the rustic that can, readin', see
> Sweet Peggy skiffin' ow'r the dewy lee;
> Or, wishfu' stealing up the sunny howe
> To gaze on Pate, laid sleeping on the knowe;
> Or hear how Bauldy ventur'd to the deil,
> How thrawn auld carlines skelpit him afiel',
> How Jude wi's hawk met Satan i' the moss,
> How Skin-flint grain't his pocks o' goud to loss;
> How bloody snouts an' bloody beards war gi'en
> To smith's and clowns at "Christ's kirk on the Green";
> How twa daft herds, wi' little sense or havings,
> Din'd by the road, on honest Hawkie's leavings;
> How Hab maist brak the priest's back wi' a rung,
> How deathless Addie died, an' how he sung;
> Whae'er can thae (o' mae I needna speak)
> Read tenty ow'r, at his ain ingle-cheek;
> An' no fin' something glowan thro' his blood,
> That gars his een glowr thro' a siller flood;
> May close the beuk, poor coof! and lift his spoon[15]

Irony is replete in the context of such characterisation of Scots poetry. Fergusson, so venerated by Wilson, is a highly classical poet, which we see both in his range of cultural reference and in his pastoral modes, among

other aspects. Fergusson continues from Ramsay as a tradition-bearer of the
ideological assumptions of Scoto-Latinity or Scottish humanism, generated
in the early eighteenth century in the cultural circles of writers, editors
and publishers such as Archibald Pitcairne, Thomas Ruddiman (uncle of
Fergusson's patron, Walter) and James Watson. The Jacobite, anti-union-
ist, aristocratic outlook of such men opposed the Scottish Whig (assumed
to include Calvinist and Unionist) cultural formations in early eighteenth-
century Scotland. Ruddiman et al. venerated the high literary traditions of
the past, including Scottish and English vernaculars as well as the canon of
ancient Latin literature. This predilection took on an ideological inflexion
as it was vaunted in the face of what was presumed, with justification up to a
point, to be the puritanical, anti-aesthetic credentials of the Scottish Whigs.
We see here, in fact, the political and cultural divides of the seventeenth-
century British Civil War perpetuated. A succinct example of this is provided by the fact that one of Allan Ramsay's Edinburgh bookshops featured
a sign with two heads, these being Ben Jonson and William Drummond
of Hawthornden. Thus a famous cross-border cultural connection is celebrated and an outlook identified, which is associated with allegiance to
the Stuart court (albeit that in actual fact this is not entirely historically
straightforward in the case of either of these writers). The Puritan-bashing
of Jonson and the refined, neo-classical sensibility of Drummond, taken
together, symbolise the range of pleasurable texts that a Cavalier, Stuart-
Loyal political mentality reserved for itself against a more plebeian, theo-
logically austere, dissenting, parliamentarian and, in particularly Scottish
terminology, Whiggish set of cultural allegiances. Latinity, or classicism
in general (including pastoral predilections), was part of the cultural self-
badging of the Cavalier grouping, as was enjoyment of a wide range of other
forms of expression extending to bawdry, drinking-songs, folk material and
work in Scots. Ramsay's *The Gentle Shepherd*, celebrating the Restoration of
1660, is a good case in point here of the new pastoralism in Scotland in the
early eighteenth century, bringing together pro-Stuart allegiance, folk song
and the Scots language.

Therefore, while Wilson's anti-classicism in the passage quoted above
retains pastoral and folk elements for his positive definition of eighteenth-
century Scots poetry (including the enjoyment of supernatural features that
The Gentle Shepherd essentially ridicules), it also witnesses a dilution, to
some extent a splitting, of an old compact of Scots language and classicism. This had been pioneered in creative terms for the eighteenth century
by Ramsay, drawing inspiration, especially, from the linguistically eclectic
publications sponsored by the Jacobite, Catholic publisher James Watson,
in his *Choice Collection of Comic and Serious Scottish Poems* (1707, 1709 and
1711) and the Episcopalian editor, Thomas Ruddiman, who published, for
instance, both the Latin productions of George Buchanan and the poems
of Ramsay. A key text for the inspiration of Wilson's anti-scholastic and

anti-materialist themes in the passage quoted is, clearly, Burns's 'Epistle to Davie' with its idea that happiness is not to be found 'in books' nor 'in Lear' (K 51, I, 67, 61). In terms of surface attitude, 'Epistle to Davie' and many other Burns texts license Wilson's subsequent anti-classicism, or what we might even call anti-historicism. Burns draws on the Scots humanist movement of the eighteenth century, employing its stanza forms (including, in the case of 'Epistle to Davie', a stanza form named after the poem *The Cherrie and the Slae*, a work of Catholic apologetics by Alexander Montgomerie, disinterred for the eighteenth century principally by Allan Ramsay). The use of this rather sophisticated verse vehicle in 'Epistle to Davie' does not sit entirely easily alongside the poem's voicing of the relegation of sophisticated cultural outlook. Across his oeuvre, Burns also utilises much of the thematic outlook of Scots Humanism, including Jacobitism, anti-Unionism and Puritan-bashing. It is a nice irony, then, that Burns (in a process we see beginning with Alexander Wilson) begins to make Scotland forget to a large extent the ideological and cultural contexts that had birthed eighteenth-century poetry in Scots.

One factor in promulgating such amnesia was Burns's own primitivist 'heaven-taught ploughman' persona, with which he played along and which he had himself essentially created in advance of Henry Mackenzie bestowing the actual epithet. Another was the long ideological flowing of the eighteenth into the nineteenth century, or the creation, especially following the revolutionary 1790s and the Napoleonic Wars, of a conservative, eventually imperial British identity. The effect of this was such that the anti-Unionism of Scots humanism, which Burns had certainly kept intact in several iterations, was dissolved through the nineteenth century, as he came to be viewed in many quarters as a loyal, 'British' poet.[16] Up to a point one might 'blame' Burns for helping foster Scotland's amnesia about the neoclassical, politically oppositional underpinnings of the Scots 'vernacular' revival as it increasingly became known during the nineteenth century (a description in itself that creates distance not only between Scots and English but also between Scots and all learned languages). It is the broad political national history of Britain, however, that largely drives this process.

Exemplary of the process I have just been generally identifying is David Irving's *Lives of the Scottish Poets* (1801). The first edition of Irving's work includes, principally, Ramsay, Alexander Ross (1699–1784), Alexander Geddes (1737–1802), Fergusson and Burns. A hugely popular book, reprinted through the first part of the nineteenth century, from the second edition onwards it completely excises the large-scale sections on Ross and Geddes, to leave us essentially the holy trinity of Scots poetry. What Irving's book witnesses is the situation where Ramsay, Fergusson and Burns can be safely read in their primitive 'vernacular' qualities, while Ross and Geddes are more awkward and best excised. This awkwardness is in one sense, perhaps, straightforward: neither of the two is as simply readable or as entertaining as Ramsay, Fergusson or Burns. However, at the same time, the situation is not quite so straightforward since, for readers of some classical knowledge, Ross and Geddes might be thought in other ways to be as exciting, sometimes, as the other three writers. Ross was the author of the longest published poem in Scots of the eighteenth century, his *Helenore, or the Fortunate Shepherdess* (1768), a marathon 4,154 liner. The poem was admired by Burns, even though its celebration of country life and custom, the pastoralism *in extenso* of *Helenore*, including a long and often serious narrative adventure, seems to be at odds with the new Scots poetry sensibility of Burns's own time, with its altogether couthier, occasion-centred accents and incidents. One might expect that the same diminishing popularity might also accrue for *The Gentle Shepherd* as for *Helenore*, but this does not happen. This is largely because Ramsay's text elicits a late eighteenth-century tradition of countryside performance, and its numerous folk songs are accessibly at the forefront of this local, theatrical reception and those things for which *The Gentle Shepherd* is most celebrated from the latter part of the eighteenth century onwards.

Alexander Geddes is, if anything, even more awkward for nineteenth century Scotland than Ross – and so, as we see in the later editions of Irving, to be excised from the post-Burnsian canonical story of eighteenth-century Scots poetry. Geddes was a Roman Catholic priest from Aberdeenshire and was inspired, principally by Burns, to publish Scots poems and songs, especially of a radical reformist nature, in the periodical press during the 1790s. Geddes had previously dabbled in Scots, most especially in his early song-writing, but it is the appearance of Burns that reinvigorates his confidence in the Scots language. We might in a sense say that Geddes had been waiting to adopt this stance, primed by his origins from within part of the heartland – Thomas Ruddiman was also an Aberdeenshire man originally – and from within part of the (non-Presbyterian) religious community predisposed to be positively receptive to Scots language literature from the beginning of the eighteenth century, as well as from even earlier times. Paradoxically, although essentially Whiggish in his politics (like Burns himself), Geddes, a strong classical scholar, humorous poet and enjoyer of song, drew expressive inspiration from the aesthetic predilections of North-East and East country Scots Humanism, set up largely in opposition to the Scottish Whig sensibility. The appearance of Burns allows Geddes to be optimistic in his *Dissertation on the Scoto-Saxon Dialect* (1792), in which he argues for the superior expressive possibilities of Scots over English. He hymns Burns as well as other Scots writers in a long accompanying poem, 'Epistle to the President, Vice-Presidents and Members of the Scottish Society of Antiquaries', demonstrating that Scots verse remains able to narrate a long sweep of Scottish cultural history from medieval times until Geddes's own. It is not difficult to see why Geddes, a Catholic priest (of revolutionary sympathies to boot) was cut out, literally so in the case of Irving's book, of the nineteenth-century version of eighteenth-century Scots poetry: one, broadly, of Presbyterian identity tied up in British imperial volition. It is only in recent years that Geddes, a hugely significant figure on a number of fronts, biblical scholar, linguistic theorist, political agitator (for abolition-ism, removal of all religious discrimination and for women's rights) as well as a poet (Burns's most able Scots contemporary in the 1790s) has begun to become firmly noticed again.[17]

Another Scots language poet little noticed in even the first edition of Irving's *Lives of the Scottish Poets* is John Skinner (1721–1807). Along with many others, Burns admired especially his song, 'Tullochgorum'. Skinner had produced Scots poetry earlier in the century, including an excellent poem in the 'Christ's Kirk' tradition, 'The Monymusk Christmas Ba'ing' (1739). Styled 'in imitation of Christ-kirk o' the Green', this is a good poem but, as a genre-piece, it is, to some extent, a conscious antiquarian exercise. Generally, aside from his Scots language songs, Skinner's writing is more concertedly in English or even Latin. A similar story to the one we have noted for Alexander Geddes emerges with Skinner, however, as his Scots language poetry impetus is re-energised by the publishing success of Burns. Tellingly, he writes his 'Epistle to Robert Burns' in 1787. In paying trib-ute to having read *Poems, Chiefly Scottish in the Scottish Dialect*, Skinner's epistle includes the following stanza:

> Your bonnie Bookie, line by line
> I've read, and think it freely fine:
> Indeed I dare na ca't *divine*,
>   as others might,
> For that, ye ken, frae pen like mine
>   wad no be right. (19–24)[18]

Skinner here alludes, obviously enough, to the fact that he is a clergy-man (an Episcopalian in this instance), but there is another implicit reason for his stance that Burns's inspiration does not fall from the sky. Aberdeenshireman Skinner is well aware that Burns's poetic antecedents emanate from the Scots-Humanist traditions that his locality cradles. Interestingly, yet another verse epistle exchange develops when Andrew Shirrefs publishes his two verse epistles to Skinner in the former's *Poems, Chiefly in the Scottish Dialect* (1790). Shirrefs, clearly an admirer of Burns, is, however, at some pains to depict more accurately the canon of eight-eenth-century Scots verse. Having earlier in his text paid tribute to Allan Ramsay, he now includes Alexander Ross (although for some reason Robert Fergusson is omitted from the story):

> For *Robie's* nae the first, ye ken,
> Whase birn *She's* gi'en a heeze;
> Whare's honest Ross. (163–5)

In his own 'Epistle to Andrew Shirrefs', Skinner reflects somewhat wryly on Burns's reception in the North East by the Duchess of Gordon, wishing that he (Shirrefs) might enjoy the patronage that the Ayrshireman has enjoyed:

> Ye Patron Gods of Robie Burns,
>   And all the rare *Nonsuches*,
> Look north, and see where Shirrefs mourns,
>   In BONACCORD on *crutches*,
> O send poor Andie friends in curns,
>   Or but one "*bonny* Dutchess",
> To free him from Misfortune's turns,
>   And Poverty's fell clutches,
>   Some lucky day.[19]

Skinner is one of the more reasonable 'loyalist' poets writing verse against the French Revolution in the 1790s – and here we might make the observation that poetry in Scots is as prevalent on this side of the political divide as it is in the cause of reform and revolution, and perhaps even more so. Alexander Geddes and Alexander Wilson are among the most outspoken poets of a Paineite, pro-revolutionary stamp. Burns was more encoded in his utterances, so that 'Is there for Honest Poverty' or 'Bruce's Address at Bannockburn' or 'The Dumfries Volunteers' can all be read in ways that also offset their reformist possibilities, if Burns had ever been too closely interrogated on these texts. Prominent contemporary reformist Scottish poets, such as James Thomas Callender (1758–1803) or James 'Balloon' Tytler' (1745–1804), composed their reformist texts largely in English (Callender is particularly concerned to reflect the ideas of George Buchanan, extending to writing sometimes in Latin, and so giving us a glimpse of an alternative Whig tradition of Humanist creative writing in eighteenth-century Scotland). Much work remains to be done on Scots language poetry, especially, in the periodical press during the 1790s and after, not least to test the lazy assumption sometimes made that this language automatically betokened (in its demotic accents) a left-leaning trajectory. Very recently, the reformist poetry (sometimes in Scots) of the Airdrie poet William Yates (no dates) has been disinterred, but the fact remains that however many Scots poets of such 'radical' outlook emerge, the most popular Scots poet alongside Burns and into the early nineteenth century was the politically reactionary Hector Macneill (1746–1818).[20] The contemporary situation of Scots poetry in Robert Burns's time was a complicated affair, less easy to read than has often been assumed.

Notes

1. See also J. C. Ewing, ' "Poor Mailie's Elegy": an early manuscript', *Burns Chronicle*, 1932, pp. 25–7, which raises the possibility of a version of this text which dates from

1783. This variant addresses 'Ye Bardies a', in cantie Kyle' (27), providing a wider and also more northern area of land, generally, than we have with merely the River Doon; clearly, across the two versions of the text, Burns was not precisely sure as to how to centre his Ayrshire bards.

2. The poetic exchange generated by Burns *a propos* Sillar continues elsewhere as the naval officer, Lieutenant Charles Gray, produces his 'Epistle to Mr David Sillar' (1808). With Sillar, Gray was an enthusiastic participant in the early Burns Club activities of the early nineteenth century (see James Paterson, *The Contemporaries of Burns, and more recent poets of Ayrshire* (Edinburgh: High Paton, Carver & Gilder, 1840), pp. 58–62).

3. One remaining collaboration, of some importance, does, however, remain as Burns credits Sillar as the author of the tune to the fine lyric, 'The Rosebud' (1788). Here again is an example of the argument advanced in the essay above, that from Ayrshire it is in the context of songwriting rather than in poetry that Burns draws much more valuable creative capital.

4. *Select Scottish Songs, Ancient and Modern*, ed. R. H. Cromek, 2 vols (Edinburgh and London: Cadell and Davies, 1810), vol. II, p. 253. This essay gives credence to William Simpson's authorship of 'Burns's' reply to Walker, though it has to be noted that so distinguished a modern Burns editor as James Kinsley accepts Burns's hand; more detective work requires to be done on the text in the future.

5. Burns complains very eloquently in a letter to the Reverend Carfrae of 27 April 1789 that, because of his many imitators, 'Scots Poetry [now] totters on the brink of contempt', in Robert Burns, *The Letters of Robert Burns*, ed. J. De Lancey Ferguson and G. Ross Roy, 2nd edn, 2 vols (Oxford: Clarendon Press, 1985), I, p. 400.

6. Colin Affleck, 'Windows of opportunity: the Scottish-English career of Robert Kellie Douglas', *The Drouth* 38, Winter 2010/2011, p. 40.

7. Cited in Paterson, *Contemporaries of Burns*, p. 143.

8. A usefully accessible extract is published in Donald Low (ed.), *Robert Burns: The Critical Heritage* (London and Boston: Routledge & Kegan Paul, 1974), pp. 93–4.

9. For a sample see Pebbles's text, 'Burns Renowned', reprinted in Low (ed.), *Burns*, pp. 249–51.

10. Low (ed.), *Burns*, pp. 83–4.

11. Janet Little, *The Poetical Works of Janet Little, The Scotch Milkmaid* (Blackmask online, 2002), 54, http://www.munseys.com/diskone/janelitt.pdf (accessed 22 January 2011).

12. For a more generous view of Janet Little, however, see Valentina Bold, 'Janet Little "The Scotch Milkmaid" and "Peasant Poetry"', *Scottish Literary Journal* 20.2, 1993, pp. 21–30.

13. Paterson, *Contemporaries of Burns*, p. 91.

14. Alexander Wilson, *The Poems & Literary Prose of Alexander Wilson*, ed. Alexander B. Grosart (Paisley: Alex Gardner, 1876), p. 17.

15. Ibid., pp. 19–20.

16. Exemplary of the process is one text among many, a poem by Thomas Campbell, 'Ode to the memory of Robert Burns' (1815), which, in its expansive British view features the lines, 'Encamp'd by Indian rivers wild, / The soldier resting on his arms, / In Burns's carol sweet recalls / The scenes that bless'd him when a child', *Poems of Thomas Campbell*, ed. Lewis Campbell (London: Macmillan, 1904), p. 202.

17. The recent reappraisal of Geddes finds strong expressions, for instance, in William
    Johnstone (ed.), *The Bible and the Enlightenment. A Case Study: Alexander Geddes,
    1737-1802* (London and New York: T&T Clark, 2004).

18. John Skinner, *Collected Poems*, ed. David M. Bertie (Peterhead: The Buchan Field
    Club, 2005), p. 252.

19. Ibid., p. 401.

20. See Ian Reid, 'In search of William Yates of Airdrie, contemporary of Burns',
    Scottish Studies Review 9.1, Spring 2008, pp. 27–48.

CHAPTER 5

'To a Mouse': Burns, Power and Equality

Freya Johnston

According to Joseph Addison in *Spectator* no. 500 (1712), 'nothing is more gratifying to the Mind of Man than Power or Dominion'.[1] In the guise of a happily married correspondent, Philogamus, Addison was describing the role of a patriarch in the family – but he could as easily have been talking about mankind's relationships with animals. Alexander Pope's *Guardian* no. 61 (1713) opens with the comment that human beings are as 'accountable for the ill Use of their Dominion over Creatures of the lower Rank of Beings' as they are 'for the Exercise of Tyranny over their own Species. The more entirely the Inferior Creation is submitted to our Power, the more answerable we should seem for our Mismanagement of it.'[2]

Burns's lines 'To a Mouse, On turning her up in her Nest, with the Plough, November, 1785' (K 69, I, 127) have a mercurial sense, not quite akin to Pope's, of what it means to be 'answerable' to 'the Inferior Creation'. What is 'Mismanagement' from one point of view (the mouse's) is good husbandry from another (the farmer's), which is perhaps why Burns prefers to treat the relationship between man and beast as a matter of sheer mobility, of showing 'unbounded good-will to every creature rational and irrational' (K, III, 968). 'To a Mouse' begins with an act of naming which is jokily reminiscent of Adam in Genesis. Having been made in the image of God, Adam is next granted 'dominion over the fish of the sea, and over the fowl of the air, and over the cattle, and over all the earth, and over every creeping thing that creepeth upon the earth'. He proceeds to confer a title on 'every beast of the field, and every fowl of the air . . . and whatsoever Adam called every living creature, that *was* the name thereof'.[3] Burns's speaker does things the other way round, and in so doing redefines the gratifications of power experienced by Addison's ideal father. He hails the mouse with an affectionately overloaded moniker which is also a nod to his new-found companion's vulnerability – 'Wee, sleekit, cowran, tim'rous *beastie*' – and only then seeks to make amends for 'Man's dominion', without which this one-sided conversation would not be taking place. Fiona Stafford writes that:

> Naming, as made clear by Adam's prelapsarian duties, is a way of asserting power, which means that failure to give a proper name may suggest

diminished authority. The more names Burns fires at the Deil, then, the less certain does his command of the situation appear.[4]

Giving more than one name to the mouse, while it also involves diminution and authority, has a different effect. Burns isn't dealing with a supernatural opponent, but with a creature who is at once his victim and 'companion'; even one of 'my Compeers, the rustic Inmates of the Hamlet'.[5] There is a hint of prelapsarian language in the fact that Burns's 'sleeket' is not intended 'in the main Scots sense, artful, sly; but English sleeked, glossy' (K, III, 1092):

> Wee, sleeket, cowran, tim'rous *beastie*,
> O, what a panic's in thy breastie!
> Thou need na start awa sae hasty,
>   Wi' bickering brattle!
> I wad be laith to rin an' chase thee,
>   Wi' mur'dring *pattle*!
>
> I'm truly sorry Man's dominion
> Has broken Nature's social union,
> An' justifies that ill opinion,
>   Which makes thee startle,
> At me, thy poor, earth-born companion,
>   An *fellow-mortal*! (1–11)

'*Beastie*', 'breastie' and 'hasty' draw attention to the poet's exuberant idiom because 'beast', 'breast' and 'haste' could do the work of rhyming in themselves. There is a lightness and generosity of spirit in the resulting sense of overspill, a feeling that the poet has more than enough to spare – in spite of the fact that it is winter, not harvest time, and in spite of the fact that 'Mouse self-interest and farmer self-interest do not run along similar lines: mice eat what farmers raise'.[6] The poem's complex effects spring from competing self-interests which are temporarily overlooked; its charm, energy and sadness have to do with our knowledge that equality between farmer and mouse cannot last. The occasional, happenstance immediacy of these lines, as of those 'To a Louse, On Seeing one on a Lady's Bonnet at Church' makes them feel in some ways as transient as a song.

Burns's tone in the opening lines of 'To a Mouse' implies that the status of such lofty topics as tend to be aligned with formal, elevated modes of address is open to question; it returns us to the Preface to the Kilmarnock volume, whose first sentence claims that 'The following trifles are not the production of the Poet, who, with all the advantages of learned art, and perhaps amid the elegancies and idlenesses of upper life, looks down for a rural theme, with an eye to Theocrites or Virgil' (K, III, 971). 'To a Mouse' seems to assert that its subject is no trifle, but it forgets that subject towards the end of the poem; it presents us with a speaker who, in the midst of work, 'looks down' with an eye to the scene before him and discovers in rural life a theme which is of universal applicability, but who closes by dwelling on himself. In language which suggests how he viewed his own descent to literary trifles and lesser creatures, Burns wrote to Frances Dunlop in 1787 that 'I trust I have too much pride for servility, and too little prudence for selfishness'.[7] As is evident from 'To a Mouse' and other Burns poems, however, it is possible to be at once imprudent and not entirely lacking in selfishness. The conversational diminutives in which the mouse is initially celebrated build each succeeding line on foundations of ease and affection. A cosy, domestic sturdiness is built into Burns's accretions and donations; and yet, given the time of year, there is little real comfort on offer to the mouse. That sense of proffering inadequate comfort – in fact, of making poetic use of the animal, having first rendered it homeless – gives rise to the second stanza, in which Burns ascribes its fear of him to conscious dislike, rather than to instinctive terror. In a letter of 1786, he argued that he 'would not have a dissocial word . . . with any one of God's creatures'.[8] Not just unsocial but positively dissocial, the word captures that sense in which a bond has been suddenly, unwittingly broken, only for Burns to try to restore it. The poem also suggests, however, that the mouse would be justified in retaining an 'ill opinion' of the voice which addresses him.

Henry Mackenzie praised Burns for delineating nature 'with the precision of intimacy', a phrase which captures the handling of language and perspective in the opening lines of 'To a Mouse'.[9] In his *Account of the Life and Character of Robert Burns* (1811), Josiah Walker understood that 'precision of thought' might be arrived at via several kindred epithets, such as those bestowed in the first line of 'To a Mouse' and in the first line of 'To a Mountain-Daisy, On turning one down, with the Plough, in April, 1786', 'Wee, modest, crimson-tipped flow'r' (K 92, I, 228):

> A number of words which are little else than synonimes, to persons who are at no pains, or who have no power to define and discriminate, convey to one more anxious for the enjoyment produced by variety and precision of thought, different shades of significance, which he separates with ease.

The negative version of this *copia verborum* is mere accretion of similitudes; the positive version is not only the power of definition or discrimination, shared by poet and reader, but also 'the protecting shield of his genius' which Burns's names seem to offer the creature or flower he describes.[10] What makes Walker's perception valuable is the way it follows Burns in associating the 'enjoyment' of poetic language – Burns himself described 'Love and Poesy' as 'my highest enjoyment'[11] – with 'pains' and anxiety as well as with 'ease'. If there is generosity and vigour in 'To a Mouse', there is also a great deal of fear.

Francis Jeffrey observed that, 'before he had ever composed a single stanza', Burns was 'intimately acquainted with Pope, Shakespeare and

Thomson'. The freshness of his voice derives from his creative responses to other poets, as well as from his proximity to nature, as John Logan recognised as early as 1787: 'In his serious poems we can trace imitations of almost every English author of celebrity'; 'He is better acquainted with the English poets than most English authors that have come under our review'.[12] Although it has echoes of Thomson, 'To a Mouse' shows Burns's acquaintance with, above all other writers, Pope. James Kinsley noted Burns's debt in 'To a Mouse' to the third epistle of *An Essay on Man* (1733–4), in which 'Union' is 'the bond of all things' and rational man imitates 'forms of social union' in the animal kingdom (K, III, p. 1093).[13] Pope depicts in that section of the *Essay* a state of nature in which 'Man walk'd with beast, joint tenant of the shade; / The same his table, and the same his bed' (III.152–3). Burns's mouse is envisaged in similar terms as the speaker's peer and has in common with human beings the condition of mortality; 'etymologically, the mouse is a companion (*com-panis*) in that it eats the speaker's bread – or grain. It is a companion because it lives in the same place and undergoes similar experiences.'[14] Burns let Epistle III of Pope's essay sound through other of his poems; it provided him with the epigraph to 'Nature's Law': 'Great Nature spoke; observant Men obey'd' (K 126, I, 296, 9).[15] A personified Nature here counsels man to be 'observant' not only in the sense of abiding by her commands but also by attending to and discovering in the natural world models for human society:

> Thy arts of building from the bee receive;
> Learn of the mole to plow, the worm to weave;
>
> …
>
> Here too all forms of social union find,
> And hence let Reason, late, instruct Mankind[.]
> (*Essay on Man*, Epistle III.175–6, 179–80)

Yet Burns, while he may pick up on the connections made in these lines between 'the arts of building' ('Thy wee-bit *housie*', 19), the 'plow' and 'forms of social union' which 'instruct Mankind', is no conventional physico-theologian. Just as he refashions Genesis in the opening lines of 'To a Mouse', so in the rest of the poem he derives from his own observations and from Pope's Nature a set of lessons quite different from those in *An Essay on Man*. Pope, following John Ray and William Derham, finds in the natural world – especially in the bee's cell – a model of strength, durability and good housekeeping (Epistle III.175–90, n.175). In contrast, Burns finds in the mouse's loss of shelter images of human weakness and of the unpredictability of the world. What his speaker learns from the encounter is how security is lost, not gained or preserved; the mouse's well-planned domestic economy is exploded by a wholly unforeseeable event. In calling the mouse's dwelling 'thy cell', which he immediately redescribes as 'That wee-bit heap o' leaves an' stibble' (30–1), Burns indicates the discrepancy between his poem and such responses to the bee's cell as that of John Ray:

> The *Bee*, a Creature of the lowest form of Animals, so that no Man can suspect it to have any considerable Measure of Understanding, or to have Knowledge of, much less to aim at any End, yet makes her Combs and Cells with that Geometrical Accuracy, that she must needs be Acted by an Instinct implanted in her by the wise Author of Nature . . . Moreover, the Combs being double . . . must needs contribute to the strength and firmness of the work. These Cells she fills with Honey for her Winter Provision[.][16]

Ray interprets the bee while she constructs her hive and prepares for winter as, by turns, possessed of and lacking in foresight – although it is no more than a '*seeming* Prudence', according to the author, which makes the bee act as she does, because she has no knowledge of the future. Perhaps Burns's mouse, laying up her winter provision, similarly proves that '*foresight* may be vain' (37); she demonstrates a moral truth to the eyes of a human beholder, but that truth cannot be known by or remotely useful to the creature herself. There is a curious hint in all this of what would happen to Burns's reputation soon after his death: the poet's biography and name were used to point a moral about suffering and imprudence. If Burns thought that 'There is not among all the Martyrologies that ever were penned, so rueful a narrative as Johnson's Lives of the Poets.—In the comparative view of Wretches, the criterion is not, what they are doomed to suffer, but how they are formed to bear', Scott's 1812 scrap of autobiography asserted from a far cooler and loftier perspective that 'From the lives of some poets a most important moral lesson may doubtless be derived, and few sermons can be read with so much profit as the Memoirs of Burns, of Chatterton, or of Savage.'[17] For Carlyle, 'it is not chiefly as a poet, but as a man, that he interests and affects us . . . To the ill-starred Burns was given the power of making man's life more venerable, but that of wisely guiding his own life was not given.'[18] If 'To a Mouse' represents Burns's own 'comparative view of Wretches', then the mouse is 'formed to bear' her misfortune through knowledge of the present only:

> To each unthinking being, Heav'n a friend,
> Gives not the useless knowledge of its end:
> To Man imparts it; but with such a view
> As, while he dreads it, makes him hope it too[.] (*Essay on Man*, Epistle III.71–4)

But the mouse's '*foresight*' is, in another sense, mere '*seeming*': this industrious creature is characterised as a thief and a chancer even before she turns out, at the end of the poem, to live solely in the here and now. In this sense, the division between human beings and animals is once again collapsed.

Rather than enforce, in the manner of a physico-theologian, the view that proofs and sound arguments for God's existence may be derived from studying nature, Burns suggests the disturbing possibility that what nature shows us is that we live in a world of random pains and cruel accidents, perhaps even one in which God toys with us as we toy with animals. Samuel Johnson imagined such a place in his bitterly comic review of Soame Jenyns's *Free Inquiry into the Nature and Origin of Evil* (1757):

> As we drown whelps and kittens, [some beings above us] amuse themselves now and then with sinking a ship, and stand round the fields of Blenheim, or the walls of Prague, as we encircle a cockpit. As we shoot a bird flying, they take a man in the midst of his business or pleasure, and knock him down with an apoplexy. Some of them, perhaps, are virtuosi, and delight in the operations of an asthma, as a human philosopher in the effects of the air pump. To swell a man with a tympany is as good sport as to blow a frog. Many a merry bout have these frolic beings at the vicissitudes of an ague, and good sport it is to see a man tumble with an epilepsy, and revive and tumble again, and all this he knows not why.[19]

'To a Mouse' set off by emphasising that both mice and men were liable to fate's sudden, unwelcome incursions; neither of them could know how or why things happened. When Burns relinquishes this attitude to the mouse in order to announce that the creature is blessed, 'compar'd wi *me*' (43), we begin to lose sight of the animal's 'wee-bit *housie*' and the fearful prospect without it of winter's '*sleety dribble*' (19, 35). The illusion of equality has itself now been broken; unions have been restored only to be again discounted. The poem has once again made it clear that this was only a mouse's nest, not an ideal of security common to human beings and other animals. Why does Burns, the 'sentimental egalitarian', veer off in this direction?[20] If the '*present* only' affects the mouse, how can it be said in the previous lines to possess 'schemes' akin to those of human beings (44, 39)?[21] Perhaps the poem cannot resist puncturing its own claims to finality, including the moral of the penultimate stanza.

Susan Manning has spoken of how Burns's language accommodates 'contrary dictions' which can 'compromise' the integrity of the verse when deployed 'without edge'.[22] And Christopher Ricks observes with reference to 'the meeting of a willed likemindedness' between Burns and Pope that 'Burns is stagnant when there is no crepitating discrepancy between what he takes and what he makes'.[23] Such discrepancy, contrariness or sudden averseness to the precedent of *An Essay on Man* appears to animate the closing lines of 'To a Mouse', in which Burns prises apart the slick unities which occupy the last couplet of the third epistle: 'Thus God and Nature link'd the gen'ral frame, / And bade Self-love and Social be the same' (*Essay on Man*, Epistle III.317–18). The closing stanza of 'To a Mouse' is not about sameness, but difference; self-love elbows social union out of the picture.

Many of the bird and animal poems are about safety and obligation.

Burns glances in the third stanza of 'To a Mouse' at Deuteronomy 24.19 when he promises to leave behind him in the field the odd, stray ear of corn ('A *daimen-icker* in a *thrave*', 15), but he is also once again remembering *An Essay on Man* (itself paraphrasing Deut. 35.4):

> Is thine alone the seed that strews the plain?
> The birds of heav'n shall vindicate their grain:
> Thine the full harvest of the golden year?
> Part pays, and justly, the deserving steer:
> The hog, that plows not nor obeys thy call,
> Lives on the labours of this lord of all. (*Essay on Man*, Epistle III.37–42)

The harvest mouse from this point of view becomes 'the stranger' to whom the Bible enjoins generosity.[24] If 'dominion' over the earth and all its creatures is, according to Genesis, man's inheritance, charity is his duty. Authority must be weighed against kindness. Burns's poems readily turn from the perspective of a governing human consciousness to that of the helpless observer or victim (as, for instance, in 'A Poet's Welcome to his love-begotten Daughter', which salutes a 'wee' creature whose appearance, like that of the mouse, is the result of 'Mischanter', or mishap, K 60, I, 99, 13–14, 1). In one of his earliest works, 'Song, composed in August', Burns alternates between scenes of love and death as he heralds the arrival of 'waving grain', 'Peggy dear' and the 'charms o' Nature' (K 2, I, 5, 5, 25, 30) on the one hand and a host of soon-to-be-slaughtered birds on the other. As in 'To a Mouse', Burns seems to have both Pope and Thomson in mind here: the poem recalls the delicate landscapes and lonely, fluttering birds who fall prey to 'slaught'ring guns' in *Windsor-Forest* (1713), as well as lines in 'Autumn' which rehearse 'the sportsman's Joy' and the 'sounding Pinions' of his victims (K, III, 1005–6). But whereas 'To a Mouse' for the most part construes human 'dominion' as an unexpected severance of nature's 'social union' – in other words, as something which disrupts an instinctive bond between mouse and man – here, 'Tyrannic man's dominion' is part of a scene in which the fracturing effects of difference and power are ever present:

> Thus ev'ry kind their pleasure find,
>   The savage and the tender;
> Some social join, and leagues combine;
>   Some solitary wander:
> Avaunt, away! the cruel sway,
>   Tyrannic man's dominion;
> The Sportsman's joy, the murd'ring cry,
>   The flutt'ring, gory pinion! (K 2, I, 5, 17–24)

The first half of this stanza considers the natural order as made up of two 'kinds', perhaps four – depending on whether we see the savage as

belonging to the same group as the solitary, and the tender to the same
group as the social. Burns's poems tend to ask such questions about the
meaning of 'social union' without answering them. Grammatically, the first
four lines cohere in a way in which the second four do not; apart from the
phrase 'Avaunt, away!', lines 21–4 consist of single abstract images and
sounds, culminating in the synecdochic 'flutt'ring, gory pinion!'. This realisation of what 'Tyrannic man's dominion' amounts to – a paltry, broken
prize – enacts the same play of great against small and height against low-
ness as do 'To a Mouse' and 'To a Mountain-Daisy'. Incidentally, Shelley
rhymes musical 'dominions' with spiritual 'pinions' in *Prometheus Unbound*
(1820), and leads us in the opposite direction – upwards, rather than down-
wards.[25] This is typical of Shelley, who heads for sublimity where Burns
heads for pathos and sometimes bathos. Although he could write in a letter
of 1788 of a poet trying 'the strength of his pinion', the wings of his own
verse are best when clipped or bedraggled or in some other sense apparently
not quite soaring to order.[26] Scott makes a related point when he writes
that 'although in these flights [Burns] naturally and almost unavoidably
assumed the dialect of Milton and Shakespeare, he never seems to have
been completely at his ease when he had not the power of descending into
what was familiar to his ear, and to his habits.'[27] To construe descent as a
'power' rather than as (say) a humiliation, or accident, suggests Burns's
command of language in situations which present themselves as wholly
ungoverned and immediate.

   Like 'To a Mouse', 'To a Louse' is concerned with modesty, partly by
virtue of its yet more diminutive and contemptible addressee. The mouse,
seeking refuge, has sought concealment, and appears comparable to the
poet in being solitary and at once exposed to and withdrawn from the world.
But the louse also affronts decorum by seeming not to know where he
belongs:

> Swith! in some beggar's haffet squattle;
> There ye may creep, and sprawl, and sprattle,
> Wi' ither kindred, jumping cattle,
>   In shoals and nations;
> Whare *horn* nor *bane* ne'er daur unsettle,
>   Your thick plantations. (K 83, I, 193, 13–18)

The recent likelihood that Burns, like other Scots, might exile himself to a
plantation means that the use of that polysyllabic word in 'To a Louse' is
more than a joke about outsized Latinate vocabulary.[28] These lines, with
their play on scale and degradation, have a flavour of *Gulliver's Travels*
(1726) and of Swift's poems on female pomp and squalor.[29] There is a
comparable reference to plantations in 'A Beautiful Young Nymph going to
Bed' (1731), a poem which doesn't take a young lady down a peg or two so
much as remove the pegs which underpin her.

> She takes a *Bolus* e'er she sleeps;
> And then between two Blankets creeps.
> With Pains of Love tormented lies;
> Or if she chance to close her Eyes,
> Of *Bridewell* and the *Compter* dreams,
> And feels the Lash, and faintly screams;
> Or, by a faithless Bully drawn,
> At some Hedge-Tavern lies in Pawn;
> Or to *Jamaica* seems transported,
> *Alone, and by no Planter courted; (37–46)

> *—*Et longam incomitata videtur / Ire viam*—[30]

If Burns's 'plantations' are fraught with the threat of genuine exile, Swift too enlivens metaphor with a harsh, glittering reality in the word 'transported' (45). In both cases, the safety of verse or of metaphoric language is paper-thin. Both poems have a chatty intimacy and partial sympathy with someone revolting; each is governed by a speaker who repeatedly and variously suggests himself as that revolting someone's equal. Even the mock-outraged, abusive voice at the opening of 'To a Louse' is ready, by the fifth line of the poem, to express a sympathetic fear that the creature dines 'but sparely' in such an elevated 'place'; Swift's speaker may be thinking of poetic 'Arts', among others, when he exclaims in mock-despondency, 'But how shall I describe her Arts / To recollect the scatter'd Parts?' (67–8). But each speaker also indicates the many ways in which that equality cannot hold, which accounts perhaps for the magic and horror of each work, and for its delicate sense of social propriety. What in another poem might point us towards the otherworldly has been collapsed by Swift into the brutalities of a world that is hyper-real, crowded out with names and places ('*Bolus*', '*Bridewell*', 'the *Compter*', '*Fleet-Ditch*', 'Hedge-Tavern', '*Jamaica*', 37–45) and slangy urban parlance ('Toast', 'Rake', 'Bully', 'Cully', 4–5, 43, 50). A 'Crystal Eye' in this context really is made of glass, and hence detachable as well as sparkling; the 'Pains of Love' or amorous transports suffered by other literary lovers are here the physical pangs of venereal disease and the threat of being actually 'transported' to another location (the word suggests either that Corinna goes to Jamaica in her imagination, or that she has been sent there as a punishment). The fact that Swift then introduces a Virgilian allusion, and signposts it in a footnote (the excerpt translates as 'She seemed to be going on a long journey alone', from Virgil's *Aeneid*, IV.467–8), places Corinna in a newly incongruous setting: that of epic. These lines come shortly before Dido's suicide, and were chosen by Addison as the epigraph to *The Spectator* 241 (1711) on the distresses of virtuous love. Swift may be suggesting that Dido's amorous fits and suicide are, in truth, no better or more dignified than Corinna's urban prostitution, suffering and disgrace. Johnson's verdict on Pope's *Elegy to the Memory of an Unfortunate Lady*

(1717) springs to mind: 'Poetry has not often been worse employed than in dignifying the amorous fury of a raving girl.'[31]

There is, then, an equalising element at work in Swift, flattening out the apparent discrepancy between modern grime and ancient nobility – while at the same time we sense that Virgil is in 'A Beautiful Young Nymph' precisely because the reference is intended to remain incongruous. It is meant to be out of place, in order to reveal the high in glaring contrast with the low. So it is in 'To a Louse' that the miniature invader of Jenny's hair is not exactly the equal of a human being, even if the 'shoals and nations' of lice sound like human populations, and even if this individual louse represents an opportunity to poke fun at Jenny's pride in her beauty. The speaker's mock-horror at witnessing the louse in the act of social climbing is an overstated recognition of that creature's actual lowly status. There is a sense in which levels of recognition and kinds of value and resemblance are being tested out in Burns, as in mock-epic, through repeatedly over- or understating the case. A norm is being arrived at through establishing what lies on either side of it.

Carol McGuirk has argued that, when Burns addresses himself to louse, mouse or mountain daisy, he is overtly mimicking the conduct of senti-mental heroes such as Mackenzie's Harley and Sterne's Yorick: an acute sensibility is able to pump significance out of the least attractive of objects.[32] In a sense, this kind of sentimental writing might be said to revive the sixteenth-century paradoxical encomium, a rhetorical form adapted from classical oratory whose best-known example is Erasmus's *Moriae Encomium* (*The Praise of Folly*, 1511) – the challenge being to generate an argument from the least promising of cues. Indeed, one of the classical models on which Renaissance encomia of this type are founded is Lucian's 'Praise of the Fly', suggesting a source for Uncle Toby's apostrophe to a fly in *The Life and Opinions of Tristram Shandy, Gentleman* (1759–67). In the para-doxical encomium, high praise is lavished ironically on low subject matter for the purposes of demonstrating the skill and extending the fame of the author. But Erasmus employed this trope and its ironies for more than mere self-aggrandisement. He turned it to moral purpose, implicating his readers in the folly he described and conducting them to self-awareness through humour – a process which applies equally to Burns's 'To a Louse'.[33]

That process works slightly differently in his tender, self-mocking 'Poor Mailie's Elegy', a poem which abides by the characteristic turns and refrains of Standard Habbie (the repeated end-line terminating in 'dead') but which, like Gray's 'Ode on the Death of a Favourite Cat' (1747) and Goldsmith's 'Elegy on the Death of a Mad Dog' (1766), splices regret with absurdity. In rehearsing his ewe's fidelity, honesty, noble lineage, good sense and good manners, and in turning the poem (like 'To a Mouse') on the figure of the poet, Burns achieves a kind of mock-epic in which a sheep is lamented as 'a friend an' neebor' (K 25, I, 35, 11), while we remain aware throughout that she is not, in fact, human. There is a subtle dispersal of implications here, a network of sympathies lightly sketched and dropped. Goldsmith's elegy is satirical where Gray's is mock-instructive; Burns, however, focuses the mock-elegy on the bard himself. His grief and his inability to recover from the death of a sheep occupy the centre of the poem. As a result, it is more sentimentally focused than are Goldsmith and Gray's mock-elegies. It is both grateful to a dead companion and archly self-gratifying.

In eighteenth-century sentimental fiction the observer, as McGuirk has noted, tends to be socially alienated, but to place his interpreting sensibility above the wretchedness which he is fervently describing and heightening.[34] We know that Burns liked to read this kind of thing:

> My favorite authors are of the sentim[l] kind, such as Shenstone, particularly his Elegies, Thomson, Man of feeling, a book I prize next to the Bible, Man of the World, Sterne, especially his Sentimental journey, M[c]pherson's Ossian, &c. these are the glorious models after which I endeavour to form my con-duct, and 'tis incongruous, 'tis absurd to suppose that the man whose mind glows with sentiments lighted up at their sacred flame—the man whose heart distends with benevolence to all the human race—he 'who can soar above this little scene of things'—can he descend to mind the paulty conccerns about which the terrae-filial race fret, and fume, and vex themselves? O how the glorious triumph swells my heart![35]

Burns, who is in fact a master at 'descending to mind the paulty conccerns' (albeit not in the sense in which they are described and dismissed here), gives a very convincing impersonation of the distending, benevolent heart in relation to the natural world in one early letter. He writes with the inten-tion to seduce:

> 'Twas a golden moment for a poetic heart.—I listened the feathered Warblers, pouring their harmony on every hand, with a congenial, kindred regard; and frequently turned out of my path lest I should disturb their little songs, or frighten them to another station.—'Surely,' said I to myself, 'he must be a wretch indeed, who, regardless of your harmonious endeavours to please him, can eye your elusive flights, to discover your secret recesses, and rob you of all the property Nature gives you; your dearest comforts, your helpless, little Nestlings.'[36]

Here, we find that same sense of being 'congenial, kindred' to little crea-tures which appears in 'To a Mouse', but what makes this letter sickly and unpleasant where the poem is not is that in the latter Burns has openly iden-tified himself with those who 'disturb' and 'frighten'; he has become a man who recognises that, in discovering nature's 'secret recesses', he also robs the mouse 'of all the property Nature gives you'. Such language is particu-larly stomach-churning in the letter insofar as it bears on what 'property' Burns hopes to find and plunder in his female addressee. The selfish heart which lurks in Sterne's imitators comes into view here, with Burns the 'old hawk' setting out to capture a 'mounting lark'.[37]

His letters of the late 1780s show a pronounced reluctance to discuss the future – 'I am still undetermined as to the future; and, as usual, [ne]ver think of it'; 'I look down on the future as I would into the bottomless pit'; 'I am still "dark as was Chaos" in respect to Futurity' – alongside a remarkably strong awareness of 'where I stand, both as a Man and a Poet', as he put it in 1787.[38] In an early letter to his father, he commented that:

> I dare not, either review past events, or look forward into futurity; for the least anxiety, or perturbation in my breast, produces most unhappy effects on my whole frame.—Sometimes, indeed, when for an hour or two, as is sometimes the case, my spirits are a little lightened, I glimmer a little into futurity; but my principal, and indeed my only pleasurable employment is looking backwards & forwards in a moral & religious way.[39]

Written in 1781, this is in some ways a draft prose version of 'To a Mouse'; the diminutives which 'lighten' the 'spirits' and the fears concerning futurity are already linked. And when Burns speaks of the 'unhappy effects on my whole frame' of considering past or coming events, we might ourselves look forward to the final stanza of 'To a Mouse', in which the 'whole frame' of the poem is unhappily affected by the final stanza, where the speaker laments his peculiar affliction of looking back and fearing the future, and thus dismantles the sense of equality between man and beast – the latter being suddenly confined to the present alone. Burns differentiates curiously, in the letter to his father, between two forms of casting the mind backwards and forwards: the one is personal, the other 'moral & religious'. But how is it possible to steer a course between them? Perhaps only via allusion and the remaking of his literary sources: a form of looking backwards and forwards, 'morally' speaking, without directly 'reviewing past events'.

Burns's brother Gilbert wrote that 'every attentive reader of Burns's Works, must have observed, that he frequently presents a caricature of his feelings, and even of his failings – a kind of mock-heroic account of himself and his opinions'.[40] Such works as 'To a Mouse' acknowledge the failings of the Bardie, while also suggesting for those failings a perspective of common weakness in which all creatures are equal – 'the comparative view of Wretches', as he put it, in which there are no winners and losers – even if that perspective cannot hold good for ever. In 'The Ordination', a personified Morality is seen 'Embracing all opinions' before he is 'banish'd our dominions' (K 85, I, 216, 100–8). Such brief moments of equality are also entertained in 'To a Louse', which warns against pride by emphasising the salutary effects of seeing 'oursels as others see us!' (44). Part of this useful but frequently unpleasant possibility are the games with scale and importance which Burns plays at the physical level, as in his 'Address to the

Tooth-Ache': a poem which makes us understand that, on the one hand, human beings are the same everywhere; on the other, that what is 'wee' from one point of view may appear vast from another. 'You see, Sir,' Burns wrote to Robert Graham in July 1789, 'with what freedom I lay before you all my little matters—little indeed to the World, but of the most important magnitude to me'.[41]

Notes

1. *The Spectator*, ed. Donald Bond, 5 vols (Oxford: Clarendon Press, 1965), vol. IV, p. 273.
2. Alexander Pope, *The Prose Works of Alexander Pope*, ed. Norman Ault and Rosemary Cowler, 2 vols (Oxford: Basil Blackwell, 1936–86), vol. I, p. 107.
3. *The Bible: Authorized King James Version*, ed. Robert Carroll and Stephen Prickett (Oxford: Oxford University Press, 1997), Gen. 1.26; 2.19. Further references are to this edition.
4. Fiona Stafford, *Local Attachments: The Province of Poetry* (Oxford: Oxford University Press, 2010), 191. On Burns and names, see also Christopher Ricks, 'Burns', *Allusion to the Poets* (Oxford: Oxford University Press, 2002), p. 50.
5. Robert Burns, *The Letters of Robert Burns*, ed. J. De Lancey Ferguson and G. Ross Roy, 2nd edn, 2 vols (Oxford: Clarendon Press, 1985), vol. I, p. 88.
6. Carol McGuirk, *Robert Burns and the Sentimental Era* (Athens, GA: University of Georgia Press, 1985), p. 10.
7. Burns, *Letters*, vol. I, pp. 104–5.
8. Ibid., vol. I, p. 77.
9. Donald Low (ed.), *Robert Burns: The Critical Heritage* (London and Boston: Routledge & Kegan Paul, 1974), p. 69.
10. Ibid., pp. 220, 184.
11. Burns, *Letters*, vol. I, p. 138.
12. Low (ed.), *Burns*, pp. 179, 76–7. On Thomson, imitation and first-hand observations of nature, see Burns, *Letters*, vol. I, pp. 325–6.
13. Alexander Pope, *The Twickenham Edition of the Poems of Alexander Pope*, III.1: *An Essay on Man*, ed. Maynard Mack (London: Methuen, 1950), Epistle III.150, 179. Further references are to this edition and given in the text. On Burns's allusions to *An Essay on Man*, see also Nigel Leask, *Robert Burns and Pastoral: Poetry and Improvement in Late Eighteenth-Century Scotland* (Oxford: Oxford University Press, 2010), pp. 161–2.
14. David Perkins, *Romanticism and Animal Rights* (Cambridge: Cambridge University Press, 2003), p. 10.
15. Pope, *Essay on Man*, Epistle III.199; Burns changes 'Men' to 'man'.
16. John Ray, *The Wisdom of God manifested in the Works of the Creation*, 6th edn (London: for William Innes, 1714), pp. 132–3.
17. Burns, *Letters*, vol. II, p. 46. Low (ed.), *Burns*, p. 42.
18. Low (ed.), *Burns*, p. 353.
19. Samuel Johnson, 'Review of [Soame Jenyns], *A Free Inquiry into the Nature and Origin of Evil*', in Samuel Johnson, *Samuel Johnson: A Critical Edition of the Major Works*, ed. Donald Greene (Oxford: Oxford University Press, 1984), p. 535.

20. Kenneth Simpson, *The Protean Scot: The Crisis of Identity in Eighteenth-Century Scottish Literature* (Aberdeen: Aberdeen University Press, 1988), p. 194.
21. See McGuirk, *Robert Burns and the Sentimental Era*, p. 9.
22. Susan Manning, 'Burns and God', in Robert Crawford (ed.), *Robert Burns and Cultural Authority* (Edinburgh: Edinburgh University Press, 1996), pp. 113–35, 127.
23. Ricks, *Allusion to the Poets*, p. 53.
24. 'When thou cuttest down thine harvest in thy field, and hast forgot a sheaf in the field, thou shalt not go again to fetch it: it shall be for the stranger, for the fatherless, and for the widow: that the LORD thy God may bless thee in all the work of thine hands' (Deut. 24.19).
25. 'Meanwhile thy spirit lifts its pinions / In music's most serene dominions' (Percy Bysshe Shelley, *The Major Works*, ed. Zachary Leader and Michael O'Neill (Oxford: Oxford University Press, 2003), *Prometheus Unbound*, II, v, 85–6).
26. Burns, *Letters*, vol. I, p. 326.
27. Low (ed.), *Burns*, p. 33.
28. See Burns, *Letters*, vol. I, pp. 39, 42, 44, 46, 48, 49, 52, 54–5, 58, 121, 144, 293.
29. Francis Jeffrey suggests a resemblance between Burns and Swift. Low (ed.), *Burns*, p. 191.
30. Jonathan Swift, *The Poems of Jonathan Swift*, ed. Harold Williams, 2nd edn, 3 vols (Oxford: Clarendon Press, 1958), vol. II, pp. 582–3.
31. Samuel Johnson, 'Life of Pope' (1781), in Samuel Johnson, *The Lives of the Poets*, ed. Roger Lonsdale, 4 vols (Oxford: Clarendon Press, 2006), vol. IV, p. 9.
32. McGuirk, *Burns and the Sentimental Era*, pp. 3–14.
33. See Henry Knight Miller, 'The Paradoxical Encomium, with special reference to its vogue in England 1600–1800', *Modern Philology* 53.3, 1956, pp. 145–78.
34. McGuirk, *Burns and the Sentimental Era*, pp. 3–6.
35. Burns, *Letters*, vol. I, pp. 17–18.
36. Ibid., vol. I, pp. 63–4.
37. Ibid., vol. I, p. 126.
38. Ibid., vol. I, pp. 72, 73, 82, 95. Stafford notes that 'Burns's sense of his own "ground" was essential to his psyche and his songs' and that 'For all the exuberance of *Poems, Chiefly in the Scottish Dialect*, there are numerous moments when the future seems a terrifying prospect' (*Local Attachments*, pp. 179, 193).
39. Burns, *Letters*, vol. I, p. 6.
40. Low (ed.), *Burns*, p. 271.
41. Burns, *Letters*, vol. I, p. 425.

CHAPTER 6

Burns's Sentiments: Gray, Milton and 'To A Mountain-Daisy'

Mina Gorji

Robert Burns achieved poetic fame as an Ayrshire ploughman. The plough served him well: it authenticated his claim to original genius and symbolised his 'connection to the earth'; it also connected him with the world of letters.[1] According to his brother Gilbert, 'Holding the plough was a favourite situation with Robert for poetic compositions, and some of his best verses were produced while he was at that exercise.'[2] One of his modern admirers, Seamus Heaney, has written of the correspondences between ploughing and poetry – between turning a line of verse and ploughing a field – 'vowels ploughed into other, opened ground, / Each verse returning like the plough turned round'.[3] For Burns, it was often less deliberate; the plough brought him to poetry by accident. Ploughing a field in Mossgiel in April 1786, he turned down a mountain daisy, and he turned the chance encounter into verse. Although we might expect a ploughman to delight in killing a weed, it caused the poet pain:

> Wee, modest, crimson-tipped flow'r,
> Thou's met me in an evil hour;
> For I maun crush amang the stoure
>   Thy slender stem:
> To spare thee now is past my pow'r,
>   Thou bonie gem.
>
> Alas! it's no thy neebor sweet,
> The bonie *Lark*, companion meet!
> Bending thee 'mang the dewy weet!
>   Wi's spreckl'd breast,
> When upward-springing, blythe, to greet
>   The purpling East.
>
> Cauld blew the bitter-biting *North*
> Upon thy early, humble birth;
> Yet cheerfully thou glinted forth
>   Amid the storm,
> Scarce rear'd above the *Parent-earth*
>   Thy tender form. (K 92, I, 228–9, 1–18)

Burns crafts the turns of his native Habbie tenderly; turning in from the three longer lines of tetrameter to the shorter fourth line he describes the flower's 'slender stem' in a form that both corresponds with and expresses its slenderness and delicacy. Tenderness is also expressed in the poem's allusions. Although Gilbert, Burns's brother, insisted that 'To the Mountain-Daisy' was 'composed . . . while the author was holding the plough', it was shaped as much by Burns's reading; echoes of Gray's 'Elegy' and Milton's *Paradise Lost* in the first stanza call up and into play well-known literary models of sympathy. Attending to the poem's literary textures and contextures, this chapter describes how Burns draws on and enriches the reach and resources of literary predecessors. By expressing his own feelings in and through the words of others, Burns turns allusion into a literary form of sentiment.

Burns was pleased with the poem's sentiments, as he explained in a letter to his friend John Kennedy soon after it was composed:

> I have here, likewise, inclosed a small piece, the very latest of my productions.— I am a good deal pleas'd with some sentiments in it myself; as they are just the native, querulous feelings of a heart, which, as elegantly melting Gray says, 'Melancholy has marked for her own'.—[4]

Here, the word 'sentiments' is richly suggestive, offering a cue to how the poem was read and understood in its time. One contemporary definition, which had become current in the late eighteenth century, is 'refined or *tender* emotion, exercise or manifestation of sensibility' (emphasis mine). Not only would Burns's early readers have recognised its expressions of tenderness but also they would have understood the poem itself generically as an 'exercise or manifestation of sensibility'. Stooping feelingly to mourn the daisy's fate, Burns rehearsed a familiar literary posture, one that was synonymous with sentimental writing. What Carol McGuirk has termed 'benevolent condescension' was a dramatic occasion for lament and moral reflection adopted in the works of Mackenzie, Sterne and other sentimental writers.[5] Weeping for a fly, a dead horse, a mouse, a flower or other humble object was proof of a feeling heart and tenderness. Burns's lines 'To a Mouse, On turning her up in her Nest, with the Plough, November, 1785' afforded another well-known example, also couched in the Habbie stanza Burns revived and made famous. Both poems, according to Gilbert, were composed in the same field in Mossgiel, standing beside the same plough; both expressed tenderness.[6]

Burns's tenderness impressed his contemporaries. 'To a Mountain-Daisy' was first published in Henry Mackenzie's *The Lounger*, in 1786, where he praised its 'precision of intimacy' and noted its distinguishing 'tender and moral' qualities.[7] James Currie recognised these as a feature of the 'Mountain-Daisy' noting that 'to extract out of incidents so common, and seemingly so trivial as these, so fine a strain of sentiment and imagery, is the surest proof, as well as the most brilliant triumph, of original genius'.[8] What distinguished Burns's composition was its tenderness. Francis Jeffrey, writing in 1809, described the poem's 'force of tenderness and truth'.[9] 'Tender' was also a key word in Wordsworth's poetic tribute to Burns, 'Composed or suggested during a tour in the summer of 1833'. In the poem's final lines he remembers the flower that 'by the unwilling ploughshare died to prove / The tender charm of Poetry and Love'.[10]

Although 'To a Mountain-Daisy' was one of the most well known and admired of Burns's poems in the eighteenth and nineteenth centuries, it has failed to charm modern critics and readers. The poem's sentiments have been perceived as inauthentic, cloying and shrill. McGuirk singles out the 'Mountain-Daisy' as the only poem of direct address in the Kilmarnock edition that 'fails to charm'.[11] This failure results, she explains, from an overblown and unconvincing sententiousness: 'Burns tries to turn the uprooting of the weed into a combination of the "Vanity of Human Wishes" and the Sermon on the Mount, but the moralising does not sound authentic.'[12] And yet this exaggeration is itself characteristic of Burns's poetic tendencies. As his brother observed, Burns 'frequently presents a caricature of his feelings'.[13] The poem, McGuirk complains, presents a 'caricature' of sentiment, couched in a self-consciously literary idiom which has proved awkward for modern readers and critics. For McGuirk, 'When Burns abandons the search for an appropriate personal voice and relies too much on sentimental models, he retards a reader's perception of his feelings.'[14] In a more recent study, Nigel Leask has described the poem's 'burden of literary self-consciousness'.[15] And yet the poem is misunderstood if we fail to appreciate its particular and deliberate use of sentiment historically, in the context of the literary culture of its day.

The senses of sentiment alive and at play in Burns's poem are poised between personal feelings and proverbial truth. This chapter will set out to resituate the poem in a culture of sentiment and by doing so attempt to reclaim it from misunderstanding. It offers a rereading and revaluation of the poem, paying particular attention to the way in which it calls up and balances between different kinds of sentiment – tender feeling, moral expression and the sense of sentiment as a literary form. In the eighteenth and early nineteenth centuries sentiments were recognised as the epigrammatic extractable parts of literary works, lines or phrases which could be easily detached from the whole narrative. These literary quotations were exemplary of particular strong feelings, such as pity, pathos, sorrow or joy, or offered pithy moral lessons, sententious extracts. Sentiments were collected in anthologies and became an established literary form in the period, one which, I suggest, shaped Burns's art of allusion. This chapter pays particular attention to Burns's creative and sympathetic transformation of literary sources in 'To a Mountain-Daisy', suggesting that these contribute to his various and subtle engagements with literary sentiment.

Burns 'favorite authors' were 'of the sentim[ental] kind', writers 'such as Shenstone':

> Thomson, [Mackenzie's] Man of feeling, a book I prize next to the Bible, [Goldsmith's] Man of the World, Sterne, especially his Sentimental journey, M^cpherson's Ossian, &c. these are the glorious models after which I endeavour to form my conduct.[16]

They also served as models after which he formed his poetry. *The Man of Feeling*, for example, introduced Burns to new structures of sentiment. The novel was perceived as a 'touchstone of the sentimental genre', a 'litmus test of reader's sensibility'.[17] In it, Mackenzie recounts episodes from the life of Harley its hero, and presents a number of encounters that were to become set-pieces of the sentimental genre, moments of tearful communion, and evocations of feeling too full for language. Finding in the smallest, most trifling object – a mountain daisy – some significance of feeling, Burns rehearses the postures of Mackenzie's hero.[18]

Addressing the daisy, Burns does not just call on the postures of sentimental literature, he also calls on its languages. The poem is rich in literary echo and allusion, summoning lines from a number of well-known literary sources. Its final lines have a self-consciously literary feel:

> Ev'n you who mourn'st the *Daisy*'s fate,
> *That fate is thine* – no distant date;
> Stern Ruin's *plough-share* drives, elate,
> Full on thy bloom,
> Till crush'd beneath the *furrow*'s weight,
> Shall be thy doom!

The ploughshare recalls a particular literary precedent from Young's *Night Thoughts*, another example of the sentimental literature Burns admired:

> and final Ruin fiercely drives
> Her ploughshare o'er Creation[19]

Burns's phrase 'Ruin's plough-share' remembers and conflates these lines from Young. The echo contributes to a shift in tone and focus, from particular and sentimental to general and sententious. The plough which had turned down the daisy in the first stanza returns, but this time as a proverbial symbol. Burns's attention moves from particular and local to general and sententious, from a real plough to a literary and proverbial ploughshare, a particular mountain daisy to a universal symbol of mortality. These particular objects of experience, the plough and the daisy have also come to represent general truths. Burns calls on and moves between different kinds of sentiment, tender feeling in the early stanzas and sententious sonority in the final lines.

There is an affinity between the collectable quotation and the sententious, both senses are contained in the word 'sentiment'. Another contemporary sense of the word, now obsolete, was 'epigramatical expression of something striking or agreeable . . . often in the manner of a proverb or proverbial' (*OED*, 8). This kind of sentiment shares space with and shades into the Maxim; both embody feelings that could provide moral instruction. The following excerpts from Richardson's collection of *Moral and Instructive Sentiments*, drawn from *Pamela, Clarissa* and *Sir Charles Grandison*, serve as examples of this kind of sentiment:

> The man who shows tenderness for the calamities of others, gives a moral assurance that he will make a good husband.
>
> How affecting to a gentle mind are the visible emotions of a manly heart.
>
> It is the glory of the human heart to melt at another's woe.[20]

In his collection, Richardson singled out what he regarded as the timeless maxims from his novels, excising any ephemeral detail. His collection was designed to make it easier for readers to absorb the instructive sentiments embedded in his novels, extracted from the narrative. Not only did the story give occasion to the sentiment, to recall Johnson's phrase, in these collections it was abandoned altogether. Richardson was not the only author whose works were presented in this new fragmentary form. Milton and Shakespeare's sentiments were also made available in this way, and, in the eighteenth and early nineteenth centuries, such expressions were routinely culled from a wide range of literary works and gathered into collections such as *The Beauties of Sentiment* (1801).[21]

The late eighteenth century saw the emergence of new forms of reading and, with these, new structures of feeling. Reading for the sentiments became commonplace, as Barbara Benedict and Leah Price have shown.[22] Readers became adept at culling quotations or 'sentiments' themselves from favourite poems and novels, and copying these into commonplace books. Once committed to memory, these literary excerpts were ready to be deployed in conversation as a mark of refined sensibility, fashionable testimony to the reader's sensitivity. Jane Austen parodies this practice in *Northanger Abbey*, when she describes and mocks Catherine Morland's familiarity with this mode of deploying sentiment and her addiction to 'portable quotations' from which she is supposed to learn to value sensibility:[23]

> from fifteen to seventeen she was in training for a heroine; she read all such works as heroines must read to supply their memories with those quotations which are so serviceable and so soothing in the vicissitudes of their eventful lives.
>
> From Pope, she learnt to censure those who
> 'bear about the mockery of woe.'

From Gray, that
> 'Many a flower is born to blush unseen,
> And waste its fragrance on the desert air.'[24]

The list goes on: Shakespeare, Shenstone, the Bible – all furnish the young heroine's mind with popular sentiments. Austen is satirising the young Catherine's pretensions, hinting at her false sensibility and atomistic morality, and, doing so, she is criticising what had become a common way of reading in the period. Although it was Samuel Johnson, an author Austen admired deeply, who famously advised reading novels for the sentiment rather than the plot, for the moral which could be extracted rather than the story, this way of reading had, by the early nineteenth century, become part of a performance of sentiment rather than a practice of edification. The fashion for this kind of reading – encouraged, as Benedict points out, by 'profiteering booksellers' practices' – threatened to undermine the authority and the appreciation of literary form, fragmenting books into collections of what modern readers might call sound-bites.[25] And yet this kind of reading for the extracts could be put to creative use.

Burns was inspired by and drew strength from his reading of literary sentiments and incorporated extracts dynamically and tactfully into his own poetic forms. Many of Burns's early poems were drafted in his commonplace book, amid literary quotations, meditations and *sententiae*; this compositional matrix was, as Leask has pointed out, 'characteristic of a budding poet in the sentimental vein'.[26] Burns's commonplace book served as 'the crucible for his Kilmarnock poems'.[27] His artful and liberal use of poetic sentiments in 'To a Mountain-Daisy', published in that volume, deserve appraisal in this context.[28] Burns describes his own habit of reading for the sentiments in a letter to William Nicol on June 1787:

> I have bought a pocket Milton which I carry perpetually about with me, in order to study the sentiments – the dauntless magnanimity; the intrepid, unyielding independence; the desperate daring, and noble defiance of hardship, in that great Personage, Satan.[29]

Burns employs quotations liberally throughout his letters. He confessed, in one, that he liked 'to have quotations ready for every occasion. –They . . . save one the trouble of finding expression adequate to one's feelings'.[30] And yet this jocular tone belies his artful and feeling use of literary quotations. Writing to his friend John Arnot in April 1786, the same month he turned down the Daisy, he mourns another loss, and doing so, he quotes lines from Book IX of *Paradise Lost*:

> I have lost, Sir, that dearest earthly treasure, that greatest blessing here below, that last, best gift which compleated Adam's happiness in the garden of bliss, I have lost —I have lost—my trembling hand refuses its office, the frighted ink recoils up the quill—Tell it not in Gath – I have lost—a—a—A WIFE!

Fairest of God's creation, last & best!
How art thou lost—[31]

Burns describes two kinds of loss: his loss of a 'wife', Jean Armour, his preg-
nant lover, and her fall from grace. The quotation thus describes both her
fallen condition and Burns's sense of loss: In April 1786 Jean had revealed
her pregnancy to her parents and she had also shown the letter Burns had
written in which he promised to marry her. Enraged at their daughter's
situation and adamant that she should not marry such a well-known rake
and fornicator, they hid Jean away and defaced the letter, cutting both
Burns and Jean's names out so that its promise was annulled. They 'cut
my very veins', Burns had complained in another letter to a friend when
he heard of the fate of his letter to Jean.[32] She had betrayed him – and yet
she herself had been deceived – by her father, and undone, by Burns. In his
letter, Burns attempts to find a language adequate to express his feelings.
If the profusion of dashes, and the ink recoiling up the quill wielded by the
trembling hand, were recognisable figures of strong feeling, familiar tropes
of sentimental writing; his use of quotation, calling on the language of the
Old Testament and on a poignant moment from Book IX of *Paradise Lost*,
offers another. Burns remembers Adam's words to Eve on hearing that she
has picked the forbidden fruit:

> Adam, soon as he heard
> The fatal trespass done by Eve, amazed,
> Astonied stood and blank, while horror chill
> Ran through his veins, and all his joints relaxed;
> From his slack hand the garland wreathed for Eve
> Down dropped, and all the faded roses shed:
> Speechless he stood and pale, till thus at length
> First to himself he inward silence broke.
>   O fairest of creation, last and best
> Of all God's works, creature in whom excelled
> Whatever can to sight or thought be formed,
> Holy, divine, good, amiable or sweet!
> How art thou lost, how on a sudden lost,
> Defaced, deflowered, and now to death devote?[33]

Remembering these lines, Burns responds to his personal crisis creatively,
finding consolation in the kindred feelings of another, and recognising in
Eve's plight the fate of his own lover, 'defac't, defloured'.

'To a Mountain-Daisy' makes this figure of ruination literal; the undo-
ing of the mountain daisy by the plough is both perhaps a real event and
also a metaphor for fornication and the ruination of Jean. The poem is
shaped by and written in the wake of the betrayal and, like the letter, it

also invokes lines from *Paradise Lost*. Milton's 'sentiments' turn up and are turned around in the first stanza of the 'Mountain-Daisy':

> Wee, modest, crimson-tipped flow'r,
> Thou's met me in an evil hour;
> For I maun crush amang the stoure
>   Thy slender stem:
> To spare thee now is past my pow'r,
>   Thou bonie gem.

Burns's 'evil hour' recalls that 'evil hour' in Milton's poem when Eve plucked the fruit:

> So saying, her rash hand in evil hour
> Forth reaching to the fruit, she plucked, she ate:
> Earth felt the wound, and nature from her seat
> Sighing through all her works gave signs of woe,
> That all was lost[34]

Calling on this sentiment, Burns transforms and answers it, turning Milton's perspective around, so that nature's sympathy with man becomes, in his lines, a moment when man sympathises with and for nature. Recalling the phrase 'evil hour', Burns also remembers his own ruined lover and her betrayal. The Miltonic allusion is also, in part, a creative response to his own situation, to the deflowering of Armour, so that the daisy, ruined by the plough, represents personal circumstances as well as more general sentiments. The allusion also plays with his own reputation as an innocent, unlettered genius, and disrupts it, knowingly and playfully.

Not only was this passage in Milton's poem personally evocative for Burns but it was also a well-known example of literary sentiment. The lines he remembers from *Paradise Lost* would have been familiar even to those who had not read the whole poem – it is a passage which Addison had singled out in *The Spectator* 351 (Saturday, 12 April 1712) as an exemplary manifestation of 'very natural sentiments'. This is the moment where, he explains, 'all Nature' was 'disturbed upon *Eve's* eating the forbidden Fruit: "earth felt the wound and all of nature sighed"'. This, Addison explained, was a great literary moment of sympathy:

> As all Nature suffer'd by the Guilt of our first Parents, these Symptoms of Trouble and Consternation are wonderfully imagin'd, not only as Prodigies, but as Marks of her Sympathising in the Fall of Man.[35]

It is fitting that Burns should turn to this moment of sympathy when he himself is sympathising with the fallen flower – it serves as both an example of and testament to his art of sentiment.

Burns knew *The Spectator* from an early age, and we can conjecture that this might have been the first place he encountered Milton's lines.

The magazine was an early favourite: 'My knowledge of modern manners, and of literature and criticism', he explained, 'I got from the Spectator.'[36] Addison's *Paradise Lost* essays are credited with drawing critical attention to the Miltonic sublime. But they also introduced readers to Milton as a sentimental poet, prized for sympathy and human drama.[37] Milton's 'evil hour' was also singled out as a key sentiment by a number of Burns's contemporaries. His friend and literary encourager Hugh Blair, Professor of Rhetoric at Edinburgh University, in his *Lectures on Rhetoric and Belles Lettres* chose the same Miltonic lines as an example of the most striking personification and as the turning point of the whole poem. He was not alone; in his *Observations on Pope*, Gilbert Wakefield argued that these lines had 'perhaps, no equal for sublimity and pathos'.[38] So it is apt then that feeling for words to express his own sentiments Burns should turn to this Miltonic sentiment.

Mourning the daisy's fate, Burns turns to and reworks another well-known sentiment. His 'bonie gem' remembers a popular and often quoted stanza from Gray's 'Elegy Written in a Country Churchyard':

> Full many a gem of purest ray serene
> The dark unfathomed caves of ocean bear:
> Full many a flower is born to blush unseen,
> And waste its sweetness on the desert air.[39]

By calling on Gray's lines to describe the ruined daisy, Burns was evoking familiar sentiments. The 'Elegy' was a set-piece of literary pathos. One of the best-known and widely anthologised poems of the late eighteenth and early nineteenth centuries, it was, to recall Johnson's famous pronouncement, a poem which 'abounds with images which find a mirrour in every mind, and with sentiments to which every bosom returns an echo'.[40] It seems appropriate then that Burns should call on these sentiments in his poem, since they provided a universal language of feeling. For Burns, the sentiments were also personal and particular.

Describing the daisy as a 'bonie gem', Burns brings together in one phrase two images from Gray's stanza, images that represented the unknown rustics buried in the churchyard. Doing so he transforms the general to the particular, metaphorical flower and gem to real-ruined daisy. In Burns's lines, the fleeting blush of Gray's unnamed flower becomes the particular, red tips of the mountain daisy. Throughout the poem, Burns plays with and tests Gray's analogy between humble rustic and blushing flower. A figure for humble rustics in Gray's poem, in Burns's lines it is 'unassuming' and in 'humble guise'. In the fourth stanza, he echoes Gray more exactly; his daisy is 'unseen, alane'. Reworking Gray's sentiments, Burns makes them more specific. Where the object of Gray's sympathies are general, Burns's are particular. Gray's 'Elegy' begins with a plodding ploughman wearily trudging home, in Burns's poem the ploughman takes centre stage. Gray presents an idyllic portrait of evening, with its gentle twilight fading; Burns locates the poem in a particular place and time: Mossgiel, April 1786. Whereas Gray's narrator mourns unknown rustics, Burns attends to a particular, named, flower, a mountain daisy, with crimson-tipped petals. These crimson petals alert us to the poem's undertones of sexual ruination, the plough, the ruined flower. Whereas Gray celebrates neglect as a guarantee of innocence, Burns infers its ruination. Gray celebrates the flower's innocence – being unseen and unknown is compared implicitly to being innocent; in Burns's poem being unseen proves fatal. Playing with Gray's sentiments, Burns is knowingly describing the dangers of cultivation. Whereas for Gray, refinement and sophistication would corrupt the innocence of the flower, and the innocent, primitive rustics it represents, in Burns's lines it is a literal form of cultivation – ploughing – that destroys the flower. Calling on Gray's lines, Burns is complicating the image of himself as an uncultivated original genius, an image he himself propagated.[41]

For all his famed originality Burns called on literary sentiments artfully. Doing so need not invalidate or undermine his poem: it also served to enforce and to summon up a bond of shared feeling. In the poem echoes of Gray and Milton are chosen deliberately, as well-known moments of pathos and tenderness, sentiments in a double sense, both examples of tender and feeling and well-known and widely circulated literary extracts. As such, these sentiments offer in literary form that 'charm of recognitions' Wordsworth saw in his writing. Reading Burns, Wordsworth constantly found himself in 'the presence of human life' as the poems struck home with the 'charm of recognitions'.[42] Reading the 'Mountain-Daisy', we recognise not only the presence of human life, as Wordsworth did, but also the presence of literary sentiment.

One of Burns's arts as a poet was to draw on and transform other people's words, to give new life to old sentiments in and through allusion.[43] Calling on well-known phrases from favourite authors helped Burns to express his own sentiments in a language which his readers could recognise. Doing so he extended the reach of sentiment as it was understood as a literary form. For Richardson and many of his contemporaries, the sentiment was a timeless example, universal in tenor, extracted from the ephemeral and local. Burns's daisy is a particular example that speaks of the general and universal fate. This bringing together of the local and the universal is an aspect of Burns's art which Fiona Stafford has discussed in her recent study.[44] And in part he does this by calling on and transforming sentiments artfully, describing his particular experiences in the words of others, making what was ephemeral and individual universally available. In the 'Mountain-Daisy', the flower is both particular and an emblem of purity and innocence lost.

In a letter to John Moore of 1787 Burns insisted that he was not vain enough to hope for poetic fame in the language of literary sentiment:

I know very well, the novelty of my character has by far the greatest share in the learned and polite notice I have lately got; and in a language where Pope and Churchill have raised the laugh, and Shenstone and Gray drawn the tear; where Thomson and Beattie have painted the landskip, and Littleton and Collins described the heart; I am not vain enough to hope for distinguished Poetic fame.[45]

He did not hope for fame in this language, nothing so singular. Instead he sought a language of sentiment, expressing his own feelings in and through the words of others. In the preface to his very first commonplace book Burns expressed a hope that readers might be curious to know how 'a ploughman thinks, and feels, under the pressure of Love, Ambition, Anxiety, Grief with the like cares and passions'. He goes on to explain that these passions, 'however diversified by the Modes, and manners of life, operate pretty much alike, I believe, in all the Species'. Calling, in his poems, on the words of his literary compeers to express his own feelings thus embodies and reveals a deep-held egalitarian belief in the possibility that men from all stations and all manners of life shared common feelings. When he writes in the preface to the Kilmarnock poems that he intended to express the 'sentiments' of his rustic compeers 'in their native language', he was attempting to authenticate his claim to genius. But he might also be inviting readers to extend their sympathies, to acknowledge the possibility that a ploughman might feel like other men. He also hoped that this 'native language' might call on and extend literary sentiment. It was, Burns explained, one of the great privileges attending poetic genius, that we can give our 'woes, cares, joys loves, &c an embodied form in verse'. [46] It was one of Burns's great sensitivities and achievements as a poet to recognise his own feelings in other poets' words, and to embody other poets' words in his own.

Notes

1. As Fiona Stafford has recently suggested: *Local Attachments: The Province of Poetry* (Oxford: Oxford University Press, 2010), p. 129. See also Nicholas Roe's discussion of Burns's playful engagement with the 'Heaven taught Ploughman' myth in 'Authenticating Robert Burns', *Essays in Criticism* xlvi.3, 1996, pp. 195–218.

2. Gilbert Burns to James Currie, in James Currie, *The Life of Robert Burns* (London, 1826), Appendix No. III, p. 531.

3. Seamus Heaney, 'Glanmore Sonnets II', *Field Work* (London: Faber, 1979), p. 34.

4. Robert Burns, *The Letters of Robert Burns*, ed. J. De Lancey Ferguson and G. Ross Roy, 2nd edn, 2 vols (Oxford: Clarendon, Clarendon Press, 1985), vol. I, p. 32, 20 April 1786.

5. Carol McGuirk, *Robert Burns and the Sentimental Era* (Athens, GA: University of Georgia Press, 1985), p. 7.

6. The two poems were often reproduced alongside one another. Mackenzie included the text of 'To a Mountain-Daisy' in his important review in *The Lounger*, 9

December 1786, and they both appeared in later editions of Vicesimus Knox's popular anthology, *Elegant Extracts*.

7. Henry Mackenzie, cited in Donald Low (ed.), *Robert Burns: The Critical Heritage* (London and Boston: Routledge & Kegan Paul, 1974), pp. 67–71, 69.

8. James Currie, cited in Low (ed.), *Burns*, p. 140.

9. Francis Jeffrey, cited in Low (ed.), *Burns*, p. 188.

10. William Wordsworth, *Sonnet Series and Itinerary Poems, 1820–1845*, ed. G. Jackson (Ithaca and London: Cornell University Press, 2004), p. 599.

11. McGuirk, *Robert Burns and the Sentimental Era*, p. 11.

12. Ibid., p. 12.

13. Gilbert Burns, cited in Low (ed.), *Burns*, p. 271.

14. McGuirk, *Robert Burns and the Sentimental Era*, p. 53.

15. Nigel Leask, *Robert Burns and Pastoral: Poetry and Improvement in Eighteenth-Century Scotland* (Oxford: Oxford University Press, 2010), p. 159.

16. Burns, *Letters*, vol. I, pp. 17–18.

17. Maureen Harkin, 'Mackenzie's *Man of Feeling*: embalming sensibility', *ELH* 61.1, 1994, pp. 317–40, 319.

18. McGuirk suggests that the poem is 'reminiscent of Mackenzie's Harley at his most lachrymose' (*Robert Burns and the Sentimental Era*, p. 14).

19. Edward Young, *Night Thoughts*, in Edward Young, *The Complete Works of Rev. Edward Young*, ed. John Doran, 2 vols (London: William Tegg, 1854), vol. I, IX.167–8.

20. Samuel Richardson, *A Collection of Moral and Instructive Sentiments, Maxims, Cautions and Reflections, Contained in the Histories of* PAMELA, CLARISSA, and Sir CHARLES GRANDISON (London, 1755), pp. 155, 361, 362.

21. *The Beauties of Sentiment; Or Select Extracts from the Best Authors*, 2 vols (London, 1801).

22. Beauties and Sentiments are related forms of literary extract, but whereas the Beauty exemplified aesthetic achievement, the Sentiment could also embody literary feeling and a moral lesson. For discussion of the extract as an emerging literary form in the eighteenth century, see Barbara Benedict, 'Reading by the book in *Northanger Abbey*', *Persuasions On-Line* 20.1, http://www.jasna.org/persuasions/on-line/vol20no1/benedict.html (accessed 22 March 2011); and also her 'The "beauties" of literature, 1750–1820: tasteful prose and fine rhyme for private consumption', *1650–1850: Ideas, Aesthetics, and Inquiries in the Early Modern Era* 1, 1994, pp. 317–46. See also Leah Price, *The Anthology and the Rise of the Novel from Richardson to George Elliot* (Cambridge: Cambridge University Press, 2000).

23. Benedict, 'Reading by the book in *Northanger Abbey*'.

24. Jane Austen, *Northanger Abbey*, in Jane Austen, *The Novels of Jane Austen*, ed. R. W. Chapman, 6 vols, 3rd edn (Oxford: Oxford University Press, 1933–69), vol. V, pp. 15–16.

25. Benedict, 'Reading by the book in *Northanger Abbey*'.

26. Leask, *Robert Burns and Pastoral*, p. 81.

27. Ibid., p. 3.

28. See John Guillory's discussion in 'Mute, inglorious Miltons: Gray, Wordsworth and the vernacular canon', in John Guillory, *Cultural Capital: The Problem of Literary Canon Formation* (Chicago: University of Chicago Press, 1993), pp. 85–133.

29. Burns, *Letters*, vol. I, p. 123, 18 June 1787.

30. Ibid., vol. I, p. 207, 14 January 1788.

31. Burns, *Letters*, vol. I, p. 34, April 1786; quoting *Paradise Lost*, IX.896, 900.

32. To Gavin Hamilton, in Burns, *Letters*, vol. I, p. 30, 15 April 1786.

33. John Milton, *Paradise Lost*, ed. Alastair Fowler (Longman: London and New York, 1968), IX.888–901.

34. Ibid., IX.780–4.

35. Joseph Addison, *The Spectator* No. 351, ed. Donald Bond, 5 vols (Oxford: Clarendon Press, 1965), vol. III, p. 311.

36. Robert Crawford, *The Bard: Robert Burns, a Biography* (London: Jonathan Cape, 2009), p. 67.

37. In the introduction to his 1750 edition of *Paradise Lost*, John Newton points out that the poem is full of 'that kind of writing which the French critics call *tender*, and which is in a particular manner engaging to all sorts of readers'. He goes on to point out that Adam and Eve, in Book X, 'are likewise drawn with such sentiments, as do not only interest the reader in their afflictions, but raise in him the most melting passions of humanity and commiseration. When Adam sees the several changes in nature produced about him, he appears in a disorder of mind suitable to one who has forfeited both his innocence and his happiness' (*Paradise Lost* (1750), p. 283, 720n.).

38. Gilbert Wakefield, *Observations on Pope* (London, 1796), p. 146. William Cowper also quoted the passage in his letters, and Fuselli depicted the scene in picture IX of his Milton Gallery (Luisa Cale, *Fuseli's Milton Gallery: Turning Readers into Spectators* (Oxford: Clarendon Press, 2006), p. 94).

39. *The Poems of Thomas Gray, William Collins, and Oliver Goldsmith*, ed. Roger Lonsdale (London: Longman, 1969), p. 127.

40. Samuel Johnson, 'Gray', *Lives of the Poets*, ed. Roger Lonsdale, 4 vols (Oxford: Oxford University Press, 2006), vol. IV, p. 184.

41. The 'Elegy', as I have argued elsewhere, became associated with peasant poets: 'Lines from the poem were often quoted in the prefaces to editions of self-taught poet', offering 'an interpretive framework for evaluating the work of the humble poet' (Mina Gorji, *John Clare and the Place of Poetry* (Liverpool: Liverpool University Press, 2008), pp. 36–56, 36).

42. Cited by Stafford in *Local Attachments*, p. 125.

43. On Burns's allusions see Christopher Ricks, 'Burns', in Christopher Ricks, *Allusion to the Poets* (Oxford: Oxford University Press, 2002), pp. 43–82; Seamus Heaney, 'Burns's art-speech', in Robert Crawford (ed.), *Robert Burns and Cultural Authority* (Edinburgh: Edinburgh University Press, 1997), pp. 216–33.

44. Stafford, *Local Attachments*, p. 191.

45. Burns, *Letters*, vol. I, p. 88, January 1787.

46. 'To Agnes McLehose', in Burns, *Letters*, vol. I, p. 207, 14 January 1788.

CHAPTER 7

House and Home in Burns's Poems

Claire Lamont

'House and Home' in Burns's poems seems an unlikely topic, since relatively few of his poems are set in the home, or make much reference to it. The phrase 'house and home' was, however, known to Burns in its Scots form 'house and hald' (K 69, I, 128, 34). This phrase is more commonly 'house and haud', where 'haud' means 'property held, a holding; a habitation, dwelling-place'.[1] In 'To a Mouse' the poet laments that the mouse whose nest he has destroyed is 'But [without] house or hald' (K 69, I, 128, 34). Burns's poems are mostly set out of doors, and if they take us inside a building it is not usually a home but a place of social meeting like a church or a pub. His songs are often set in the countryside, which is not surprising since many are love-songs and there was not much privacy for young lovers within a rural cottage–witness the awkwardness with which the boyfriend is first introduced to the family in 'The Cotter's Saturday Night'. What justifies the topic, I hope, is that although there are not many poems by Burns about houses, those that there are are among his best known and best loved. Any temptation to add 'and his most sentimental' should be left to take its chance in the argument that follows. It is worth remembering that Robert Fergusson, not usually accused of sentimentality, is best known for 'The Farmer's Ingle'.

It is often said that one's childhood home shapes one's sense of what a house ought to be like. Burns lived in three homes in his childhood, Alloway, Mount Oliphant and Lochlie, all modest farm cottages with outhouses, typical of rural Ayrshire in the late eighteenth century. It is the first of these which dominates Burns's later recollection. He was born there, and lived there until the age of seven. The cottage at Alloway, which still survives despite various restorations, is a one-storey thatched house with two rooms for the family, for use as a kitchen and a bedroom, and, beyond a partition, a byre. The most celebrated aspect of this house is that it was built by Burns's father, William Burnes.[2] Burns was born in this cottage on 25 January 1759, and within ten days the gable end had been blown out in a storm. Burns alludes to this event in the song starting 'There was a lad':

> Our monarch's hindmost year but ane[3]
> Was five-and-twenty days begun,

'Twas then a blast o' Janwar' Win'
Blew hansel in on Robin. (K 140, I, 321, 9–12)

This story of building and destruction takes fuller shape when Burns's brother Gilbert recounted it in a letter to the biographer, James Currie:

> When my father built his 'clay biggin,' he put in two stone jambs, as they are called, and a lintel, carrying up a chimney in his clay gable. The consequence was, that as the gable subsided, the jambs, remaining firm, threw it off its centre, and, one very stormy morning, when my brother was nine or ten days old, a little before day-light, a part of the gable fell out, and the rest appeared so shattered, that my mother, with the young poet, had to be carried through the storm to a neighbour's house, where they remained a week till their own dwelling was adjusted. That you may not think too meanly of this house, or of my father's taste in building, by supposing the poet's description in the Vision (which is entirely a fancy picture) applicable to it, allow me to take notice to you, that the house consisted of a kitchen in one end, and a room in the other, with a fire-place and chimney; that my father had constructed a concealed bed in the kitchen, with a small closet at the end, of the same materials with the house, and, when altogether cast over, outside and in, with lime, it had a neat, comfortable appearance, such as no family of the same rank, in the present improved style of living, would think themselves ill-lodged in.[4]

The poem which picks up this story is, of course, 'To a Mouse, On turning her up in her Nest, with the Plough, November, 1785'. The mouse has toiled to build her own house: 'That wee-bit heap o' leaves an' stibble, / Has cost thee monie a weary nibble' (K 69, I, 128, 31–2) and though it was the coulter of the plough which caused the primary damage, the loss is completed by the weather: 'Thy wee-bit *housie*, too, in ruin! / It's silly wa's the win's are strewin!' (19–20). The '*housie*' raises the issue of the meaning of the term 'house and home'. If the house is the architectural aspect of the concept, be it made of clay, brick, stone, leaves or stalks, home is the domestic reality which the house enables and on which it becomes imprinted. Burns's mouse is female; her nest is 'cozie' and carries with it the idea of future young ones. As Gaston Bachelard has pointed out, the human home has often been likened to a nest because it is the nurturing place of the young and because it, metaphorically at least, reflects the body-shape of the creature who made it.[5] The house as nest is an intimate place, conflating the concepts of house and home.

Robert Crawford has described 'The Cotter's Saturday Night' as a 'celebration of William Burnes's home life'.[6] It is the Alloway cottage that is recalled in the setting of the poem, although it is family life rather than architecture that is celebrated. The house is described in terms of space, its only interior features being the hallan beyond which their cow 'snugly chows her cood' (K 72, I, 148, 94) and the fireplace. The fireplace is the most important part of the house. The poem starts at the end of a November day when the Cotter walks wearily home:

> At length his lonely *Cot* appears in view,
>   Beneath the shelter of an aged tree;
> Th' expectant wee-things, toddlan, stacher thro'
>   To meet their *Dad*, wi' flichterin noise and glee.
> His wee–bit ingle blinkan bonilie,
>   His clean hearth-stane, his thrifty *Wifie*'s smile (19–24)

This scene may have happened often in Burns's childhood; but it is also in a long tradition of cottage description. It has been traced back to classical writers; and would be best known to Burns from Gray's 'Elegy' and Scottish renderings of it by Allan Ramsay, James Thomson and Robert Fergusson. The topos is recognised by two features: the cottage is seen through the eyes of the man entering it and the first object seen is the fire, the 'wee-bit ingle, blinkan bonilie'.

Both Lucretius and Virgil give descriptions of the husband returning home to be greeted by his wife and children, Virgil's being specifically a ploughman.[7] Horace adds the fire: writing on the pleasures of living in the country he adds a fire of seasoned wood to the wife's preparation for the return of her weary husband.[8] All these were available to those without Latin in Dryden's verse translations.[9] Thomson, in his *Winter*, follows Lucretius in lamenting one who will not return home. His lament is for a shepherd who died buried in deep snow in a landscape evoking the poet's youth on the Scottish Border:

> In vain for him th' officious Wife prepares   [busy]
> The Fire fair-blazing, and the Vestment warm;
> In vain his little Children, peeping out
> Into the mingling Storm, demand their Sire,
> With Tears of artless Innocence.[10]

The stanza in Gray's 'Elegy' (1751) which describes the returning labourer is concerned with death in a different way. The poet is looking at the graves in a churchyard and Thomson's 'In vain' is replaced by 'no more':

> For them no more the blazing hearth shall burn,
> Or busy housewife ply her evening care:
> No children run to lisp their sire's return,
> Or climb his knees the envied kiss to share.[11]

Burns's stanza about the returning labourer, drawing on the memory of his father as it does, may be nostalgic, but is not elegiac. It is indeed possible for the tradition to be drawn on cheerfully. Peggy, in Ramsay's *The Gentle Shepherd* (1725), envisages ways in which she will please a future husband:

At even, when he comes weary frae the hill,
I'll have a' things made ready to his will.
In winter, when he toils thro' wind and rain,
A bleezing ingle, and a clean hearth-stane.
And soon as he flings by his plaid and staff,
The seething pot's be ready to take aff.[12]

The poem which is the closest predecessor to Burns's 'The Cotter's Saturday Night' is Fergusson's 'The Farmer's Ingle' (1773). In that the farmer and his workers return to the house on a winter's evening:

Weel kens the gudewife that the pleughs require   [ploughmen]
  A heartsome meltith, and refreshing synd   [meal, drink]
O' nappy liquor, o'er a bleezing fire:
  Sair wark and poortith douna weel be join'd.[13]   [poverty]

In comparison with Burns's poor cotter, who appears to work his land single-handedly, Fergusson's 'gudeman' has employees both male and female.[14] The household seems less benign than that of the cotter. The gudeman, approaching the house, 'o'er the halland flings his een' (15) to check that everything is as clean and orderly as he likes it.[15] Although the simple evening meal is satisfying and accompanied by cheerful local gossip, we notice that before it the children had been crying with hunger (57–8). After the meal the old grandmother tells an 'auld warld tale', which sounds not unlike 'Tam o' Shanter' (60–4). The telling of supernatural stories is replaced in 'The Cotter's Saturday Night' by prayers and the reading of the Bible. Fergusson explains that regression to old superstitions is a feature of age:

O mock na this, my friends! but rather mourn,
  Ye in life's brawest spring wi' reason clear,
Wi' eild our idle fancies a' return,   [age]
  And dim our dolefu' days wi bairnly fear;
The mind's ay cradled when the grave is near. (68–72)

'The Farmer's Ingle' shares with 'The Cotter's Saturday Night' simplicity, work and patriotism, but it is not a religious poem: its mental world seems formed between 'reason' and 'idle fancies', closed off from the imaginative range of the Cotter's visionary religion.

Poets writing about the returning labourer often write about shepherds because, like Ramsay, they are writing in the pastoral tradition or, like Thomson, gained their inspiration from a farming environment which was more pastoral than agricultural. In Gray's 'Elegy' the famous opening stanza makes the ploughman stand for all who plod wearily home at night. Shepherds have symbolic status gained from both classical and biblical sources. The ploughman's symbolic status is not as far-reaching; but can be traced to the humble dedication to work and virtue in *Piers Plowman* and Chaucer's Ploughman, providing a tradition in which Burns places his hard-working father in 'The Cotter's Saturday Night'. A poet who takes Burns's description of rural home-coming from the ploughman and gives it back to the shepherd is Wordsworth in his 'Michael' (1800), whose protagonist also enters his cottage to be welcomed by his wife and a good fire.[16] The criss-crossing of influence among poets on this theme continues. Features of the cottage scene in 'Michael' owe something to Burns. Scott, in a further twist in the story of the labourer and his cottage, compares the ploughman and the shepherd on a stormy night, when the issue is not returning to the cottage but leaving it. 'When the tir'd ploughman, dry and warm, / Hears, half asleep, the rising storm', the shepherd by contrast has to go out to gather his flock to safety:

> The blast that whistles o'er the fells,
> Stiffens his locks to icicles;
> Oft he looks back, while, streaming far,
> His cottage window seems a star,—[17]

The cottage seen as a star is a Wordsworthian image, and best known from 'Michael'.[18]

Asked to define a house, those of us in northern latitudes would be likely to mention the roof. We value 'a roof over one's head', and are distressed to see any house rendered roofless. Anthropologists, however, who consider the matter historically and globally, are more likely to give primacy to the fire in establishing the idea of a household. The importance of fire is that it is necessary for cooking, and therefore signifies that cultural evolution traced by Richard Wrangham in his *Catching Fire*.[19] The fire also gathers people round it to enjoy its heat and light. The Cotter forgets his toil when he sits by the fire with a small child on his knee. After the fire's use for cooking is over, the family forms a circle round it for prayers, just as in 'The Farmer's Ingle' the children listen to the grandmother's tales 'before the ingle's low' (59), clustered round the glow of the hearth.

Psychology also has something to say about this scene. In mentioning the fire in 'The Cotter's Saturday Night' one should not overlook 'His clean hearth-stane' and 'his thrifty *Wifie*'s smile' (K 72, I, 146, 24). The topos of the returning labourer describes the man resuming control of space which during the day has been the realm of women and children. The poem calls the fire 'His' – the Cotter's – despite the hearth's being clearly associated with the woman. It is a measure of her efficiency as a housewife that her hearthstone should be well-swept. Freud, writing on the symbolism of houses, associates the room or the inside of a house with the woman, seeing such spaces as womb-like.[20] Of fire he writes, 'Flame is always a male genital, and the hearth is its female counterpart.'[21] In 'The Cotter' the man enters the female space of the interior, as the fire penetrates the hearth.

Fire occurs also in 'Tam o' Shanter', in the contrast between Tam's home, which is not welcoming, and the inn which is. It is the inn that has the blazing fire, welcoming the working man into its cosiness: 'Ae market-night, / *Tam* had got planted unco right; / Fast by an ingle, bleezing finely' (K 321, II, 558, 37–9). The wife is replaced by the landlady, with whom Tam 'grew gracious' (47). Kate, his 'sullen dame' is at home 'Nursing her wrath to keep it warm' (10, 12). This plays on two expectations, first that if nursing she should be nursing a child and, secondly, that what needed to be kept warm was the hearth not 'her wrath'. In this case one might say that it is the inn that is being sentimentalised rather than the cottage – a Scots tradition, I suggest.

In the poems I have just mentioned, the description of the house, or the inn as a house substitute, is from a male perspective, and that a married man. Domestic comfort seems less successful for a man alone in Burns; for him fires do not 'bleeze finely'. In 'The Vision' the poet describes himself after a hard day threshing:

> There, lanely, by the ingle-cheek,
> I sat and ey'd the spewing reek,
> That fill'd, wi' hoast-provoking smeek,   [cough-provoking]
>   The auld, clay biggin;
> And heard the restless rattons squeak
>   About the riggin. (K 62, I, 103, 13–18)

These are no doubt the lines which Gilbert Burns had in mind when, in the passage quoted above, he assured Currie that 'the description in the Vision' was not based on the family home at Alloway. James Kinsley suggests that the 'auld, clay biggin' here may reflect aspects of the house at Lochlie (K III, 1075). A smoking fire again accompanies Burns's loneliness when first at Ellisland before his wife joined him. In the 'Epistle to Hugh Parker' he describes himself as 'ambush'd by the chimla cheek, / Hid in an atmosphere of reek' (K 222, II, 412, 7–8). It seems to take a wife to make a decent fire.

Poems by Burns which show the house from the woman's perspective are scarce; but more can be gleaned from his songs.[22] Most of the songs have male speakers, and the major theme is love and sexual pursuit, usually without expectations of marriage – so there is seldom any mention of a house. Duncan Davison, trying to tempt the lively Meg, says 'We will big a wee, wee house, / And we will live like king and queen' (K 202, I, 391, 17–18); but that is a rare statement. A male singer wishing to offer shelter to his lass usually thinks his plaid the best option:

> Oh wert thou in the cauld blast,
>   On yonder lea, on yonder lea;
> My plaidie to the angry airt,
>   I'd shelter thee, I'd shelter thee (K 524, II, 813, 1–4)

There are, however, songs by female singers. Girl singers, mostly unmarried, are just as eager and wistful about love as the young men; but slightly more aware of a domestic future. Interestingly, the songs do not mention keeping the fire in – perhaps because the singers are not wives. What is found in the songs is the folk-song motif of making the bed. The young woman in 'The Ploughman' seems cheerful about domestic tasks:

> I will wash my Ploughman's hose,
>   And I will dress his o'erlay;
> I will mak my Ploughman's bed,
>   And chear him late and early. (K 205, I, 394, 13–16)

There is also the folk-song trope of making a bed *to* someone. Spoken by a woman this is a sexual invitation, as in the song 'The bonie lass made the bed to me' in which 'She made the bed baith large and wide' (K 571, II, 855, 13). Young men in Burns's songs are described as 'rantin' and 'rovin' (K 140, I, 320, 5–8). The young women sing approvingly of these dashing qualities, leading too often to sad songs like 'The rantin laddie', in which a girl who had had a 'bastart babie' is confined to her father's kitchen (K 575, II, 859, 4), and 'Duncan Gray', in which the singer's vitality has no outlet other than rocking the cradle with her toe (K 204, I, 393, 6–7). The wife in 'The Cotter's Saturday Night' gets satisfaction from seeing her children well turned out and from the quality of her cheese, gratifications which do not figure in the songs. Instead we have the rebellious wife in 'The weary Pund o' Tow' (K 360, II, 623) referring to the tedious business of spinning flax, which was a daily obligation of a wife in a poor household.

So far nothing has been said about the political aspect of Burns's description of houses. There is an issue about politics and the home. 'Homeless' is a frightening word, and it is a straightforward radical position to support housing the poor. In contrast, 'staying at home' is usually a conservative position, perhaps indicating self-satisfaction and lack of concern for others, or a lack of a sense of adventure. Housing is a radical issue; actually living in a house may not be. So, what happens to the politics when Burns writes about houses?

'To a Mouse' is a story of homelessness at the onset of winter, the homelessness of a provident creature who had made appropriate preparation. The beginning of the poem does not stress the destruction of the nest. The poet instead wants to reassure the mouse that he will not chase her 'Wi' murd'ring *pattle*' (6), that is, the spade used to remove mud from the plough. Why should the poet be suspected of wanting to murder the mouse with his spade? Well, mice ate corn, but not much, and the poet recognises that he can spare that small amount. Yet the poem suggests that he might have wanted to destroy the homeless little thief *utterly*. We read this as a human story, and a terrifying one, implying that it is in the nature of man to act vindictively at the expense of the poor. The mouse's being turned out is the fault of 'Man's Dominion', here in having made the agricultural advances which led to farming and ploughs. The least the poet can do is reinstate 'Nature's social union' by letting the mouse have its small portion of corn. There is no such healing gesture in the face of 'Man's Dominion' over housing, as is seen again in other poems about homelessness.

Burns's poem 'A Winter Night' has as its epigraph Shakespeare's great lines on destitution from *King Lear*:

> *Poor naked wretches, wheresoe'er you are,*
> *That bide the pelting of this pityless storm!*
> *How shall your houseless heads, and unfed sides,*
> *Your loop'd and window'd raggedness, defend you*
> *From seasons such as these–* (K 130, I, 303)[23]

The poet asks that question on a stormy winter night. Poorly housed himself, he thinks how the animal world is faring, before hearing a 'plaintive strain' (34) urging those who are 'sunk in beds of down' (73) to reflect on the poor man as

> Stretch'd on his straw he lays himself to sleep,
> While through the ragged roof and chinky wall,
> Chill, o'er his slumbers, piles the drifty heap! (78–80)

The rich man's 'down' is the poor man's snow. As often in Burns, nature and the poor are linked against the thoughtless rich. The natural world knows this, as he claims in a 'Scotish Song':

> The lavrock shuns the palace gay,   [lark]
>   And o'er the cottage sings (K 470, II 753, 5–6)

Poor housing is one abuse; another is the threat of dispossession. In 'The Twa Dogs' the rich man's dog, Ceasar, describes the vindictive treatment of poor debtors:

> Poor *tenant-bodies*, scant o' cash,
> How they maun thole a *factor*'s snash;
> He'll stamp an' threaten, curse an'swear,
> He'll *apprehend* them, *poind* their gear,
> While they maun stand, wi' aspect humble,
> An' hear it a', an' fear an' tremble! (K 71, I, 140, 95–100)

These lines describe circumstances similar to those which had threatened Burns's own family at Lochlie.[24] He was equally able to write about such abuse further from home. In his 'Address of Beelzebub' he has that luminary write from Hell to the Earl of Breadalbane, President of the Highland Society in London, concerning attempts by the Society to prevent five hundred Highlanders from leaving Scotland to settle in Canada – the clearances in reverse, and a situation not uncommon in the decades after

Culloden. The poem contains a devastating exposure of the conditions of the Highlanders in Scotland, as Beelzebub encourages the Earl to oppress them even further:

> But smash them! crush them a' to spails!   [splinters]
> An rot the DYVORS i' the JAILS!   [bankrupts]

After a tirade in that mode the Devil turns politely to his correspondent:

> Go on, my lord! I lang to meet you
> An' in my HOUSE at HAME to greet you;
> Wi' COMMON LORDS ye shanna mingle,
> The benmost newk, beside the ingle
> At my right hand, assign'd your seat (K 108, I, 255, 39–40, 53–7)

Hell clearly has more comfortable housing than anything offered to the Highlanders.

In that poem *home* belongs to the Devil; what the Highlanders wanted was liberty and those freedoms which Burns associated with North America. There were still some freedoms to be found in Scotland, however, and one of them might be freedom from houses and domesticity. Burns got satisfaction from family life when settled with his wife and children at Ellisland; in his verse letter to Dr Blacklock he reflected

> To make a happy fireside clime
>   To weans and wife,
> That's the true *Pathos* and *Sublime*
>   Of Human life.– (K 273b, I, 491, 51–4)

That does not deny other occasions on which he recognised the appeal of life lived on the unsettled margins of society. He could relish the freedom of the beggar or vagrant. In the 'Epistle to Davie, a Brother Poet', after reflecting on the unequal distribution of riches and its relation to happiness, Burns makes this claim for the two poets, Davie and himself:

> To lye in kilns and barns at e'en,
> When banes are craz'd, and bluid is thin,
>   Is, doubtless, great distress!
> Yet then *content* could make us blest;
> Ev'n then, sometimes we'd snatch a taste
>   Of truest happiness. (K 51, I, 66, 29–34)

This is seriously argued, and lacks the insouciance of Burns's most celebrated poem about the homeless, 'Love and Liberty–A Cantata'. Vagrants drinking, singing and dancing in the warmth and shelter afforded by an inn, join in a chorus which shows that they not only do not miss the conventional comforts of a home but also actively disparage them:

With the ready trick and fable
   Round we wander all the day;
And at night, in barn or stable,
   Hug our doxies on the hay.
     A fig for &c.

Does the train-attended Carriage
   Thro' the country lighter rove?
Does the sober bed of Marriage
   Witness brighter scenes of love? (K 84, I, 208, 262–9)

'House and home' is a cliché, threatening to lull the critical faculty with trite alliteration. The terms are, however, complex in their overlapping meanings. The poems cited above show Burns's writing about houses to be often angry and sardonic, forcing outrages on the reader. Why then is he thought to write sentimentally about houses? 'Sentimental' in such a context implies that feelings for which there is some justification have been treated disproportionately, and that the disproportion is the result of some weakness in addressing the issues. Sentimentality often deals in the diminutive. Setting aside the Scots usage of words which misleadingly appear diminutive, there is no doubt that the mouse is 'wee'. But Swift has taught us that altering size is a technique of satirical vision. We have no difficulty in seeing the housing issue from the perspective of the Lilliputian mouse, and to the extent to which the disproportion is Swiftian we will not be tempted to call it sentimental. What, however, about the Cotter? He is no smaller than we are; yet treacherously somehow the reader is being invited to look down on him. Because he lives a more simple life than that of our complicated selves? Because his life represents the old-world style of the poet's father, and perhaps the reader's grandfather? Even if there is something diminishing about these characters, it is not shared by their houses. The mouse's nest and the Cotter's house, like Burns's other houses, are functional; they are not prettified or picturesque.

It appears that a home is something Burns tends to see in a diminished context, inviting the term 'sentimental'. When we turn to houses, however, the situation is different. Homes may invite sentimentality; but houses are political.

Notes

1. *The Concise Scots Dictionary*, ed. Mairi Robinson (Aberdeen: Aberdeen University Press, 1985), p. 271, col. 2.
2. James Mackay, *A Biography of Robert Burns* (Edinburgh: Mainstream Publishing, 1992), pp. 29–30; Robert Crawford, *The Bard: Robert Burns, a Biography* (London: Jonathan Cape, 2009), pp. 28, 30.
3. George II died in 1760, the year after Burns was born.
4. Robert Burns, *The Works of Robert Burns*, ed. James Currie, 2nd edn, 4 vols

(London, 1801), Appendix III, I, 372–3. Currie's edition, first published in 1800, starts with an account of the poet's life. In response to it Burns's brother, Gilbert, sent the letter from which this passage is taken to Currie on 24 October 1800, and it was first published in Currie's second edition of 1801.

5. Gaston Bachelard, *The Poetics of Space*, trans. Maria Jolas (Boston: Beacon Press, 1994; first published in French in 1958).

6. Crawford, *The Bard*, p. 131.

7. Lucretius, *De rerum natura*, III.894–6; Virgil, *Georgics*, II.513–15, 523–34.

8. Horace, *Epodes*, II.39–40, 43–4.

9. John Dryden, *John Dryden*, ed. Keith Walker (Oxford: Oxford University Press, 1987): Lucretius, 'The Latter Part of the Third Book', 76–9, 276–7; 'Virgil's *Georgics*, Book II', 760–2, 499; 'The Second Epode of Horace', 58–60, 64–8, 306–7.

10. James Thomson, *The Seasons* [1746], ed. James Sambrook (Oxford: Clarendon Press, 1981), p. 218, ll. 311–15.

11. Thomas Gray, 'Elegy Written in a Country Churchyard', ll. 21–4, in *The Poems of Thomas Gray, William Collins, Oliver Goldsmith*, ed. Roger Lonsdale (London: Longman, 1969), pp. 121–2. For the classical examples of the 'returning labourer' topos mentioned above I am indebted to Lonsdale's note on p. 121.

12. Allan Ramsay, *The Gentle Shepherd*, ll. 177–82, in *Poems by Allan Ramsay and Robert Fergusson*, ed. Alexander Manson Kinghorn and Alexander Law (Edinburgh: Scottish Academic Press, 1974), pp. x, 52–3.

13. Robert Fergusson, 'The Farmer's Ingle', ll. 19–22, in *Poems by Allan Ramsay and Robert Fergusson*, p. 162.

14. For the difference between the cotter and the gudeman with reference to these poems, see Nigel Leask, *Robert Burns and Pastoral* (Oxford: Oxford University Press, 2010), pp. 216–20.

15. The halland is here 'an inner wall, partition, or door-screen erected between the door and the fireplace' (*Concise Scots Dictionary*, p. 262).

16. William Wordsworth, 'Michael', ll. 97–111, in William Wordsworth, *The Major Poems*, ed. Stephen Gill (Oxford: Oxford University Press, 2000), p. 227.

17. Walter Scott, *Marmion*, 'Introduction to Canto Fourth' (1808), in Walter Scott, *Scott: Poetical Works*, ed. J. Logie Robertson (London: Oxford University Press, 1904), 124, cols 2–125, col. 1.

18. For the cottage 'named the Evening Star' see Wordsworth, 'Michael', ll. 136–46.

19. Richard Wrangham, *Catching Fire: How Cooking Made Us Human* (London: Profile Books, 2009), pp. 11–14.

20. Sigmund Freud, 'Symbolism in dreams', in Sigmund Freud, *Introductory Lectures on Psycho-Analysis*, trans. James Strachey, *The Standard Edition of the Complete Psychological Works of Sigmund Freud* (London: Vintage, 2001, first published 1963), vol. 15, p. 163, and *Civilisation and Its Discontents* in vol. 21, p. 91.

21. Freud, 'Symbolism in dreams', p. 162.

22. There are both textual problems and questions of authorship concerning the songs traditionally attributed to Burns. All those mentioned here are included in James Kinsley's edition.

23. William Shakespeare, *King Lear*, III, iv, 28–32.

24. For William Burns's legal entanglement with his landlord, originating in pursuit for unpaid rent, see Crawford, *The Bard*, pp. 124–37.

CHAPTER 8

'The Real Language of Men': Fa's Speerin? Burns and the Scottish Romantic Vernacular

Murray Pittock

William Wordsworth's 1802 Preface to *Lyrical Ballads* famously stated that it was the poet's intention to write of 'the real language of men in a state of vivid sensation' and 'to chuse incidents and situations from common life, and to relate or describe them . . . as far as was possible, in a selection of language really used by men'. The men in question were to be the products of 'low and rustic life', and Wordsworth assured his reader that, 'aukward' as his attempts at poetry in this vein might seem, he was nonetheless intending to ensure that these men's language would be 'purified indeed from what appear to be its real defects, from all lasting or rational causes of dislike or disgust'. What these significant shortcomings are in a language Wordsworth claims as more valid for poetic experience than that of his predecessors, he does not specify: but it is safe enough to conclude from their ensuing absence that representations of Cumbrian voicing or language are among them. Wordsworth barely uses regional dialect words, though he does occasionally utilise Scots: he also stands at a distance from the dialect-speaking classes he so often describes, and is – possibly as a consequence – painfully oblique about sexual passion. Given his aspiration towards a 'purified', if quotidian, English, register inevitably circumscribes the realm of Wordsworth's Romantic subject, and even variety of pronunciation can be difficult to detect, as it is not in Byron for instance.[1]

Nonetheless, Wordsworth promises his readership to preserve the 'plainer and more emphatic language' of 'low and rustic life'. How can this circle be squared? By approaching to the condition of one literary kind in particular: the ballad, 'artless' and yet 'admirable', already conveniently authenticated as possessing *volkisch* verity by a collecting process controlled by those from outside the group identified as producing the tradition, and often modified in its range of register or reference by those who collected it, a process which was already deemed acceptable, even normative. It was this external control in the arrangement of popular tradition which led to the editorialising of ballads and of the wider range of traditional materials, a process which – as I have argued – Burns had already protested against in 'Tam o' Shanter' (1791).[2]

Hazlitt commented on Wordsworth's deep and rich northern accent, while the poet himself subscribed to dialect poetry, such as Robert Anderson's *Poetical Works* of 1820. It follows, then, that the nature of the 'real language of men' was an ideological choice on Wordsworth's part, not a gentleman's misprision of provincial realities, although these realities were very decidedly present in Wordsworth's lifetime and afterwards. As late as 1861, the Royal Commission on Mines sitting at Westminster employed interpreters for the Northumbrian witnesses; and it is hard to imagine that the everyday speech of Cumberland or Westmorland was more penetrable seventy years earlier. Vast areas of the United Kingdom spoke in mutually incomprehensible ways: Wales was 90 per cent Welsh-speaking in the eighteenth century; monolingual speakers of Gaelic were widespread in Scotland and Ireland; Scots itself was widely spoken, while in England areas from Yorkshire and Devon used a thesaurus of terms unknown in the metropolis. As late as the 1940s, the dialect of the Clee Hills in south Shropshire contained hundreds of words which rapidly dropped out of use in the wake of the growing presence of electronic media.[3]

This mutual incomprehensibility, combined with strong regional and national divergence in elements such as pay rates and confessional loyalties (to say nothing of cultural or political nationalism), made of these islands – as I argued in *Inventing and Resisting Britain* (1997) – a far less unified polity than that posited by Linda Colley in *Britons* (1992). Understanding this is the only way to understand the need contemporaries saw for the Enlightenment imperative of 'a non-localised, supra-regional "standard"' language argued for by Thomas Sheridan, James Beattie and many others, promoters of 'linguistic homogeneity' throughout the British Isles. This was not just a question of Anglicising the Scots tongue, as some narrower literary histories might claim, but a widespread 'provincial anxiety' about how far one could participate in the new British state without using the metropolitan version of its language. Sheridan was an advocate of standardisation of the basis that studying and speaking English will make Englishmen of all the islands, and this was simply an overt example of a goal which was frequently present implicitly.[4]

Enlightenment Scotland, from David Hume to Sir John Sinclair, tended to embrace the march of such conformity. James Sibbald regretted that Allan Ramsay and others had deserted the good example of Drummond of Hawthornden's English verse to write 'in the familiar dialects of the meanest vulgar', and claimed that – barring some differences in orthography – Scots and Yorkshire dialect were indistinguishable. Even James Currie, Burns's editor and biographer, opined that 'since the Union, the manners and language of the people of Scotland have no longer a standard among themselves, but are tried by the standard of the nation to which they are united'. Scots, in other words, was slipping closer and closer to standard English: any other view of the matter was mere obfuscation. A few sturdy defences were mounted against this position: J. Runcole in an essay 'On Scottish Songs' in *The Bee* arguing that 'had we retained a court and parliament of our own, the tongues of the two sister-kingdoms would . . . have differed like the Castilian and Portugueze . . . each would have had its own classics', while Francis Jeffrey forcefully declared that Scots was 'not to be considered a provincial dialect' but 'the language of a whole country . . . it is an ignorant, as well as any illiberal prejudice, which would seek to confound it with the barbarous dialect of Yorkshire or Devon'. But on the whole, the role of Gramscian cosmopolitanism in creating an anxiety which alienated Scots 'from their social experience and cultural traditions' was far more normative. Indeed, as so often happens in such situations, Scots were among the sturdiest defenders of the need 'to identify themselves with the dominant culture'. Paradoxically, the strengths of their own education system enabled them to become among the most sophisticated theorists of the adoption of alien models in other walks of life.[5]

Scotland's response to the provincial dilemma over linguistic conformity was thus both the most articulate and the most focused, owing to the fact that its professional and intellectual infrastructure survived the Union of 1707 intact, and indeed continued to develop in a distinctive way. University courses and professional and associational society alike responded in a structured fashion to the agenda of standardisation of language, while the wider Scottish Enlightenment welcomed this linguistic dimension of its teleology of civility as underpinning both the general ability to communicate a new generation of generally applicable ideas and the development of a civil society on a unified if not unitary British model, to which the emergent Scottish public sphere aspired in the aftermath of the 1745 Rising. The universities supported the dissemination of these developments, which in turn led to the rise of 'English' as university subject in Scotland, and it was in this context perhaps no coincidence that, as Ruriko Suzuki argues, Wordsworth's concept of the 'real language of men' may have been influenced by the theories of Hugh Blair, who from 1762 was the first professor of what came to be English at the University of Edinburgh. This 'English', under the guise of 'Rhetoric and Belles Lettres', was the metropolitan middle-class speech championed by Joseph Addison at the beginning of the eighteenth century: as Thomas Miller points out, 'the first university professors [in Scotland] to teach English taught the English of the *Spectator*', which Burns admired while regretting it was 'so thoroughly and entirely English'. Education and standardisation were believed to go together, with the 'essay as a univocal instrument' for instilling sensibility. What was called 'delicacy of sensibility and exactness of propriety' had their objective correlative in a single language through which both could be expressed. 'Delicacy' and 'exactness', like Wordsworth and Coleridge's 'talent', 'severe thought' and 'best models' are terms of rhetorical aspiration to unitary standards of excellence and taste. Thus Wordsworth's 'real language of men' paradoxically has its origins in the framework of conformity to Enlightenment civility against which it appeared to rebel. The solitary, native and local is set against the urban, cosmopolitan and rhetorical, but only as part of an argument the same set of intellectual assumptions are having with themselves, not with the Enlightenment paradigm that underpins them both.[6]

Adam Smith was one of the most prominent major Enlightenment figures engaged in supporting the goal of a standard language of civility. In his *Theory of Moral Sentiments* (1759, 6th edn 1790), violent events and images (implicitly linked to Scotland's past) were converted into the structures of sympathy, where mutual recognition was greatly aided by mutually recognisable language, both of word and body. This requirement implied shared notions of civility and a shared standard language. It might be doubted whether anyone could truly sympathise with a Gaelic or even a Scots speaker: incomprehensible language might invoke the colonisation of pity but not sympathy. Smith's moral sentiments implied a unitary public space and language, and in a telling passage Smith associates sympathy with commonality of language, not only social development:

> The rules of justice may be compared to the rules of grammar; the rules of the other virtues, to the rules which critics lay down for the attainment of what is sublime and elegant: composition . . . A man may learn to write grammatically by rule, with the most absolute infallibility; and so, perhaps, he may be taught to act justly.

Consistency and uniformity of language are thus just as important to the 'impartial spectator' of conscience as is sympathy itself, for who can be an impartial spectator while ignorant of the syntax of justice? Smith 'valorised the virtues of assimilation' and by the sixth edition of *Moral Sentiments* was trying to objectify refinement in these terms. Refined sentiments belonged in 'the expanding domain of print literacy', and this of course had less and less room for non-standard forms of English. Just as – as Alexander Broadie has argued – Smith was indebted to the Aristotelian mean in his doctrine of sympathetic exchange, so too he sought the occupation by syntax, vocabulary and grammar of a shared middle ground, alike remote from the party language of the seventeenth century or the provincial or Irish and Scottish tongues which reflected a lack of political and cultural assimilation in his own day.[7]

Burns was deeply influenced by *Moral Sentiments* (Smith returned the compliment by ordering four copies of the Edinburgh edition of Burns's poems), first reading the book before 1783, possibly as early as 1777. In 1789, Burns read *Wealth of Nations*, and his own library contained the sixth edition of Smith's text. Burns mentions Smith explicitly in 'Epistle to Glenconner' and uses *Moral Sentiments* implicitly in 'Address to the Unco Guid' and the 1787 Woods Prologue, paraphrasing from it in 'To a Louse' ('O wad some Pow'r the giftie gie us / *To see ourels as others see us!*', K 83,

I, 194, 43–4). It has been long recognised that Smith's *Moral Sentiments* –
indeed, like Mackenzie's *Man of Feeling* – was an important text for Burns.
But in order to fulfil his role as a poet, Burns had to find the space to inter-
rogate and resist such influential texts – a condition Andrew Noble notes in
the Canongate notes on 'To a Louse', and which Raymond Bentman also
articulates in saying that 'running in and out of Burns's works is a desire
both to agree with and to question the Enlightenment thinkers' reliance on
reason'.[8]

This was the root of Burns's version of 'the real language of men', for his
Scots in its varied registers and local dialects exists in a dialogic relationship
to the Enlightenment quest for civility and a British golden mean in language, derived from English models and free of Irish bulls and Scotticisms
alike. Burns is complex in his use of Scots for reasons of thematic reference
and depth of connotation and argument: he crosses register between English
and Scots, and between light and heavy Scots, but also uses historic Scots
words and dialects from different parts of Scotland (principally his father's
north-eastern and mother's Ayrshire Scots) to offer potentially significant if
not radically distinctive readings of the same poem. In other words, Burns
turns the Enlightenment paradigm on its head while celebrating it: the
exact opposite of Wordsworth's practice.

Celebrating it? In what way does Burns appear to celebrate the
Enlightenment? I will deal with this issue first before going on to examine
'To a Louse''s precise use of Scots, which reveals the sheer sophistication of Burns's practice, and considering 'Halloween', which uses shifts in
register and a metropolitan English paratext to provide, within the context
of the poem's Scots, a parodic example of the collector's art in making out
of a living tradition a curiosity of what Joep Leerssen has termed 'auto-
exoticism'. The key fresh position put forward for consideration in this
essay is this: we have read Burns too much through glossaries, and not
enough through dictionaries, thesauruses and histories.[9]

Burns has both a local rustic and an official Enlightenment persona. He
seems to tell his readership that he writes in the standard terms of English
which Sheridan and Smith promoted, but this is only his reversal of the
Wordsworthian paradox, adopting a set of poetic values which run athwart
the reality of his practice. In a letter of January 1787, Burns describes his as
'a language where Pope and Churchill have raised the laugh, and Shenstone
and Gray drawn the tear; where Thomson and Beattie have painted the
landskip; and Littleton and Collins described the heart'. Yet at once the
perfect periods should give us pause. This is Burns telling us how Burns
writes in a manner in which he does not write, just as he does in a different
fashion when expressing the view that 'part of the machinery, as he called
it, of his poetical character' was 'to pass for an illiterate ploughman who
wrote from pure inspiration'. In other words, Burns's Science of Man was
to appear less Enlightened than he was. Although many Burns critics have

read him so carelessly as to be taken in by this, he was more accurately described in *The Bee* in 1791 as combining the elements of 'soaring sweetly on the muse's wing' and being down at 'old Coila's rustic streams', both a universal and abstract and a realised local writer.

The frontispiece image of the shepherd and shepherdess which graced the first appearance of the *Scots Musical Museum* (*SMM*) bore that stylised quality of classical pastoral (though with two tell-tale Gothic ruins, one of which disappeared in later volumes) which indicated a status for Scottish pastoral on a level with Vergil or rather Theocritus: great but unconstrained by register. Yet the realisation of the vernacular and apparently authentic served up in the book which followed was itself framed by the collectors' paradigmatic cabinet of curiosities, enshrined in the term 'Museum'. This representation escaped the pressure of its own paradoxicality through the relieving inheritance of a vernacular poetry which could aspire to gentility of register and genre while nonetheless remaining politically unthreatening in its 'Museum'. Sets adapted to voice, harp and pianoforte had been advertised in *SMM* from the first volume onwards, and in Volume VI (1803), published after Burns's death, the 'original Simplicity of our ancient national Airs is retained unincumbered with useless Accompaniments & Graces', yet come supplied 'with proper Bases for the pianoforte', which presumably the reader was to understand Scotland's song had always enjoyed, rather than being the product of a hybridisation of traditional airs with the drawing room which only went back to the 1720s . Only in Scotland could the inheritors of the Enlightenment have their vernacular Herderian cake and eat it with artsong confections. Herder's view of the 'intimate dependence of thought on language' and his emphasis on 'moral sentiments' at the expense of 'system-building' and 'abstract theorising' invited the confluence of *volkisch* expression with authentic sentiment which Wordsworth, in adopting a linguistic plainness of style unaffected by regional variation, pretended to, but Burns – enabled by the closeness of Enlightenment discourse to Scottish associational life and even the basics of its education – achieved.[10]

If morality is based on sentiment, and sentiment is based on authentic feeling, and authentic feeling requires authentic language, the Smithian premiss of linguistic convergence as denominating successfully convertible sympathetic exchange is turned on its head. The Theocritan Doric *locus amoenus* and the speech that goes with it becomes the mark of true feeling, and heteroglossic hierarchies are overcome by the process of a dialogism that does not rank Scots below English, but sets them in competition with each other. Among Romantic uses of genre, Burns's is both unusual and profound: but the subject at hand is language. Burns used 'over 2,000 words in Scots' besides a few dozen in Gaelic, a language which had only recently disappeared from Ayrshire.[11]

In 'To a Louse', Burns voices the words of the Smithian spectator, disinterested and impartial, one who should '*see ourselves as others see us*' (K 83, I, 194, 43) but is in reality voyeuristically ogling a young woman: his is no grammar of justice but a frank sexual interest and class envy posing as egalitarianism. The 'Louse' simultaneously stands in the tradition of a number of eighteenth-century insect poems, and Donne's 'Flea', a poem about Smithian sympathy and sexual intimacy, and this is represented in the slipperiness of its Scots. As Nigel Leask points out, there are a number of more recent exemplars for Burns's poems, notably Fergusson's 'The Bugs' and Peter Pindar (or John Wolcot)'s anti-monarchical poem, *The Lousiad*. A range of parodic, political and sexual reference already exists for Burns on the generic threshold of the poem. Before we even reach the language's 'starting lines', the allusive range is complex enough to suggest to us a certain fluidity of approach.[12]

The difference in rank between the louse, lady and speaker is of course easily recognised as primarily present in a distinction between local language and a cosmopolitan standard, whose very fashion represents a citizenry of the world rather than Ayrshire. The louse is addressed (presumably in terms it will understand, like the local Scots employed in dialogue with the Ayrshire mouse in another poem) as the 'crowlan ferlie' (creeping wonder, with possible overtones of contempt in Burns's glossary). Such a creature might settle on an 'auld wife's *flainen* toy' (flannel cap, not glossed by Burns who, as with earlier writers in Scots, used the glossary not to explain meaning simply but rather to provide an additional filter for it) or 'squattle' in a 'beggar's haffet' (nestle in a temple, though neither are glossed). At the same time, 'Miss's fine *Lunardi*, fye !' brings us much closer to the world of Scottish 'standard' English, the language of the 'Misses' of Burns's world and their latest fashions. Lunardi's hot air balloon was a contemporary sensation, its flight in Scotland being described by Robert Arnot in the *Scots Magazine* in October 1785. The 'Lunardi bonnet' in the shape of a balloon appeared shortly afterwards, and since Burns probably wrote the poem before the beginning of 1786, the 'Miss Jenny' of the poem is indeed setting the fashion (K, III, 1148).[13]

By contrast, locality is poverty. The louse sits at the bottom of the class pile without speech – living in 'plantations' as do the speechless slaves transported under (as Nigel Leask has pointed out) 'the guinea stamp', but different from them in that he is free to roam beyond the limits – 'horn' (outlawry, not glossed) and 'bane' set by society – the language of the comb is also the language of legal outlawry and social rejection. The louse is a 'ferlie', a wonder, because, despite being such an outsider, he has in one sense escaped the class system to which the gazer is limited in terms of the lack of precisely that social mobility and free intimacy which the insect can command. To caress a young woman of position would be to take a 'freedom' with her: part of the puzzle for the speaker is that the lowest of the low, the louse in its overcrowded plantations, exiled from all society by 'horn' and 'bane', 'Detested, shunn'd, by saunt an' sinner', has that freedom, and can 'strunt rarely'. So Burns here challenges Smith's idea of moral sentiments as a proxy for a standard universalisable humanity, able to communicate as well as spectate, thus converting Scottish and social difference into British unity: class and language in their different ways divide the speaker from both louse and lady. Yet the louse enjoys the lady in a shady, miry different kind of 'union', desired but not achieved by the poetic voice.

So far so good. Burns's Scots creates a double world of domestic interiority which challenges the universalisable abstracts of Enlightenment decorum by breaking open register's voicing of class in the insect's favour. But does it do more? If we look carefully at the use of language in 'To a Louse', we can break further into the nested meanings of Burns's 'plantations' of language and situation.

The poem begins with the speaker in church, ignoring the minister to focus on the lady, sitting ahead of him in a front pew which presumably her family can afford to hire: rather like Jean Armour's father in fact, and a physical demonstration of the inequalities of class, situation (and language) in a place where all should be equal. Even were this not a kirk service, the speaker cannot readily speak to the lady directly in a world where they are so separated by convention, so he looks at her instead. His gaze is driven by instinct (not unlike the louses's); it is voyeuristic; and the louse's role on one level is to be the bug as sexual avatar, where the insect travels intimately over a body the onlooker wishes to occupy. Here the meaning of the relationship between speaker and louse rests on the vernacular address and Scots vocabulary, combined with much deeper nested meanings (taking MS rather than Kilmarnock textual readings makes little difference to this, though there are arguably some shifts in emphasis). The 'Lady' makes no appearance until line 10, and there appears in the English not the Scottish form ('leddy'). We may have guessed as much when we saw in line 4 that she was dressed in 'gawze and lace', fancy apparel far removed from the patriot garb of Ramsay's 'Tartana, or the Plaid' or Burns's own 'hodden gray': these are surely the 'base foreign fashions' commented on in the Ramsayan tradition, the essence of pretension and a defiance of the community reinstated by the louse's forcible communion with dress, hair and flesh. 'Crowlan', from the north-eastern Scots verb 'crowl' (did this come from Burns's father's family?) on one level means 'crawling', but 'crowl' is also a stunted, small or undersized body (cf. creepy-crawlie). In Ayrshire Scots it is recorded (somewhat later than Burns admittedly, though there is no reason to think it a nineteenth-century neologism as far as I'm aware) as a term of derision or contempt, which would redouble the contemptuous implications of 'ferlie' noted by Burns in the Kilmarnock glossary. 'Ferlie' as a wonder or marvel with implications of contempt may be a term which rebounds on the speaker: Burns may have known the proverb 'fools wonder ay at farlies' recorded in 1721, so by identifying the louse – a parasitic insect of unimpressive dimensions – as a 'ferlie', the speaker may only be showing himself to be a gowk, or fool. 'Ferlie' is also news, gossip or scandal, and thus provides an indication of the barely suppressed licentiousness of the poem.

The louse 'strunts', another term unglossed by Burns. The verb means on one level to walk about in a stately or affected manner, and this is how the *Scottish National Dictionary* (henceforward *SND*) sees Burns as using it here. However, this far from exhausts 'strunt', which can be a fit of pique or pettishness or a sulk: 'ta'en the strunt', to be in a huff, is found in Ramsay. Here the louse's act may once again reflect the viewer's priorities, not the insect's, for the viewer is annoyed that the louse can be where he cannot go. 'Gawze' may not only suggest the material but also could be at odds with the disgruntled threat of the speaker that the louse will dine 'but sparely' – for 'gawsie' (also spelt with a z) is a description of a plump good-looking person or a showy place: 'sic a place' may refer to both a lovely, well-fed lady and the showy place she sits and the clothes she wears. The closing phrase of the first stanza may thus exert pressure on the speaker's assumption of the louse's poor dining, mediated through a double or triple connotation for 'gawze'. It is tempting to go down this route, as it develops the range of the poem's meanings very neatly within the frame of reference they have already established. Indeed, the second stanza, with its envious outrage that the louse presumes to dine on the 'Lady', strongly suggests that the insect's presumption is focused on a dinner preferable to that found on 'some poor body' by virtue of its plenitude not sparseness. 'Blastet', descriptive of a stunted or withered creature (glossed as 'worthless' by Burns), not only reinforces 'crowlan' earlier but also contains the idea of cursing, which the speaker is doing. 'Creep afore ye gang' is proverbial: the 'creepan' louse, taking things one step at a time, has accomplished more than the impotent desire of the onlooker, who seeks to grab at and characterise everything at one gaze. 'Wonner' evokes both the meaning that the louse is marvellous and that it is small and contemptible ('wonder, a term of contempt' is Burns's gloss): 'a nasty, unpleasant, mischievous or insignificant creature' in the *SND*. It thus perfectly sums up the divided view of the speaker, simultaneously envying and condemning the louse's licence: and if one both envies and condemns in a word, where is the disinterested spectator to whom the poem so obviously alludes, a role moreover the speaker puts himself in the frame for with his closing miniature sermon ('O wad some Pow'r the giftie gie us')? Robert Crawford[14] points out that this apostrophe is a sermon; its brevity is an implied rebuke to the length of Presbyterian sermons (which in this case quite possibly are contributing to the speaker's inattention), and imply that he is putting himself in the minister's place, just as he has been envying the louse's. The dramatic irony lies in the fact that the speaker has spent the entire poem neglecting the church service, and thus is equally liable to be seen 'as others see us' with louse or lady.

'Swith', quickly, rapidly, with the sense of clearing off ('get away' is Burns's gloss, clearly pointing to its use in this poem), is the speaker's next attempt, to shoo the louse away if he cannot shame it, and to despatch it to a beggar as being more in line with what ought to be its social position. The louse should go and 'squattle' (unglossed) in a beggar's 'haffet', a word signifying temple ('haffet-locks' are in Ramsay), but also interestingly the upright end of a church pew. 'Sprattle' (unglossed) suggests scrambling, struggling and sprawling, indicating that the louse may have to move more quickly on the beggar, as he faces competition from 'kindred, jumping cattle' there. 'Squattle' (recorded from the south-west) suggests sprawling too: it can also be a verb for swallowing, swilling and gulping, suggesting haste also is necessary, as there is a lot of competition on a beggar for a much worse meal than that available on the 'Miss'. It's hard to see what the incentive is for switching to the beggar, where the louse will have to move quickly and gobble his food. The sense of ceaseless hard work goes well with the double meaning of 'plantations', while 'horn' is the process not just of outlawry, but specifically of outlawry for debt: 'his siller's gane, he's drowned in debt, / An' putten to the horn' – a reference to horn spoons may also be implied, a point on which I am indebted to Cameron Goodall. Hence the reference to the louse's dining on the beggar suggests both the ceaseless work of slaves on 'plantations' and being put outside the law for debt, a situation hardly alien to Burns's own experience. Competing to dine on a beggar is a fit outcome for the lowest of the low; but the louse's sturdy independency resists the fate imagined for him by the jealous onlooker.

'Fatt'rels' are ribbons, or anything loose and trailing ('ribband ends', Burns says, with contempt again glossed as a connotation); but 'fatter' is also a Dumfriesshire verb in south-western Scots meaning to thresh the beards of barley: connotatively, this may be the louse's harvest. 'The vera tapmost, towrin height / O' *Miss's bonnet*' seems a simple enough description in Scots English: but then 'tap' as an adjective can refer to a crest or feathers on a hat or to a plant tuft: thus even here the idea of harvest, the metonymic vanity of the Lunardi bonnet and perhaps an outlying association with theme of beggary (as in the verb 'to tap' for borrowing money) may be being squeezed out.

'Grozet' (unglossed) is a gooseberry, but 'grozet fairs' were also held in Kilmarnock and Ayr in gooseberry season, so Burns may have had in mind the connotations of trading, carnival and carnality. The 'rozet' and 'smeddum' which the speaker wishes he could visit on the louse would 'dress your droddum' ('give you a thrashing'): this is again North-Eastern Scots. 'Rozet' (unglossed) is resin, but particularly that resin used on a fiddle-bow: an interesting conceit about poetic or song composition as exorcising the louse hovers on the edge of the range of available meanings here, while although 'red smeddum' is a specific insecticide, 'smeddum' itself (under-

glossed by Burns as 'powder of any kind') is primarily used of ground bar-
ley-meal or malt, extending the feeding / harvesting metaphor. But there
is another meaning too: the 'red smeddum' the speaker wishes to thrash
the louse with is a mercury compound, and mercury was the treatment for
syphilitic infection (I am indebted to Sir Kenneth Calman for this point).
The louse sexually possesses the lady as well as feeding off her, contrasting
his freedom to act with the speaker's.

The 'flainen' is usually glossed as 'flannel', and this is correct: but it is
instructive to note that the word is used in compound to describe a meal
('flannen-broth', 'flannen-bannock') in North East Scots. 'Toy' is a married woman's head covering, and a woman who had been found guilty of
fornication might be married sewn into it, as Burns very likely knew: thus
the speaker indicates to the louse that he would be quite unsuprised to see
it dine on a woman who has sexual experience, and is preferably 'auld' into
the bargain, but he should keep off the maiden 'Jenny'. Suddenly, it is
not social class which the speaker sees as violated by the louse, but virginity: crudely, he wants to have the woman first but the louse has got there
before him, though the ambivalent characterisation of this 'Miss' as both
untouched by men but not by the louse and at the same time so available the
louse may catch venereal disease remains. The 'wylecoat' (flannel under-
coat) of a 'duddie boy' (a ragged one, 'duds' being glossed by Burns as 'rags
of clothes') would also be a suitable destination for the daring insect: here
the class marker returns, but only where sexual interest is absent. 'Duddie'
can also mean rags of meat adhering to a bone, and this deepens the frame
of reference once again back to feeding.

'Blastie' makes a return in line 40, uniting woman and louse in a common
destiny of withering and fading. Burns was probably aware that 'Jenny' was
the common name for a Scottish girl in the broadside ballads, frequently
one on whom her 'Jocky' urged the ancient temptation of *carpe diem*. The
'*winks* and *finger-ends*' of the congregation are signs of their taking notice
and pointing (K, III, 1148): but they are also language which carries further
connotation about the lady's nature and character. 'Finger' in Scots implies
being pampered and delicately reared, which we already know to be true of
this '*Jenny*'. 'Wink', apart from the obvious flirtatious hint it connotes, also
means closing one's eyes, which is what the woman is doing with respect to
both the pride and the louse: hence the prayer of the last stanza to open her
eyes and 'see', which, Smithian as it is, emanates from a source so sexually
absorbed in her as to be only incrementally more credible than Willie Fisher
in 'Holy Willie's prayer'. It may also be relevant that 'winkit milk' is milk
that has gone sour, untasted: *carpe diem* is again hinted at without being
spelt out. Even in the last stanza, 'air', which seems so obvious, can mean
'taste' as a verb, which once again invokes the devouring metaphor of the
poem.

Reading Burns through the Scots he used cannot be done by reading the

English closely and deeply as established by New Critical and subsequent practice, and allowing to the Scots only the flat denotation of a glossary, and 'To a Louse' becomes much more clearly a poem about class, fertility, food and appetites once it is read through a full encounter with the frame of reference of the language in which it is written.

In the case of 'Halloween' (K 73, I, 152), Burns adopts a deliberately anti-quarian frame, which he glosses with what Nigel Leask terms 'rationalizing paratexts',[15] a description which parallels Burns's approach with the 'auto-exoticism' attributed by Joep Leerssen to Maria Edgeworth and Sydney Owenson in Ireland. The antiquarian framing of a narrative provided by the narrator in 'Tam o' Shanter' is here placed as an external interpreta-tive boundary: the poet as educated Enlightenment figure commenting on the poem written by the same poet as impenetrable heaven-taught plough-man. Like 'Tam', the theme is a Gothic one, the search for a spouse by supernatural means, sometimes an approach which – as in the encounter of Leonella and Antonia with the gypsy in Matthew Lewis's *The Monk*, or in the attempt to seek out a spouse by similar means in Charles Maturin's 'Leixlip Castle' – brings little luck to those who pursue it.

The poem is set in the vicinity of '*Cassilis Downans*', associated with the traditional tale of the abduction of Lady Cassilis by the gipsy king Johnie Faa, which in its turn gave rise to a whole subgenre of gipsy and highland laddie abduction and seduction songs, where sexual directness more than makes up for want of money or position in the suitor. As in these songs, there are slight references in Burns to the equation of supernaturalism with political dissent: for example, in two references to the year 1715 (127, 240), the date of the Jacobite Rising which, Burns believed, his grandfather had fought in. Stanza XV looks back to 'Ae Hairst afore the *Sherra-moor*', the great battle of the 'Fifteen, with the implied suggestion of the now vanished fertility of a lost national past (itself a commonplace trope of Jacobite refer-ence). These are also the scenes (in the second stanza) 'Where BRUCE ance rul'd the martial ranks / An' shook his *Carrick* spear', and such fertility has – in the aftermath of the 'Fifteen – departed in some degree, so 'uncle *John*' who has desired '*wedlock's joys* / Sin' *Mar's-year*' is perpetually to be disappointed of his natural fruitfulness, which now he is in any event inca-pable of enjoying (Stanza XXVII). On a site ('*Cassilis Downans*') long asso-ciated with a song cycle of sexual and political directness, an antiquarian collector comments obliquely on customs which clearly evince the former and express occasional nostalgia for the latter as linked to it through the common metaphor of fertility. As in 'Tam o' Shanter', native traditions and native authenticity are different sides of the same coin: in a classic example of the Fanonesque literature of combat, the supernatural and localised is a badge of native authenticity and a resistance to the wider world to which the colonist seeks to seduce it. 'Hearts leal' (Stanza III, 'loyal, true' in Burns's gloss) are to be found in such places.[16]

The introduction to the poem subscribes fully to the deservedly repressed condition of Gothic manners within the paradigm of Enlightenment stadialism, noting that 'The passion of prying into Futurity makes a striking part of the hiſtory of Human-nature, in it's [sic] rude state, in all ages and nations; and it may be some entertainment to a philosophic mind . . . to see the remains of it, among the more unenlightened in our own' (K 73, I, 152). Thus Burns places his own poem (and by implication the 'Readers' by whom it will be 'well enough understood' to whom he first addresses his introductory paratext) within the realm of a barbaric and provincial survival; he then counterweights that with a threshold quotation from Goldsmith in favour of 'The simple pleasures of the lowly train' and their 'native charms'.

The paratexts provide a gazeteer of the area and a detailed summation of the various activities of Halloween night; the Scots is partly glossed in these notes, which adopt the detached tone of the enlightened antiquarian: for example, the physical sexual activity alluded to in 'But her *tap-pickle* maist was lost' in the sixth stanza, lives in the gloss only as a description of what may be foretold by custom, not accomplished by action. The editor is looking the other way, as he is when Nell and Rob 'In loving bleeze they sweetly join, / Till white in ase [glossed as 'ashes'] they're sobbin' in Stanza X or when 'an aizle [spark, with a nice double meaning, brought out in Burns's gloss of 'red ember'] brunt / Her braw, new, worset apron' in Stanza XIII. We begin to notice at this stage that the editor is beginning to be too involved with his material, as he begins to seem as superstitious as what he is documenting ('Whoever would, with success, try this spell, must strictly observe these directions'). The suspicion grows that the antiquarian is collecting and explaining traditional customs, but the poem he is glossing is describing universal activities. While the editor gets more and more engaged in supernatural ways of discerning a future husband ('Take a candle, and go, alone, to a looking glass: eat an apple before it, and some traditions say you should comb your hair all the time: the face of your conjugal companion, *to be,* will be seen in the glass, as if peeping over your shoulder', I, 157), more and more of the subjects of the poem are arguably engaging in more direct relations and not the metaphors for them. When Rab M'Graen 'gat *Eppie Sim* wi' wean' in Stanza XVI , the editor chooses to gloss yet another charm:

Steal out, unperceived, and sow a handful of hemp s*eed;* harrowing it with any thing you can conveniently draw after you. Repeat, now and then, 'Hemp seed I saw thee, Hemp seed I saw thee; and him (or her) that is to be my true-love, come after me and pou thee.' Look over your left shoulder, and you will ſee the appearance of the person invoked, in the attitude of pulling hemp. Some traditions say, 'come after me and shaw thee,' that is, show thyself; in which case it simply appears. Others omit the harrowing, and say, 'come after me and harrow thee.'

The paratext and its antiquarian paradigm seem almost a displacement activity of curiosity in the face of carnality. The editor is not only glossing the supernatural customs of a locality (and the locality may be more pan-Scottish than the poem allows, for Kinsley notes that a number of the traditions (in the third, eleventh and twelfth stanzas) cited were from or endured longest in Burns's ancestral north-east (K, III,1119)), but also bowdlerising them. On the surface, the author of the paratext gets more and more involved in the beliefs he is apparently documenting from a superior and more Enlightened perspective, but there is a deeper suggestion. Is supernaturalism itself – as perhaps in 'Tam o' Shanter' – merely a bowdlerising antiquarian's way of turning rampant sexual licence into charming local custom? And, if so, is the distance between what happens and what is recorded the distance between Scots and English? As Burns puts it in the Kilmarnock glossary, 'Houghmagandie' is 'a species of gender composed of the masculine and feminine united' . But rather than being Scots for a hermaphrodite, it is the real language of men and women in a state of vivid sensation.

Burns's extraordinary linguistic range gives him many voices. Like John Clare, he can appear a labouring-class poet to whom dialect comes naturally; like Maria Edgeworth and Sydney Owenson from upper-middle and upper-class backgrounds, he can comment on his own text through paratexts. His use of Scots can reveal a different, deeper and richer way of reading a poem; it can range for thematic reasons across different dialects of the language, or it can nest a nagging subtext underneath an ostensibly humorous tone, like the doughty and violent peasant lurking just under the parodic surface in 'To a Haggis'. If there is one thing this essay sets out to do, it is to change the way we read Burns. Alive to a language close to that *really* used by men, Burns's use of Scots and its implications is extraordinary, and largely unrecognised. We must stop reading him through glossaries and start reading him through dictionaries, thesauruses and histories.

Notes

1. ('Fa's Speerin?', Anglice, 'Who's Asking?'). William Wordsworth, *William Wordsworth*, ed. Stephen Gill, The Oxford Authors (Oxford: Oxford University Press, 1990 (1984)), pp. 595, 596, 597, 610, 613; Michael Baron, *Language and Relationship in Wordsworth's Writing* (London and New York: Longman, 1995), pp. 30, 85, 143–9.

2. Murray Pittock, *Scottish and Irish Romanticism* (Oxford: Oxford University Press, 2008), ch. 8; see William Bernard McCarthy, *The Ballad Matrix* (Bloomington: Indiana University Press, 1990), for the bowdlerisation of the politically direct in ballad collection.

3. Wordsworth, *William Wordsworth*, pp. 591, 614; [William Wordsworth and S. T. Coleridge], *Lyrical ballads with a Few Other Poems* (Bristol: Biggs and Cottle, 1798), p. iii; Bernard Jones, 'Wordsworth, Hardy and "the real language of men":

a centenary note', *English Studies* 80.6 (1999), pp. 509–17, 511; Murray Pittock, *Inventing and Resisting Britain: Cultural Identities in Britain and Ireland, 1685–1789* (Basingstoke: Macmillan, 1997), pp. 118–19; Raphael Samuel (ed.), *Patriotism: The Making and Unmaking of British National Identity*, 3 vols (London and New York: Routledge, 1989), vol. I, p. xv; vol. III, pp. xi, 18. For Shrophire dialect, see A. E. Jenkins, *Titterstone Clee Hills* (Orleton: privately printed, 1992 (1983)).

4. Pittock, *Inventing and Resisting Britain*; Linda Colley, *Britons: Forging the Nation, 1707–1837* (New Haven: Yale University Press, 1992); Lynda Mugglestone, *Talking Proper* (Oxford: Oxford University Press, 2003), pp. 15, 258; Thomas Miller, *The Formation of College English* (Pittsburgh: University of Pittsburgh Press, 1997), pp. 11, 17, 100, 136–7, 170; Jeremy Smith, '*Copia Verborum*: the linguistic choices of Robert Burns', *Review of English Studies* 58.233 (2007), pp. 73–88, 78.

5. For Sinclair see Charles Jones, *A Language Suppressed* (Edinburgh: Edinburgh University Press, 1995), p. 5; James Sibbald, *Chronicle of Scottish Poetry*, 4 vols (Edinburgh: J. Sibbald, 1802), vol. IV, p. xlv; Robert Burns, *The Works of Robert Burns*, ed. James Currie, 3rd edn, 4 vols (London: William Allason, 1819), vol. I, p. 25; J. Runcole, 'On Scottish Songs', *The Bee II* (1791), pp. 208–9; Francis Jeffrey, *Edinburgh Review* 26 (1809), p. 259, cited in Nigel Leask, *Robert Burns and Pastoral* (Oxford: Oxford University Press, 2010), p. 295; Thomas Miller, *The Formation of College English: Rhetoric and Belles Lettres in the British Cultural Provinces* (Pittsburgh: University of Pittsburgh Press, 1997), p. 11.

6. Robert Crawford, *The Bard: Robert Burns, a Biography* (London: Jonathan Cape, 2009), p. 260; Ruriko Suzuki, 'The idea of "the real language of men" in the 1800 "Preface" to Lyrical Ballads; or Enfield's idea of language derived from Condillac', *Romanticism on the Net* 11 (1998), http://www.erudit.org/revue/ron/1998/v/n11/005814ar.html (accessed 29 June 2011), p. 2; Miller, *Formation of College English*, pp. 11, 17, 137.

7. Adam Smith, *Theory of Moral Sentiments*, ed D. D. Raphael and A. Macfie (Oxford: Clarendon Press, 1979), pp. 25, 175; Pittock, *Scottish and Irish Romanticism*, pp. 21, 65–6; Alexander Broadie, 'Aristotle, Adam Smith and the virtue of propriety', *Journal of Scottish Philosophy* 8.1 (2009), pp. 79–89. I am indebted to Luke Gibbons for first suggesting the hidden historical narrative in Adam Smith, *Theory of Moral Sentiments*.

8. Robert Burns, *Robert Burns's Common Place Book*, ed. Raymond Lamont Brown (Edinburgh: S. R. Publishers Ltd, 1969 (1872)), p. 7; Robert Burns, *The Canongate Burns*, ed Andrew Noble and Patrick Scott Hogg (Edinburgh: Canongate, 2001), p. 132; Raymond Bentman, *Robert Burns* (Boston: Twayne, 1987), p. 45; Murray Pittock, 'Nibbling at Adam Smith', in Gerry Carruthers and Johnny Rodger (eds), *Fickle Man: Robert Burns in the 21st Century* (Dingwall: Sandstone Press, 2009), pp. 118–31.

9. For the concept of 'auto-exoticism' see Joep Leerssen, *Remembrance and Imagination* (Cork: Cork University Press/Field Day, 1996).

10. Robert Burns, *The Letters of Robert Burns*, ed J. De Lancey Ferguson and G. Ross Roy, 2nd edn, 2 vols (Oxford: Clarendon Press, 1985), Vol. I, p. 88; Crawford, *The Bard*, p. 252; 'Oran Ussaig–To R. Burns', *The Bee* II (1791), pp. 317–19; for Wordsworth's 'linguistic primitivism' see David Duff, *Romanticism and the Uses of Genre* (Oxford: Oxford University Press, 2009), p. 61; Johann

Gottfried von Herder, *Philosophical Writings*, ed. and trans. Michael N. Foster (Cambridge: Cambridge University Press, 2002), pp. vii, x, xii–xiii, 380. For bibliographical details of the *Museum* see J. W. Egerer, *A Bibliography of Robert Burns* (Edinburgh and London: Oliver and Boyd, 1965 (1964)), pp. 18–25.

11. Theocritus, *Idylls*, trans. Anthony Verity, ed. Richard Hunter (Oxford: Oxford University Press, 2003 (2002)), p. xiv; Mikhail Mikhailovich Bakhtin, *Dialogic Imagination: Four Essays*, ed. Michael Holquist, trans. Carl Emerson and Michael Holquist (Austin: University of Texas Press, 1981), p. 273; Leask, *Burns and Pastoral*, p. 75; Roderick MacDonald, 'Robert Burns and Gaelic', *Scottish Language* 9 (1990), pp. 17–33.

12. Alexander Broadie (ed.), *The Scottish Enlightenment* (Edinburgh: Canongate, 1997), p. 285; Leask, *Burns and Pastoral*, pp. 169–70; Duff, *Romanticism and the Uses of Genre*, pp. vii–viii. For 'starting lines' see Fiona Stafford, *Starting Lines in Scottish, Irish, and English Poetry from Burns to Heaney* (Oxford: Oxford University Press, 2000).

13. References to the glossary are to Robert Burns, *Poems, Chiefly in the Scottish Dialect* (Kilmarnock: John Wilson, 1786); the *Scottish National Dictionary* and the online synthesis of the *Dictionary of the Older Scottish Tongue* and *The Scottish National Dictionary* at <http://www.dsac.uk/>.

14. Crawford, *The Bard*, pp. 206–7.

15. Leask, *Burns and Pastoral*, p. 200.

16. Frantz Fanon, *The Wretched of the Earth*, trans. Constance Farrington, intr. Jean-Paul Sartre (London: MacGibbon-Kee, 1965), p. 44.

CHAPTER 9

'Merry Ha'e We Been': The Midnight Visions of Brian Merriman and Robert Burns

Patrick Crotty

Cúirt an Mheán Oíche and 'Tam o' Shanter' are two of the best-known poems in Irish Gaelic and Lowland Scots, without doubt the best-known eighteenth-century poems in the respective literary traditions of those languages. Each is a comic narrative which engages with questions of gender relations and explores the boundaries between liberty and licence. The copious critical response to both works is lacking in consensus to an unusual and even striking degree. The present essay attempts neither a comprehensive reading of the two texts nor a survey of the secondary literature they have provoked. It seeks rather to sketch the remarkable parallels and correspondences between these almost contemporary products of one of the Celtic and one of the Teutonic cultures of the 'British' Isles, written in a period when the four nations of the archipelago were drawing close to an unprecedented and, as it turned out, not altogether long-lived political unity. It is hoped that discussion of each poem in the light of the other may serve both to resolve persistent cruces of interpretation and to illustrate the rich and still largely unexplored possibilities of a comparative approach to the literatures of Ireland and Scotland.

Hugh MacDiarmid, that eminent Caledonian hibernophile, cautioned in 'Advice to Young Writers' that watertight compartments are useful only to a sinking ship.[1] Most of the scholarly responses to Brian Merriman's poem have come from practitioners of Celtic Studies, a discipline that can invoke restrictive and even reductive notions of tradition, and one moreover that characteristically brings a philological and archaeological rather than a literary critical approach to the objects of its attention. A consequence of this is that the *Cúirt* has tended to be discussed exclusively in relation to the poetic patrimony of Irish Gaelic and to the immediate political and economic circumstances of 1780s Munster, with little regard for the poem's broader literary and intellectual contexts or for the demonstrably hybridised nature of its author's cultural experience. Just as watertightly, if perhaps more understandably, the leading commentaries on Robert Burns's last major poem evince almost no awareness of the contemporary non-Teutonic literatures of the archipelago, or even of so frequently translated an example of those literatures as the work entitled 'The Midnight Court' in almost all of its many English versions. No critic, so far as I am aware, has perforated the watertight partitions by explicitly connecting one poem to the other, though two Irish writers (neither of whom was a professional scholar) have remarked on the Burnsian qualities of the *Cúirt*, and one of them, by implicitly suggesting a link between Merriman's poem and 'Tam o' Shanter', has provided the impetus for the present article.

In his introduction to Percy Arland Ussher's 1926 translation of the *Cúirt*, W. B. Yeats noted that Merriman's praise of bastardy was almost contemporary with what he called Burns's 'beautiful defiant "Welcome to his love-begotten daughter"'.[2] More daringly, Frank O'Connor observed in 1959, in the preface to *Kings, Lords, & Commons*, his compilation of translations of Irish poetry from 600 to 1800, that Merriman 'was deeply influenced by the ideas of the Enlightenment and particularly by Burns's.[3] He acknowledged that Gaelic scholars have gone along with the *Cúirt*'s dating of its own composition to 1780 but insisted that they are wrong: '[T]he thing is impossible. [Merriman] must derive from Burns.'[4] Fourteen years earlier O'Connor's translation had appeared as a separate volume, which promptly and notoriously fell foul of the Censorship of Publications Act in Ireland – a fate one might be tempted to interpret in terms of support for the translator's contention that the poem incorporates enlightened and non-native ideas. O'Connor's spirited introduction to the 1945 volume, however, made no reference to Burns. Rather it identified Merriman's key influences as 'Savage, Swift, Goldsmith and, most of all, Rousseau'. It ascribed a neoclassical aesthetic to the *Cúirt*, implicitly linking it to the high Augustan ideals of the English mid-eighteenth century: 'What Merryman aimed at was something that had never even been guessed at in Gaelic Ireland; a perfectly proportioned work of art on a contemporary subject, with every detail subordinated to the central theme.'[5]

By 1959, however, Burns had become central to O'Connor's understanding of Merriman's artistic lineage. Why? I think by far the most persuasive answer is that sometime between 1945 and 1959 O'Connor read or reread 'Tam o' Shanter' and was overwhelmed by a sense of its kinship with *Cúirt an Mheán Oíche*. The similarities and parallels between the poems are multiple and in some respects profound, as I hope to show, and O'Connor is to be commended for being the first to notice them. Having noticed them, however, he made the mistake of thinking of them as intertextual rather than contextual in nature. Once he had made that mistake, he was stubborn and fearless in its service.[6] His claim that Merriman was a follower of Burns may easily be discredited on grounds of historical scholarship, but it is hugely illuminating. Believing one poet to have definitively influenced the other, O'Connor was forced to choose Burns as the precursor. It is worth reflecting on how much more eccentric he would have sounded if he had argued that the Scottish poet had been inspired by the work of his Irish counterpart. For all the growing interest in the cultures of the Irish and Scottish Gaelic and Welsh languages attendant on the rise of antiquarianism, the traffic between the contemporary Teutonic and Celtic literatures of the archipelago was as much a one-way affair in the eighteenth century as it is today. The practice of Gaelic or Welsh writers could be affected by the work of their coevals in English or Scots, that is to say, but not the other way round. (The debt of James Macpherson's 'epic' texts to Ossianic ballads still current in the author's Highland youth provides a solitary and somewhat dubious exception.) The first English translation of the *Cúirt*, made by Merriman's fellow-Clareman Dennis Woulfe in the 1820s, did not see the light of day until 1880, eight and a half decades after the death of Burns, when it appeared in expurgated form in the periodical *The Irishman*. If it is inconceivable that Merriman's poem could have had an impact on the Scottish poet, it is by contrast possible, indeed even probable, that long before he died in 1805 Merriman may have heard of Burns and indeed read his poetry. There is scholarly unanimity, however, that he wrote the *Cúirt* at a point when his Scottish brother-poet had as yet produced only juvenilia. And the evidence that underlies that unanimity, as Burns might have said, is a chiel that winna ding. If the experts are right,[7] *Cúirt an Mheán Oíche* was circulating in manuscript in Munster some years before the publication of *Poems, Chiefly in the Scottish Dialect* – the so-called Kilmarnock edition – in 1786, and almost a decade before the composition of 'Tam o' Shanter': the Clare poet, consequently, cannot have 'derived' from the Ayr poet.

The similarities which appear to have prompted O'Connor's remarks relate equally to subject matter and poetic form. With regard to subject matter it may be observed that both poems have at the centre of their action a midnight gathering of women in a lighted rural church. Merriman's assembly is a Court of Women, set up in opposition to the English courts derided in a passage about the slumped state of Ireland in the Bailiff's address near the beginning of the poem; Burns's one is a Witches' Sabbath, held in defiance of the proprieties of kirk and state. A significant difference between the meetings is that the Irish one is presided over by the intensely female Aoibheal of Craglea, sovereignty goddess of Munster and still a presence in the folklife of County Clare in the eighteenth century, and the Scottish by the emphatically male Devil – 'auld Nick, in shape o' beast' (K 321, II, 561, 120) – no less a presence in the Ayrshire countryside of Burns's youth, perhaps, but also, as Nigel Leask has argued, a figure mediated here through the poet's antiquarian reading.[8] The repudiation of ecclesiastical authority by both gatherings is underscored by their taking place in church – the 'teampall' at Cnoc Maonmhaí in the one, '*Alloway*'s auld haunted kirk' (K 321, II, 558, 32) in the other.[9] A transforming supernatural light infuses both locations:

> Is deimhin go bhfaca mé ar lasadh le tóirshibh
> An teaghlach taitneamhach maiseamhail mórtach,
> Soilseach seasamhach lannamhail lómrach
> Taibhseach tathagach daingean dea-dhóirseach.[10]

> And there (I am sure) lit torches showed
> A handsome, grand, well-built abode,
> A stately, steadfast, glittering space,
> Accessible and commodious.[11]

The 'bleeze' in Kirk Alloway, too, is facilitated by torches or tapers, if of a more ghastly kind:

> Coffins stood round, like open presses,
> That shaw'd the dead in their last dresses;
> And by some devilish cantraip slight
> Each in its cauld hand held a light. – (K 321, II, 561, 125–8)

Both congregations of women celebrate a sexuality which by the religious standards of the local community is licentious – they do this mainly through discourse in the Irish poem, through dance, dress and gesture in the Scottish one. Both narratives temper a transgressive glee where sexual matters are concerned with an affectation of coyness. Thus Merriman's first witness describes her charms:

> Féach mo chom! Nach leabhair mo chnámha!
> Níl mé lom ná crom ná stágach,
> Seo toll is cosa agus colainn nach náir dom,
> Is an togha go socair fá cover ná tráchtaim.[12]

> Look at that waist! My legs are long,
> Limber as willows and light and strong.
> There's bottom and belly that claim attention,
> And the best concealed that I needn't mention.[13]

Similarly, Tam's drunken delight in the spectacle of the winsome wench's flaunting of her nether regions in her cutty sark is filtered through Burns's teasingly modest narration:

> But here my Muse her wing maun cour;
> Sic flights are far beyond her pow'r;
> To sing how Nannie lap and flang,
> (A souple jade she was, and strang),
> And how *Tam* stood, like ane bewitch'd,
> And thought his very een enrich'd . . . (179–84)

In the rhetorical economy of Burns's narrative, this admission of the limits of poetic prowess chimes with the sudden curtailment of the catalogue of abominations displayed on the altar for the Witches' Sabbath forty lines earlier:

> Wi' mair o' horrible an' awefu'.
> Which even to name wad be unlawfu'. (141–2)

(The poet's decision in 1793 to excise the four lines about lawyers' tongues and priests' hearts that follow this couplet in the early printings of 'Tam o' Shanter' makes so much sense in aesthetic terms, by reinforcing the comic impression of unspeakable dread, that arguments about self-censorship in the interest of political tact seem beside the point.)

Both poems make reference to the power of witchcraft in the surrounding countryside, though how seriously we are to take these references is debatable. In the *Cúirt* the complainant considers resorting to diabolism to secure a man, and lists some of the dark arts that may be called upon in the quest for marriage, telling of one girl who successfully followed advice to eat nothing from Shrovetide to November but 'cuile na móna dóite ar lionn'[14] (bog-flies roasted in beer). In 'Tam o' Shanter' we hear that in the years intervening between the tale and its telling Nannie grew up to be a powerful force for mischief in the locality:

> [M]ony a beast to dead she shot,
> And perish'd mony a bony boat,
> And shook baith meikle corn and bear,
> And kept the country-side in fear . . . (167–70)

The openings of the works resemble each other in that each takes the form of an ambulatory, quotidian semi-idyll set in the indeterminate hour between darkness and light (dawn in the Irish poem, dusk in the Scottish one):

> Ba ghnáth mé ag siúl le cuimhais na habhann
> Ar bháinseach úr 's an drúcht go trom,
> In aice na gcoillte, I gcoim an tslé',
> Gan mhairg, gan mhoill, ar shoilse an lae.[15]

> 'Twas my custom to stroll by a clear winding stream,
> With my boots full of dew from the lush meadow green,
> Near a neck of the woods where the mountain holds sway,
> Without danger or fear at the dawn of the day . . . [16]

> When chapman billies leave the street,
> And drouthy neebors, neebors meet,
> As market-days are wearing late,
> An' folk begin to tak the gate . . . (1–4)

There is a more emphatic parallel between their conclusions: both narratives end with the women characters turning with violent intent upon a male, the eponymous protagonist in the case of 'Tam o' Shanter', the narrating poet himself, identified by way of a punning clue as Brian Merriman, in the *Cúirt*. Though presented in both cases as a less than prepossessing representative of his sex, the male is nevertheless miraculously saved, whether through the actions of the faithful mare Meg, who carries Tam safely over the keystane o' the Brig o' Doon in the nick of time, or the schoolboy composition device of Merriman's waking from his dream. The nature of the punishment the witches would have inflicted upon Tam had they caught up with him is not made explicit – it presumably included matters too horrible and awefu' to be lawfully named. While we are given a symbolic hint at the very end of the narrative as to what it might involve, during the chase the narrator is content to enjoy the unfortunate miscreant's discomfiture, leaning out of the storytelling clouds to advise at least that his prospects are not good:

> Ah, *Tam*! Ah *Tam*! thou'll get thy fairin!
> In hell they'll roast thee like a herrin! (201–2)

The nature of the torments awaiting all men who have failed to marry by twenty-one is, by contrast, indicated at some length by Aoibheal in her summative judgement in the *Cúirt*. She gives her lascivious devotees leave to improvise the more painful details, intimating that these, too, will include roasting. (The elderly are to be spared so they can in due course provide the cover of marriage for the products of their young wives' affairs with fitter and more attractive men.) The particular sentence to be carried out on the poet-narrator – the 'blithesome and gay merry man of the name',[17] as Thomas Kinsella renders the identifying line – is that he be stripped, tied, whipped and flayed by the women whose charms he has scorned.

So much for subject matter. Where poetic form is concerned there are similarly striking correspondences between the *Cúirt* and 'Tam o' Shanter', though in enumerating them I do not wish to distract attention from a number of fundamental and perhaps no less significant differences. Both are narrative poems – by no means an unknown genre in Scots poetry, albeit one that had not been essayed with an energy comparable to Burns's since the age of the makars, an at best intermittent one in Irish Gaelic. The *Cúirt* begins and ends as a first-person narrative, with the direct speech of the major characters making up most of the body of the poem. Indeed its dramatic aspect is one of the work's most singular attributes in the context of the broader Gaelic poetic canon. There is by contrast no direct speech by the protagonists of 'Tam o' Shanter' other than the hero's climactic and calamitous expostulation 'Weel done, Cutty-sark!' (189); the constantly shifting relationship of the narrator to his material and the ever-changing distance between his consciousness and Tam's, however, lend an immediacy to the action that may be thought of as dramatic. Not only are both works narrative poems, they are narrative poems committed to tetrameter couplets. Such couplets are highly unusual in Irish,[18] while they are so common as to constitute pretty much a staple measure in Scots poetry from

The Brus in the fourteenth century to the work of Ramsay and Fergusson in the eighteenth. The 'finishing polish' of which Burns boasted in a letter to his confidante Mrs Frances Dunlop in April 1791,[19] however, links the couplets of 'Tam o' Shanter' to the civilities of English Augustan utterance as much as to the Scots couplet tradition he had himself extended so brilliantly in 'The Twa Dogs' four years earlier. Burns's recourse in 'Tam o' Shanter' to the mock form that permeated the poetic and prose literature of eighteenth-century England provides the occasion of a species of vocalisation markedly different from that of the poems of the Mossgiel period of 1784–6 which make up the core of the Kilmarnock edition. With its subtle interplay of idiomatic naturalism and artifice, the 1790 work negotiates Augustan aesthetic priorities in a way that Burns's anglophone neoclassical pieces of the intervening years had signally failed to do. Indeed it is in a shared ambiguity towards Augustan values, an attitude involving both absorption and rejection, that the key to the similarities between *Cúirt an Mheán Oíche* and 'Tam o' Shanter' is to be found. The debt of Burns's poem to the mock heroic tradition of eighteenth-century England is overt. He adapts the tradition to local conditions to come up with a work that is less mock heroic than mock ethical: if Pope's *The Rape of the Lock* is a mock epic, 'Tam o' Shanter' is a mock moral tale. The 'truth' about human behaviour that Tam 'fand' as 'he frae Ayr ae night did canter' (14) was not an improving proposition such as *Radix malorum est cupiditas* but the banal recognition that people go to the pub at the end of a market day. Tam's drunkenness and randiness remain unpunished as the poem closes, and the tailless condition of his mare is the sole, absurd reminder of the dangers of behavioural excess. Such a dénouement is Augustan to the extent that it playfully inverts the conventions of the master genre, in this case the moral tale, but strikingly un- or post-Augustan in its challenge to morality itself. The ongoing debate about Burns's radicalism should perhaps take 'Tam o' Shanter' centrally into account, as the Bard's greatest poem arguably goes further than any other in establishing his revolutionary credentials. The cumulative impact even of 'The Twa Dogs', 'Love and Liberty' and the more Jacobin among the songs offers a less thoroughgoing threat to conservative Enlightenment ideas of order than the ironisation and repudiation of the very concept of right behaviour at the libertarian heart of 'Tam o' Shanter'.

The Augustan parameters of *Cúirt an Mheán Oíche* may seem scarcely less obvious, though they have not been widely attested. The poem's status as a satire links it to the dominant poetic genre of the English eighteenth century, as do the paired end-rhymes we have already mentioned. It is only fair to point out, however, that Merriman's couplets operate very differently from their English counterparts.[20] Commentators familiar with the *Cúirt* only in translation can hear a more Augustan poem than the original, which is propelled by its assonantally and sometimes alliteratively connected stresses rather than its end-rhymes, and consequently makes a rougher, more turbulent sound than all but the most recent attempts to present it in English – those by Seamus Heaney and Ciaran Carson – manage to convey. The gentility of the couplet tradition in English can lead an ear schooled only in the poetry of that language to misplace the tonalities of Merriman's poem (which is presumably why Kinsella chose to eschew rhyme for his version). If the idiom of 'Tam o' Shanter' is of the Garden, to invoke a favourite eighteenth-century antinomy, that of the *Cúirt* is of the Wild. When I say this I mean to suggest neither that the poem lacks moments of delicacy and tenderness nor that Gaelic poetry in general has anything wild or uncivil about it. In the history of Irish literary idiom the *Cúirt* is important because of its departure from the refined and formal language in which Aodhogán Ó Rathaille (*c.*1670–1729) and Eoghan Rua Ó Súilleabháin (1748–84) – those other leading poets of eighteenth-century Munster – composed their lyrics. Their language in turn stays considerably closer to speech than the stylised idiom – as thoroughgoing an example of 'poetic diction' as anything eighteenth-century England could offer – of the classical or 'bardic' syllabic poetry that predominated in Gaelic Ireland and Scotland from *c.*1210 to *c.*1650. By comparison with Merriman's, though, the accentual style of the post-bardic lyric poets is elevated and decorous. The *Cúirt*'s repudiation of conventional poetic language in the interests of colloquial authenticity and a transgressive, politically alert naturalism gives it a proto-Romantic aspect. The plenitude, slanginess and gargantuan brio of his vocabulary represent Merriman's most radically innovative contribution to Gaelic poetic method, and it is extremely difficult for translation to communicate this aspect of his achievement. (Carson catches the vernacular exuberance of the *Cúirt*'s mode of address better than any other translator, though sometimes at the expense of its underlying passion; Heaney honours the original's thumping assonantal drive and rootedness in living speech, while Kinsella's more downbeat approach effectively communicates its matter-of-fact attitude to love and the body; O'Connor's version, still the most widely known, displays admirable vigour but can perhaps be criticised for using canonical English poetry as its sounding board and for playing up the poem's sexual explicitness in an effort to bait the mid-twentieth-century custodians of the purity of the Gael).[21] Merriman's style marks a vernacular revolution in Gaelic poetry that might have served as the foundation of an entire new literature had political and economic circumstances not conspired to bring Irish near to extinction in the nineteenth century. To draw an illustration from 'Tam o' Shanter', it might be observed that the teeming, resourceful, uncouth linguistic vitality of the *Cúirt* has more in common with Kate's sweet counsels than with the rest of Burns's poem:

> She tauld thee weel thou was a skellum,
> A blethering, blustering, drunken blellum;

That frae November till October,
Ae market-day thou was nae sober . . . (19–22)

(Intriguingly, the literary historian Kurt Wittig detected a Gaelic quality in the music of the first two of these lines.[22] The assonantal patternings of the extract as a whole bear a loose similarity to those of Merriman's poem, while the riotous alliteration of the second line sets up an acoustic that startlingly resembles the *Cúirt*'s.) In general it can be said that the vernacular energy of the Irish work calls to mind the contents of the Kilmarnock edition more readily than 'Tam o' Shanter'. The lexical richness and associated sense of release into articulation of a hitherto suppressed mode of communal being that distinguish the poems of Burns's early maturity from those of his immediate predecessor Robert Fergusson find strong parallels in the *Cúirt*, and it is possible that lexical considerations may have been among the lesser factors behind O'Connor's tantalisingly undeveloped claim with regard to the Burnsian qualities of Merriman's poem.

If Merriman's onrushing couplets simultaneously exhibit Augustan and non-Augustan tendencies, his approach to his subject matter is in at least one crucial respect deeply continuous with eighteenth-century English literary practice. The *Cúirt*'s parody of the *aisling* presents another variation of the mock heroic and should not necessarily be construed – as it has almost invariably been construed by Gaelic scholars – in terms of medieval burlesque. An *aisling* (plural, *aislingí*) is a vision poem in song metre in which the speaker encounters a *spéir-bhean* (lit., 'sky-woman'), a beautiful, distressed maiden, who pleads for deliverance from the embraces of a foreign lout or group of louts and tells of her betrothal to an overseas lover. The roots of the tradition run back through the dream vision poetry of the Middle Ages to the ancient trope of the sovereignty goddess whose marriage to the king guaranteed the fertility of the land. By the eighteenth century the *aisling* had come to dominate the lyric poetry of Gaelic Ireland, and particularly of Merriman's native province of Munster. The political allegory of the *aislingí* was an open secret, with the maiden being understood to represent Ireland, and her absent betrothed the Stuart king over the water. Long before 1780, the hope for a Jacobite saviour implicit in the mode had been reduced to the status of a mere affectation, and the exquisitely modulated but otherwise formulaic *aislingí* of his almost exact contemporary Ó Súilleabháin must have seemed to a poet of Merriman's impatiently realist temperament the very stuff of fatuity and defeatism. (Yeats's lyric 'Red Hanrahan's Song about Ireland' and his and Lady Gregory's play *Cathleen Ni Houlihan* are highly self-aware partial recuperations of the *aisling* in English. Hanrahan, protagonist of a series of six stories published by Yeats in the early 1890s, was based on Ó Súilleabháin.) We should note in passing that Burns himself wrote an *aisling* or something very like one. An alternately inventive and gauche poem in the Kilmarnock edition – called, appropriately enough, 'The Vision' – sees the despondent speaker visited by a 'bleezan bright . . . tight, outlandish *Hizzie*' (K 62, I, 104, 41) who embodies the spirit of the poet's native district of Kyle. It is presumably coincidental that one of the phrases Burns uses for his enchanting visitor, 'heavenly-seeming *Fair*' (134), is a pretty exact translation of *spéir-bhean*. Burns's poem arguably comes more directly than *Cúirt an Mheán Oíche* from the medieval dream vision tradition, albeit by way of Allan Ramsay's pseudonymous medieval pastiche of the same name, *The Vision* (1724). In Merriman's poem, at any rate, the parody of the conventional visitation by a celestial woman in the account of the speaker's entrapment by a titanic female horror lends the opening section (1–166) the status of a mock *aisling* to set beside *The Rape of the Lock*'s mock epic and 'Tam o' Shanter's' mock moral tale. The profoundly anti-idealising representations of women in the central portion of the poem continue the critique of the ethereality of the *aisling* tradition, and are congruent with the replacing of the rarefied language of the lyric poets by something much more socialised and bodily. The *Cúirt*'s inversion of the values of the *aisling* through a mock deployment of the genre is as recognisable in an Augustan context as its status as a satire and deployment of rhyming couplets. Yet it is difficult to agree that the poem is quite as representative of the eighteenth-century mainstream as O'Connor asserts. Comparison with 'Tam o' Shanter' casts doubt on the degree to which Merriman can be said to have made use of neoclassical architectonics, and the Scottish poem answers more fully than the Irish one to the translator's description of 'a perfectly proportioned work of art . . . with every detail subordinated to the central theme'.

If neither Merriman 'derives' from Burns nor Burns from Merriman, it can be said that they both derive in significant though not equal measure from Alexander Pope. The *Cúirt* and 'Tam o' Shanter' stage separate encounters between one of the old, increasingly threatened linguistic cultures of the archipelago and the ever more unignorable English one centred on London. The Gaelic world is still the more powerful partner in the canonical nuptials of the *Cúirt*, whereas the Scots vernacular and English neoclassical traditions achieve more or less exact parity in Burns's poem (which is in this sense, if in no other, a Unionist text). Pope's influence must have been well nigh inescapable not only in the Teutonic cultures of England and Lowland Scotland but in a Gaelic realm increasingly interpenetrated by English as the eighteenth century proceeded. Even the illiterate, monoglot Scots Gaelic poet Rob Donn MacAoidh (1714–78) absorbed the example of the dominant London writer of the day, whose verse was rendered orally into Gaelic for him in Sutherland by his mentor, the clergyman Murdoch MacDonald. We know that Merriman won prizes for his flax at the Royal Dublin Society in 1797 and made his living in his later years as a teacher of mathematics in Limerick. By the last quarter of the eighteenth century the East Clare area near the village of Feakle, where he grew up and was working as a farmer and schoolmaster when he wrote the *Cúirt*, was already much more anglicised than the west of the county where he had been born around 1749. It appears that the Catholic and Protestant gentry of the east of the county (the very people the narrator-poet is condemned near the end of the poem for consorting with) used English among themselves but had recourse to Irish for their dealings with the monoglot rural poor.[23] Merriman must have moved with competence – if not necessarily with ease – between the two main linguistic cultures of the south of Ireland, and it is impossible to believe he was less acquainted with the English literature of his time than the cattle drover MacAoidh.

Pope's poems, repeatedly pirated by Dublin printers throughout the eighteenth century, had considerable impact on the practice of Irish poets writing in English. Matthew Concanen's popular three-canto *A Match of Football, or The Irish Champions* (1726) is one of many works that with greater or lesser subtlety apply the mock heroic methodology of *The Rape of the Lock* to local materials, in this case a football game in north County Dublin. (Concanen in due course washed up in the second book of *The Dunciad*, ll. 299–304, where he is described as 'A cold, long-winded native of the deep', what we would now call a bottom-feeder.) Jonathan Swift's longest poem, *Cadenus and Vanessa*, is thought to have been drafted in 1712 and 1713, a period that coincided with the beginning of the author's long friendship with Pope, though the text may have been substantially reworked before appearing in print in 1726, three years after the death of Esther Vanhomrigh, the Vanessa of the title. Its martial presentation of coquetry and a number of incidental details draw on the example of *The Rape of the Lock*, the first, two-canto version of which had been published in 1712. Taking up the suggestion of the English Celtic scholar Robin Flower, W. B. Yeats declared that the *Cúirt* was 'founded upon'[24] *Cadenus and Vanessa*, which tells of a Court of Love instituted to investigate why 'Cupid now has lost his art, / Or blunts the point of every dart'.[25] Certainly Swift's poem to some degree anticipates the theme and legal setting of Merriman's, which, if it is indebted to it, repudiates its classical allusiveness and reverses its attack on women's 'gross desire'.[26] In 1981 the Gaelic poet and scholar Seán Ó Tuama exhibited a confidence equal to Yeats's when he traced the literary foundations of Merriman's poem to the Middle Ages in general and to Jean de Meung's bawdy additions to the *Roman de la Rose* in particular, though in conceding the unlikelihood of the poet's direct familiarity with the *Roman* and in concluding that the traditions deriving from the French poem could have become available to Merriman in a never satisfactorily specified 'variety of ways' he took much of the wind out of the sails of his certainty.[27] Ó Tuama's argument that the *Cúirt*'s 'debt to the general European tradition is best understood by looking at the overall shape of the poem, and noting its affiliations with various medieval literary forms'[28] is conducted without acknowledgement of the many connections between

that shape and the literature of the poet's own century. Yeats's observation that Merriman read *Cadenus and Vanessa* 'perhaps in some country
gentleman's library'[29] assumes that he was a peasant with a smattering of
learning, an assumption as complacent and misleading as the typification
of Burns as heaven-taught ploughman. Ó Tuama is similarly (if perhaps
less consciously) eager to circumscribe Merriman's intellect: his scorn for
O'Connor's argument that the author of the *Cúirt* was influenced by the
ideas of the Enlightenment[30] amounts to an insistence that he lacked alert-
ness to the ideational currents of his own time, an insistence extraordinarily
difficult to reconcile either with the little we know of the poet's bilingual
lifestyle or the very great deal his poem tells us about the quality of his
intelligence. That a writer who so adroitly negotiated the religious, cultural
and linguistic faultlines of Irish life should fall prey scores of years after
his death to the condescension alike of Anglo-Irishman and Gael may be
depressing but it is a tribute to Merriman's success in baffling the received
(and dismayingly constant) categories of his country's ethnic and political
discourse.

Where the legal aspect the *Cúirt* is concerned, the eighteenth-century
Munster *barántas* – a sub-canonical, subversively parodic arrest-warrant
genre variously in Irish prose and Irish and macaronic verse – may have had
a more decisive impact on Merriman than anything in Gaelic, English or
European high culture, as Declan Kiberd has fleetingly suggested.[31] There
is an immensely suggestive link between the *barántas* and Burns, who in
1786 wrote a spoof summons satirising the prosecution of fornicators at
the Kirk Assises in Ayr. 'Libel Summons' (K 109, I, 256–62) celebrates the
sexual enterprise of the men who impregnate local girls but condemns those
among them who lack the courage to take responsibility for their actions.
The poem, which exists in three manuscript versions and remained unpublished until long after Burns's death, shares the tetrameter couplets of the
two works under discussion and, like the *Cúirt*, concludes with a threat to
strip and bind a recalcitrant male. The connections between the *barántas*
and 'Libel Summons' and between the latter and Merriman's poem can
only be contextual, but they serve as a reminder that cultural habits and
political conditions can sometimes provide more illuminating means for
understanding individual literary works than the scrambling for textual
prototypes that unites the otherwise disparate commentaries on the *Cúirt*
of Yeats, O'Connor and Ó Tuama. In particular, 'Libel Summons' makes
it clear that in an age when parody and inversion provided standard literary modes of response to topical events and situations a poet who wished to
draw attention to injustice of any kind might have recourse to a mock court
as the framework for his poem. When that poet had little respect for the
existing system – whether legal, as in Merriman's case, or ecclesiastical as in
Burns's – he could be expected to make considerable comic mileage out of
aping procedures he considered oppressive and an affront to natural justice.

None of this is to say that poems are free of debt to other poems or that *Cúirt an Mheán Oíche* does not bear the mark of Merriman's reading. In 1945, as we have seen, the ever-perspicacious O'Connor cited Oliver Goldsmith as an influence on Merriman but left it to others, as he would do with his later citation of Burns, to identify his reasons for doing so. *The Deserted Village*, the most famous and polished of all eighteenth-century Irish poems in English, was published in 1770, a mere ten years before the composition of the *Cúirt*, and achieved immediate popularity in Ireland. Goldsmith's Athlone-based sister Mrs Catherine Hodson was among the first of many Irish readers to insist that Lissoy in County Westmeath, where the poet spent his childhood, is the model for Auburn, the village of the title,[32] though the characteristically Augustan universalising tendency of the poem makes it impossible to read naturalistically and renders more or less pointless arguments as to whether English or Irish clearances, enclosures and 'improvements' provided the historical stimulus for its protest against the flight from the land. The great interest of Goldsmith's poem where Merriman is concerned is that it supplies an answer to a question that has bedevilled attempts to historicise the *Cúirt*. The increase in population that would eventually issue in the catastrophic famines of the 1840s was already developing apace in the 1770s in Munster. Why then does Merriman's poem complain about rural depopulation? At the risk of sounding like Harold Bloom I would venture that it does so because *The Deserted Village* does so.

> Ill fares the land, to hastening ills a prey,
> Where wealth accumulates, and men decay[33]

wrote Goldsmith. Merriman's townland (rather than village) risks becoming deserted because wealth accumulates and *women* decay, their charms unappreciated and their reproductive faculties ignored by males interested only in economic advancement. Because his land, East Clare, fares ill Merriman invokes Aoibheal, traditional protectress of the territory, to set matters right. Social, political and economic conditions in late eighteenth-century Munster are registered in a number of oblique ways in the *Cúirt* but they may ultimately have no more to do with the stricken status of the poem's fictive East Clare than the author's reading – which, like that of any poet, can be presumed to have included accessible and widely discussed works in the languages with which he was familiar. Though Seán Ó Ríordáin's debt to T.S. Eliot and Gerard Manley Hopkins and Sorley MacLean's to Yeats and Hugh MacDiarmid are critical truisms in Gaelic studies, scholarly commentators have been reluctant to acknowledge contemporary non-Celtic or extra-communal influences on texts written before the nineteenth- and twentieth-century period of comprehensive anglicisation. Even poets with strong fealties to particular religious and linguistic communities tend to be more interested in poetry than in anything else, though, and no-one familiar with the curiosity of practitioners about the art would consider it eccentric to suggest that *Cúirt an Mheán Oíche* should be read as a creative response by Brian Merriman in one of his two everyday languages to a masterpiece by a compatriot and near-contemporary in the other.

What the term 'compatriot' might mean in relation to the communal divisions of eighteenth-century Ireland inevitably raises the question of religion. The young Goldsmith is said to have been interested in the language and culture of his Roman Catholic neighbours, who outnumbered Anglicans in his father's Church of Ireland parish by a ratio of nine to one.[34] The penal laws limiting the religious, economic and political rights of Catholics were enforced with varying degrees of strictness throughout the eighteenth century, and the prolonged process of reform that belatedly culminated in the Catholic Emancipation Act of 1829 began with the repeal of a few of them in the late 1770s. (The law barring Catholics from running schools remained on the statute books until 1782, two years after the schoolmaster Merriman wrote his poem.) Social intercourse between Catholics and Protestants was by no means uncommon, and politically fuelled sectarian tensions were much less marked in the decades leading up to the composition of the *Cúirt* than in the closing years of the century. The poem's proposition that Catholic priests be allowed to marry to redress the problems of depopulation and female sexual frustration has led to speculation that Merriman was some sort of apostate from Catholicism. That he was a Catholic in the first instance, however, is something of an assumption. O'Connor, who seems to have thought about the content, form and context of the *Cúirt* more deeply than any other critic, commented as follows on him:

> He was undoubtedly a man of powerful objective intelligence; his obituary describes him as 'a teacher of mathematics' which may explain something; and though his use of '*Ego vos*' for the marriage service suggests a Catholic upbringing, the religious background of *The Midnight Court* is Protestant, which may explain more.[35]

Two observations can be made which have implications for our sense of Merriman's religious identity, though firm conclusions can be drawn from neither of them. One is that the setting of the *Cúirt* is given as the 'teampall' at Cnoc Maonmhaí, Moonmoy Church. In Munster Irish a Catholic church is usually called an *eaglais*, while *teampall* indicates a Protestant place of worship.[36] The other is that Merriman is not an Irish but an English surname. Yeats calls the author of the *Cúirt* Brian Mac Giolla Meidhre, but that is an artificial Gaelicisation. The poet's forename appears not to have been *Brian* but *Bryan* – the death announcement (O'Connor's 'obituary') in the *General Advertiser and Limerick Gazette* of Monday 29 July 1805 prefixes a non-Gaelic and possibly Welsh spelling of the given name to the English surname:

Died – : On Saturday morning, in Old Clare-street, after a few hours' illness, Mr Bryan Merryman, teacher of Mathematics, etc.

True, the name is rendered as 'Brian'[37] in the poem itself, but the Irish alphabet lacks a *y*. The surname is indicated there only through a translingual pun on 'meidhreach'[38] (merry). It is possible that the psychological source both of the poem's extraordinary energy and of its thematic focus on legitimacy may be traced to uncertainties about identity and social class deriving from the status of 'Merriman' – more correctly, perhaps, 'Merryman' – as every bit as much a given name as Brian/Bryan. (I have used 'Merriman' throughout as it is by far the more common spelling in the commentaries and translations.) According to tradition, the poet was born to a single mother who on marrying a travelling mason called Merriman moved with her son from Ennistymon to Feakle. Almost as little is known for certain about the stepson as the stepfather. O'Connor's identification of Richard Savage as an influence on the former may have been based on a surmise that the *Cúirt* draws as much of its force from authorial anger over patrimony foregone as Savage's embittered, briefly scandalous but ultimately conventional (and in every respect lesser) poem 'The Bastard' (1726).

I suggested at the outset that by reading the Merriman and Burns poems against each other we can move towards a resolution of longstanding difficulties of interpretation. One of the main areas of contention in Merriman studies, as we have seen, relates to the question as to whether the *Cúirt* looks backwards or forwards, whether it is to be understood by reference to the archaic traditions of Gaelic Munster or the universalising ideals of the British and European eighteenth century. Consideration of the work beside 'Tam o' Shanter' suggests that this may be a false dichotomy and that, like Burns's poem, it looks in both directions, wittily mediating between modernity and vanishing modes of communal experience. The fact that it was composed in the remote village of Feakle – still sufficiently remote nearly two centuries later to be chosen as the location for secret talks between militant republicans and Protestant clergymen at the height of the Northern Irish Troubles in 1974 – offers no support for the argument that the author was cut off from the literary and intellectual trends of his time: the figure of Rob Donn MacAoidh should remind us that well before 1780 cultural marginality had ceased to be a corollary of geographical isolation in the rapidly modernising archipelago.

Beyond highlighting that Merriman's poem is a satire, that it is written in rhyming couplets and that it develops the characteristic eighteenth-century mock mode, reflection on the *Cúirt* in the context of 'Tam o' Shanter' draws attention to one of its quintessentially Enlightenment aspects, its participation in the widespread enthusiasm for antiquities. The debt of Burns's poem to the antiquarian movement is well known. 'Tam o' Shanter' was both an afterthought and a footnote. It had its origins in the author's request to the English antiquary Captain Francis Grose that an illustration of Kirk Alloway be included in the latter's *Antiquities of Scotland*. Situated a few hundred yards from his birthplace, the ruined church was of particular significance to Burns because of his father's burial in its grounds in 1784. He agreed to supply Grose with a witch story to accompany the illustration. In due course he came up with three, and in the autumn of 1790, in a state of sustained excitement, combined details drawn from all of them in the poem he thereafter regarded as his masterpiece. (The kirk setting was the first 'given' of Burn's poem; presumably a church near Feakle was chosen as the location of Merriman's Court to underscore the depth of the women characters' challenge to the patriarchal order.) 'Tam o' Shanter' was published both in the *Edinburgh Herald* and the *Edinburgh Magazine* in March 1791 before appearing a month later as a double column footnote in the second volume of Grose's *Antiquities*. Though not included in Grose text, the epigraph from the 'ancient' makar Gawin Douglas in the definitive 1793 version reinforces the poem's antiquarian dimension. One of the reasons I think O'Connor is wrong in seeing *Cúirt an Mheán Oíche* as exemplifying Augustan principles of decorum, whereby each detail is subsumed to an overall architecture, is that the long list of *pisreoga* in the complainant's first speech is digressive in character and distorts to some degree the overall shape of the work. *Pisreoga* are charms, or *piseogs* as they are called in the hiberno-English of my native County Cork: the girl explains that she has burnt bits of her frock, slept with a spade, stuck a flail up the chimney etc. in hope of securing a husband. These details, lovingly if somewhat too lengthily recorded, comprise a typically late-eighteenth-century antiquarian catalogue of local practices and offer yet another illustration of how centrally representative Merriman was of the archipelagic culture of his day. (The list of contemporary fashions in clothes and footwear a little earlier in the poem should be seen, I think, as a joking extension of antiquarian methodology to the latest fads rather than as an instance of subaltern Irish resistance to English ways.) By far the least neoclassical aspect of the *Cúirt* is its language, which is characterised throughout by a sense of upsurge, exuberance and refusal of the politeness of received literary idiom. There is an antiquarian connection here, too, and one that links the poem to none other than Burns's friend Francis Grose. Marilyn Butler has remarked that the emphasis of antiquarianism 'on oral, popular experience, or minority or conquered experience . . . was at odds with' the state-centred worldview of such dominant eighteenth-century figures as Samuel Johnson and Edmund Burke.[39] The repudiation of conservative cultural values with regard to language took memorable form in England in 1785, when Grose published what posterity has come to regard as his most important book, the *Classical Dictionary of the Vulgar Tongue*. This gleeful compilation of 3000 words that had been excluded from Johnson's famous *Dictionary* appeared the year after the great lexicographer's death. It shares with Merriman's poem a faith in the capacity of the unfettered deployment of language to lead to authenticity and liberation. The author of *Cúirt an Mheán Oíche* would have appreciated (and, for all we know, did appreciate) the joke in the first adjective of the title.

Merriman's poem in turn sheds light on the meaning of 'Tam o' Shanter'. Though the *Cúirt* is expressly and sustainedly concerned with gender politics, this aspect of its meaning has only come to be commented upon centrally since the rise of feminism. The testimony of the young woman who delivers two of the three long monologues that constitute the main body of the text can be construed either in terms of recognition by a male poet of the validity of female desire or of an elaboration of male sexual fantasy. The left-wing activist Máirín de Búrca took the latter view in a lecture at the Merriman Summer School in 1980, when she condemned the 'sexist not to mention ageist nonsense' of the author of the *Cúirt* who, as a man, was 'by definition . . . a member of the oppressing class'.[40] It can be pointed out at least that the young woman is presented by Merriman much more sympathetically than her detractor, the foul-mouthed old man who speaks the intervening monologue: he fetishises sexuality in terms of economic exchange, whereas she sees it as its own justification. The poem's comic gusto and gleeful debunking of the ethereality of the *aisling* might make us slow to detect a fear of women behind the description of the gigantic female Bailiff in the opening section. The concluding part of the *Cúirt*, though, when the Bailiff and young woman move to carry out on the poet himself Aoibheal's judgement on men who have remained unmarried after twenty-one, is suggestive of extreme male anxiety in the face of female licentiousness. Noting that the speaker is condemned not just for his virginity but for his poetic disposition – 'Sinm ar cheolta, spórt is aoibhneas'[41] ('Playing his tunes, on sprees and batters')[42] – Seamus Heaney has argued that the end of the poem draws on a source much older than the *Roman de la Rose*, namely, the myth of Orpheus, who was torn apart by the Thracian women he had spurned in pursuit of his art. More slyly, perhaps, Heaney recruits Merriman as a defence witness in the gender trials of contemporary poetry criticism:

> Merriman deserves a specially lenient hearing in the women's court, if only for having envisaged his own prosecution ahead of time and for having provided the outline of a case against himself. He was surely something of a progressive when it came to the representation of women. He gave them bodies and brains and let them speak as if they lived by them.[43]

All of this raises the relatively unexplored question of the gender politics of 'Tam o' Shanter' and helps sharpen our sense of the implications not only of the vengeance the witches seek to wreak on Tam but of the injury Nannie succeeds on inflicting on his grey mare Meg. The poet Kenneth White – independently of Heaney's remarks on Merriman – has suggested that 'Tam o' Shanter' constructs Burns's own poetic identity in orphic terms, though by suggesting that Shanter is a pun on chanter and that the poem as a whole rewrites the ballad of Thomas the Rhymer he overextends his argument.[44] White's essential point is persuasive, though, insofar as many details throughout the poems and songs suggest that Burns did indeed think of himself as a latter-day Orpheus. The congruence between, on the one hand, his self-representation as 'rantin' rovin' Robin' in 'There was a Lad' and as a 'rantin, drinkin' *Bardie*' in 'Address to the Deil'[45] and, on the other, Merriman's self-depiction as someone who wastes his time on music, sprees and batters, is more than striking. If Burns thought of himself as an Orpheus figure, however, it is not clear that he shared the Irish poet's sense of the high price to be paid by Orpheus for his lyric freedom.

So here, at the end of the essay, we come to what is no longer at the end of Meg, her tail, homonymic partner of the subtitle of 'Tam o' Shanter: A Tale'. The tailless condition of Meg leaves her rump exposed, rather as the cutty sark left Nannie's. To that extent the tail is connected to female sexuality. The tail was the only trophy the witches took from their attempted attack on the peeping Tam who had interrupted their all-female Sabbath, and to that extent it is connected to male sexuality. The closing verse paragraphs of the *Cúirt* heighten our sense of the seriousness of the hags' designs upon the fleeing drunk, and give powerful support to John MacQueen's often criticised suggestion that the mare's tail is ultimately and paradoxically a phallic symbol.[46] (The bawdy traditional song upon which Burns modelled 'John Anderson My Jo', it should be remembered, uses 'tail-tree' for penis.)[47] No-one who turns from *Cúirt an Mheán Oíche* to 'Tam o' Shanter' can fail to read the end of Burns's narrative in terms of castration anxiety, however genially communicated.

If this essay lacks a resonant closing paragraph I can only plead the appropriateness of its being as tailless as the sole dependable participant in Burns's 'Tale', and of its ending as suddenly as Merriman's midnight vision.

Notes

1. Hugh MacDiarmid, *The Complete Poems of Hugh MacDiarmid*, ed. Michael Grieve and W. R. Aitken, 2 vols (Manchester: Carcanet, 1993), vol. I, p. 657.

2. W. B. Yeats, 'Introduction', in *The Midnight Court and The Adventures of a Luckless Fellow*, ed. and trans. Percy Arland Ussher (London: Jonathan Cape, 1926), p. 11.

3. Frank O'Connor, *Kings, Lords, & Commons: An Anthology from the Irish Translated by Frank O'Connor*, 3rd edn (Dublin: Gill and Macmillan; London: Macmillan, 1970), p. xiv.

4. Ibid., p. xiv.

5. Frank O'Connor, 'Introduction', in Brian Merriman, *The Midnight Court*, 5th edn (Dublin: O'Brien Press, 1989), p. 10.

6. In a book completed shortly before his death in 1966 O'Connor asserted that Merriman 'seems to have studied' Swift, Goldsmith and Burns 'closely', and also ascribed the composition of the *Cúirt* to 'about the year 1790', a date which, though mistaken, has sufficient elasticity to accommodate the implication of the Clare poet's reading 'Tam o' Shanter'. See Frank O'Connor, *The Backward Look: A Survey of Irish Literature* (London: Macmillan, 1967), p. 130.

7. See, for example, Seán Ó Tuama, *Repossessions: Selected Essays on the Irish Literary Heritage* (Cork: Cork University Press, 1995), p. 64.

8. See Nigel Leask, *Robert Burns and Pastoral: Poetry and Improvement in Late Eighteenth-Century Scotland* (Oxford: Oxford University Press, 2010), pp. 270–3.

9. *Cúirt an Mheán Oíche*, ed. Dáithí Ó hUaithne (Dublin: Dolmen Press, 1968), p. 21.

10. Ibid., p. 21.

11. Seamus Heaney, *The Midnight Verdict*, 2nd edn (Oldcastle, Co. Meath: Gallery, 2000), p. 27. *The Midnight Verdict* presents two translated extracts from *Cúirt an Mheán Oíche* flanked by two from Ovid's *Metamorphoses*.

12. *Cúirt an Mheán Oíche*, p. 24. 'Cover' is one of the English words that crop up in the poem, to varyingly caustic effect.

13. O'Connor, *Kings, Lords, & Commons*, p. 143.

14. *Cúirt an Mheán Oíche*, p. 28.

15. Ibid., p. 17.

16. Ciaran Carson, *The Midnight Court: A New Translation of 'Cúirt an Mheán Oíche' by Brian Merriman* (Oldcastle, Co. Meath: Gallery, 2005), p. 19.

17. Thomas Kinsella (ed.), *The New Oxford Book of Irish Verse* (Oxford: Oxford University Press, 1986), p. 246.

18. The texts collected in *Five Seventeenth-Century Political Poems*, ed. Cecile O'Rahilly (Dublin: Dublin Institute for Advanced Studies, 1952), are sometimes said to offer precedents for Merriman's couplets. They do not. All five of these long poems in popular idiom use the same rhyme throughout (not a demanding technical feat, given the inflected nature of Irish and the dependence of rhyme on vowel rather than consonant). The poems are in rhymed tetrameters rather than rhymed tetrameter couplets. The conclusion that eighteenth-century English poetry had a decisive influence on Merriman's practice is difficult to avoid.

19. Robert Burns, *The Letters of Robert Burns*, ed. J. De Lancey Ferguson and G. Ross Roy, 2nd edn, 2 vols (Oxford: Clarendon Press, 1985), vol. II, p. 83, 11 April 1791.

20. For an argument for the Augustan character of Merriman's couplets see Declan Kiberd, *Irish Classics* (London: Granta, 2000), pp. 184–6.

21. A composite English version of the entire text, drawing on Carson, Heaney, Kinsella and O'Connor, can be found in Patrick Crotty (ed.), *The Penguin Book of Irish Poetry* (London: Penguin, 2010), pp. 322–49. Translations unmentioned in the body of the present essay include those of Brendan Behan, Bowes Egan, Lord Longford, David Marcus, Cosslett Ó Cuinn, Michael C. O'Shea and Patrick C. Power. Only fragments of the Behan version survive: the author is said to have lost the manuscript three days after reading it to an audience in McDaid's pub in Dublin.

22. See Kurt Wittig, *The Scottish Tradition in Literature* (Edinburgh and London: Oliver and Boyd, 1958), p. 218.

23. Ó Tuama, *Repossessions*, p. 71.

24. Yeats, 'Introduction', p. 5.

25. Jonathan Swift, 'Cadenus and Vanessa', in Jonathan Swift, *The Complete Poems*, ed. Pat Rogers (London: Penguin, 1983), p. 130.

26. Ibid., p. 131.

27. Ó Tuama, *Repossessions*, pp. 64–5.

28. Ibid., p. 65.

29. Yeats, 'Introduction', p. 6.

30. Ó Tuama, *Repossessions*, p. 64.

31. Kiberd, *Irish Classics*, p. 192.

32. See Gayle Baylis, 'Goldsmith's "The Deserted Village": images of *The Dispossessed*', in Joseph McMinn (ed.), *The Internationalism of Irish Literature and Drama* (Gerrards Cross: Colin Smythe, 1992), pp. 165–70, 165.

33. Oliver Goldsmith, 'The Deserted Village', in Oliver Goldsmith, *Poems and Plays*, ed. Tom Davis (London: Everyman, 1993), p. 182.

34. *Oxford Dictionary of National Biography*, www.oxforddnb.com (accessed 11 February 2011).

35. *Midnight Court*, p. 10.

36. I am grateful to Máirín Ní Dhonnchadha for drawing this to my attention.

37. *Cúirt an Mheán Oíche*, p. 50.

38. Ibid., p. 49.

39. Marilyn Butler, 'Antiquarianism (popular)', in Iain McCalman (ed.), *An Oxford Companion to The Romantic Age: British Culture 1776–1832* (Oxford: Oxford University Press, 1999), p. 330.

40. See Máirín De Búrca, 'Analysis of The Midnight Court', in Angela Bourke et al., eds, *The Field Day Anthology of Irish Writing*, Vol. V: *Irish Women's Writing and Traditions* (Cork: Cork University Press, 2002), pp. 1588–91.

41. *Cúirt an Mheán Oíche*, p. 49.

42. *Midnight Verdict*, p. 32.

43. Seamus Heaney, 'Orpheus in Ireland', in Seamus Heaney, *The Redress of Poetry: Oxford Lectures* (London: Faber and Faber, 1995), p. 55.

44. Kenneth White, '"Tam o' Shanter": an interpretation', *Scottish Literary Journal* 17.2 (November 1990), pp. 5–15, 5.

45. K 140, I, 320–1; K 76, I, 172, 116.

46. John MacQueen, *The Enlightenment and Scottish Literature*, Vol. I: *Progress and Poetry* (Edinburgh: Scottish Academic Press, 1982), p. 147.

47. See Robert Burns, *The Merry Muses of Caledonia*, ed. James Barke and Sydney Goodsir Smith, 2nd edn (London: Panther, 1966), p. 143.

CHAPTER 10

Arcades Ambo: Robert Burns and Thomas Dermody

Michael Griffin

In the summer of 1802, poverty drove the young Ennis-born poet Thomas Dermody (1775–1802) from Portpool Lane in London to a brickmaker's ruined hut in Sydenham in Kent, from where on 9 July he sent word to his patron and biographer James Grant Raymond that he was all but dead and in need of whatever assistance Raymond could afford. Raymond, accompanied by the playwright John Till Allingham, went to visit him. His description of the scene and the poet's state was harrowing. There lay Dermody,

> in a wretched hovel, leaning over a few embers which hardly gave warmth to his shivering and emaciated body, in a state of the deepest misery and dejection. He had scarce power enough left to express the grateful sentiments which their visit inspired: the words faltered on his parched lips; his eyes became filled with tears; and being unable to give expression to the strong feelings which laboured in his breast, he sunk again into the melancholy position in which they had discovered him and continued silent for a considerable time. These emotions having subsided he endeavoured to relate the particulars of his unhappy situation; but was often obliged to pause, in order to gather sufficient strength to encounter the violent and oppressive cough which momentarily returned.[1]

Raymond and Allingham discussed with the fading poet the possibility of providing him with a healthier and reviving environment, and a nurse. Dermody knew, however, that he was finished. He died that evening, on 15 July 1802, aged twenty-seven years and six months. His funeral expenses were supplied by former patrons. He was buried in Lewisham.

Dermody had left Ireland for England eight years earlier amid increased political and personal turbulence. One source of upset was the publication, early in 1793, of a now rare republican pamphlet, *The Rights of Justice; Or Rational Liberty*, a sarcastic assault on what he perceived as Edmund Burke's narcissistic dotage following the publication of *Reflections on the Revolution in France* (1790). Dermody's pamphlet was a vigorous plea that Ireland should participate more fully in the revolutionary moment:

> I am no dogmatical Stoic who shall invoke the deceased spirit of my little *Book*, on every occasion, who will sleep with my *Book*, hug my *Book*, weep over my

Book, bathe a whole Kingdom in Blood for my *Book*, and damn every other *Book* that contradicts my *Book*! Altho', were I disposed to indulge in this amiable egotism, I might readily find a precedent, and a great one too. One, whose wonderful talents are tinged with the excrescence of venality. One, whose pen never failed to convince, but at that moment, when Wit submitted to Party; and Folly, proud of her victim, came in. The apostacy of such a person from the Shrine of Freedom, is a spectacle, more lamentable than idiotism, or dotage. Indeed, they seem to be nearly allied. However, the cause is sufficiently strong, without any levies on foreign fancy, or Judgment; Taste, like the Morning Star, foreruns that Sun of Knowledge, which shall illumine the horizon of Creation, and disperse those beams of intellectual radiance around, which flash on the monkish gloom of Folly, and rouse the smothered scintillations of degraded Humanity. The French are already beginning to evince a strength of reasoning, before deemed incongruous with their national levity. They, at this moment, deal more, in practice than theory, nevertheless, Time before he has advanced very far, shall receive a pacquet for Fame, in which pacquet, Liberty, and her sister Revolution, shall inform the World, ———

That France Is A Second Rome, More Glorious Than The First, Mistress Of Very Elegant Art, Nurse Of Heroism, And Invincible On The Rock Of Union.[2]

Taking the form of 'A letter to an Acquaintance in the Country', and dated 20 February, Dermody's intervention could not have been more injudiciously timed. Following France's declaration of war just three weeks before, his sentiments would now be considered seditious; and while Burke's reputation survived the hectoring of the eighteen year-old poet, Dermody's messianic fervour cost him the support of his Irish patrons. It appeared just as the nature of revolutionary France's ambitions was becoming clear to onlookers in Dublin, where 'National Guard' Volunteerism, with its French-inspired symbolism, would be outlawed on 11 March. Such was the ferment of ideas into which Dermody brazenly stepped: his own youthful idealism was augmented and amplified in a heady mix of French, Painite, United Irish and Burnsian radicalisms.

In this essay the last of these contexts is studied. As Kenneth Simpson has argued, 'the subtlest, and arguably most effective expression of Burns's radicalism is to be found in the radical use of poetic forms'.[3] Consequently, it was when he was most under the *poetic* influence of Burns that Dermody would pen his most dangerous political prose work. Having left Ennis for Dublin at the age of ten, Dermody published his first small volume of verse in 1789, his second in 1792 and his republican pamphlet in 1793. Burns was possibly the most famous poet living and active in Britain or Ireland in these years. And so, between the ages of fourteen and eighteen, Dermody studied Burns's poetry with enough rigour to be able to absorb his forms, vocabulary and democratising influence, and even to draw upon his precursors. That Burns should be his presiding influence in these revolutionary years constitutes a fascinating moment in Scottish-Irish literary relations.

The careers of Burns and Dermody, their rapid ascents and their dissolute proclivities, have frequently been compared. Assessing R. H. Cromek's *Reliques of Robert Burns* in his *Edinburgh Review* Francis Jeffrey declared in 1809: 'Burns is certainly by far the greatest of our poetical prodigies – from Stephen Duck down to Thomas Dermody. *They* are forgotten already; or only remembered for derision.'[4] Jeffrey accused Burns of indelicacy and a lack of the old graces, and suggested that the myth of Burns's impoverished beginnings served as a poor excuse for the roughness of his work. For the most part, Dermody's writing did not have that roughness; indeed, Dermody's worst work was characterised by a sickly excess of poetic diction and aspirational sensibility. Dermody's best work was where he shared in what Jeffrey would have decried as a false notion of *force* in writing, characterised by invective, irreverence, and low comic wit. What was wayward in Burns was seen as equivalent to what was wayward in Dermody.

Jeffrey was a conservative critic who, in Andrew Noble's forceful argument, practised 'political containment by way of aesthetic discrimination'.[5] In the case of his critique of Burns, Jeffrey's political, or politicised, criticism would gradually resolve itself into an appreciation of Burns's gentler registers. In the case of Dermody, however, it might be argued that some of Jeffrey's derision was deserved. It is doubtful that Jeffrey ever studied Dermody's poetry; he would, however, like most, have known something of the legend of his self-destruction. But while his criticism of that sort of dissolution would have applied equally for both Burns and Dermody, Jeffrey might have been surprised at the ornate, delicate qualities of that verse which Dermody produced in his final wayward years at the turn of the century in London – the verse which was, in truth, his worst. By then he was completely at the mercy of a class of patrons who, like Jeffrey, were the arbiters of taste and acceptable politics in literature. Dermody, a poet of well-educated though impecunious beginnings, was a prodigy and would become a literary cult figure; he was also a legendary winner and waster of the most controlling sort of patronage. His was a potential which was never quite fully cultivated, largely because his talent for translation and for poetry was matched only by his talent for drinking and debauchery.

Dermody's failure to fulfil early promise could be attributed to his wilful profligacy; but much blame could also be laid at the door of his supporters. He was beholden to their good offices in ways which could often mitigate against the development of an independent voice. The patronage system 'functioned to guarantee political quiescence as well as personal "gratitude",' writes Alan Richardson, 'and lapses (or perceived lapses) in either could end a poet's career.'[6] This was especially true for poets of less than aristocratic origins; according to Michael Scrivener, the economy of favour 'infantilised plebeian poets'.[7]

Dermody, at times infantilised, was at other times evocative, witty and irreverent, and when he was, it was often under the influence: of alcohol, regrettably, but also, more productively, of Burns. His comic spirit shone through in the series of poems which he wrote in imitation of the Scot, when he was at his most mischievous, his most politically subversive. This is the irreverent, bardic, occasionally self-deprecating persona which disappears from his later verse, characterised as it would be by a somewhat petrified and stilted sensibility. This trajectory was understood by peers whose reputations would long outlast his. Robert Southey wrote to Coleridge on 25 July 1801: 'At Falmouth, I bought Thomas Dermody's Poems, for old acquaintance sake; alas! the boy wrote better than the man', sentiments expressed by the poet himself, who declared in 'My Own Character. To a Lady' that his 'summer of genius arrived ere its Spring'.[8]

Burns's influence came to Dermody in the midst of a general radicalisation of political and cultural life in the Dublin to which he had migrated. The edition of Burns's *Poems, Chiefly in the Scottish Dialect* with which Dermody was almost certainly familiar, was the Dublin edition of 1787, advertised in the *Dublin Evening Post* on 18 September of that year and printed for William Gilbert of Great George's Street. This edition was exactly the same, in pagination and presentation, as the contemporary Belfast edition, published by James Magee. What is interesting about these editions is that they featured the famous *Lounger* review essay by Henry MacKenzie, thereby conveying to Irish readers some of the rusticity-fetishism which attended the work's publication in Scotland. As in Scotland, however, this celebration of the rough and the rural was no mere reactionary cult. The appeal of the rustic could in Ireland and Scotland be construed as part of an appeal for national integrity and native strength in the face of a dependent and demeaning dispensation.

Given some of Dermody's own early political inclinations, it was also telling that the volume of Burns which would so influence him was published by a figure who would acquire radical associations. The United Irishmen, a new political club, had been formed by William Drennan, Thomas Russell, James Napper Tandy and Theobald Wolfe Tone in November of 1791. On 4 October 1793, one other founding member, Thomas Collins, listed William Gilbert, Burns's Dublin publisher, as a United Irishman present at a meeting of the 'radical side' of the divided Aldermen of Skinner's Alley.[9] That someone with Gilbert's leanings should have published Burns in Dublin tallies with the popular perception of Burns's politics; in *Poems, Chiefly in the Scottish Dialect*, there is plenty, in pieces such as 'The Twa Dogs' and 'The Author's Earnest Cry and Prayer', to inspire the Irish radical as much as the Scottish. The parallels go further. Like Dermody, Burns would find himself fighting against a conservative backlash after France's declaration of war in 1793, one which, according to Liam McIlvanney, 'overtook the Scottish reform movement in the 1790s'.[10] Dermody would feel more keenly than most the insecurity of the poetic vocation in the midst of a new politics: he would learn too well that convictions might render one poor if they clashed with those of one's patrons.

Dermody's most enduring, and most vexed, patron was Lady Moira; under her direction Dermody was placed in the care of the Reverend Henry Boyd of Killeigh, King's County (Offaly), a famous translator of Dante. Dermody would remain in Offaly for two years (1790–2) which were to prove very important in his development as a poet but which also greatly advanced his abilities as a drinker. Boyd noticed young Dermody's licentious leanings: 'while his talents placed him on an eminence among the great and the learned, his corrupted qualities sunk him to the low but sociable frequenter of a country alehouse'.[11]

Remembering Dermody's prodigious revelry, Boyd would, in 1805, pen 'The Woodman's Tale', a turgid Spenserian allegory on the dangers of excessive drinking, which invoked the cautionary example of Burns:

> O pride of Caledon! Milesian youth!
>   I see your sentence with prophetic eye;
> Tho' will ye knew the gen'ral breast to soothe,
>   On fire by turns with noblest minstrelsy.
>   I see you round the ample circus fly,
> Each by a seeming Muse of fire pursu'd,
>   And now ye rest, and now again ye try
> A sportive strain, or chant in mournful mood,
> Then sink in fitful pangs, by Circe's charms subdu'd.

To the first line of this stanza, Boyd footnotes: 'the author is far from meaning any comparison between the poetical powers of Burns and Dermody: he only intends to mark the similarity in their fates, as they both fell victims to intemperance'.[12] The two poets are likened, but primarily in terms of a shared flaw which was potentially a threat to the Romantics who would follow. Anya Taylor writes: 'Burns was the model, the forerunner, dazzling Wordsworth, Coleridge, Lamb, Hazlitt, Keats and Byron with his greatness and self-destructive daring, but at the same time rousing their pity and terror at the dark side of drunkenness.'[13] Boyd tried to intervene in Dermody's drinking but to no avail; while Dermody did (lamentably, it might be said) absorb some of Boyd's poetic influence, particularly his penchant for unsuccessful Spenserian stanzas, he failed to heed his moral direction. Perhaps Boyd's message at the time was as unclear in conversation as it would be in his poetry: as the *Monthly Review* would later remark, the argument of 'The Woodman's Tale' was evident only in its long prose introduction. While Boyd's intention was commendable, it was, they thought, 'not very likely to be forwarded by an obscure allegory in the Spenserian stanza'; they doubted, accordingly, 'that it will ever reclaim a single votary of Bacchus'.[14]

Alongside their shared and much-discussed dissolution, both Burns and Dermody were substantially influenced by the major pastoral works of Thomas Gray (1716–71), and Oliver Goldsmith (1728–74), the second an Irish poet who married a nostalgic monarchism to a radical concern for the rural poor. There are certainly traces of Goldsmith's politicised nostalgia in Burns. Robert Crawford writes: 'Issues of looking back and looking fearfully forward undergird a number of poems written in late 1785 and early 1786.' Poems such as 'Hallowe'en', which takes its epigraph from Goldsmith's *The Deserted Village* (1770), 'presents a lively folk idyll'. There is also a good deal of Goldsmith in 'The Cotter's Saturday Night', in which, according to Crawford, Burns 'sentimentally idealises cottage life, while drawing on his own upbringing'.[15] Dermody would also write poems in the manner of Goldsmith such as 'Memory' (1792) and 'The Retrospect' (1800). Syllogistically, Dermody thought of the Ayrshire poet not so much in terms of an anxiety but rather an affinity of influence. Perhaps this affinity explains why Dermody would have taken his edition of Burns with him to study and imitate during his spell of rural sequestration with Boyd in Killeigh.

It was after reading Burns's work and the forms which inspired him that Dermody produced in the opening years of the 1790s a sequence of poems addressed to, and describing, local characters in Killeigh. Burns's formal influence over the Killeigh series is self-evident in their prevailing use of the Standard Habbie stanza. For Stephen Dornan, the vernacular Scottish influence offered 'poetic models that could incorporate characters and language that pre-existing Anglo-Irish models could not'.[16] Thus, Dornan questions Bryan Coleborne's characterisation of the Killeigh poems – in *The Field Day Anthology of Irish Writing* – as having an 'inventive stanzaic pattern'.[17] From a Scottish perspective, he argues, these poems might in fact be considered traditional: 'The form is only inventive insofar as Dermody has transplanted it into Irish poetry.'[18] Scottish in form, and (faux-)Scots-dialect in much of the language, the content of these poems still conveys the texture of life and community for a prodigious poet and reveller in eighteenth-century Ireland. The Killeigh series features mock-elegies such as 'John Baynham's Epitaph', 'Will Gorman, the Killeigh Weaver', 'A Lamentable Elegy on Nicholas, the Killeigh Taylor', 'The Death of Poor Davie, the Killeigh Piper' and 'My Own Elegy'. Many of these pieces echo quite directly the style and tenor of Burns's verse epistles from the 1786 (Kilmarnock) *Poems*. These poems were the boozy, jocular, fraternal salutes to Burns's Ayrshire friends and assorted hangers-on.

Only two pieces in Dermody's 1792 collection, *Poems, Consisting of Essays, Lyric, Elegiac, &c. Written between the 13th and 16th years of his Age* were in the form of the Burns stanza: his 'Tam to Rab. An Odaic Epistle' and his 'Ode to the Collegians'. Dermody's poems in the mock elegy mode do not appear in this collection, and were only to appear later in *The Harp of Erin*, a posthumously produced two-volume edition of his poetry collected by James Grant Raymond. The *Harp of Erin* poems may have been considered a little too local and irreverent for public consumption while Dermody was still living; thus, while Burns had established the legitimacy of colourful verse about real people in real locales, Dermody's 1792 collection excised such poems in favour of those which were more generally influenced by Burns or which imitated him in a gentler vein. The influence is most explicitly signaled in 'Tam to Rab: An Odaic Epistle', in which the Irish poet sets himself up, in the first stanza, as a co-conspirator in bardic fraternity:

> Hail, brither Rab, thou genuine Bard,
> May Laurels be thy grand reward!
> Laurels, with gold, and siller hard,
>   To fill the purse,
> For else, they are not worth a card,
>   Or beldame's curse.

It is a little difficult to gauge the loading of the word 'genuine' here. It may be intended to distinguish between Burns and other contemporary poets who have pretended to authenticity. Or it may be a commendation which Dermody is seeking to have mirrored back onto himself. Given his self-image, it is probably the latter. Dermody subscribes here to the cult of the organic, plebeian genius with sonorous fellow-feeling. But there is also a decidedly unromantic emphasis on monetary reward, perhaps a knowing comment on genuine hardship bearing with it a worldliness not valued by these primitivist (rather than primitive) poets who can only play at impoverished rusticity. In the second stanza, however, Dermody admits honestly that, while he knows poverty, he does not have the hand-coarsening rural credentials of his Scottish counterpart. Admitting a discrepancy between their backgrounds, he extends the bases of their camaraderie from poetry to a shared propensity for attracting women through poetry:

> Arcades Ambo! baith are ready,
> T'invoke, and woo, each tuneful Lady,
> But thou, sweet friend, has got a trade, I
>   Ken no such thing,
> Though can'st even drive the ploughshare steady;
>   I can but sing.

Like the first verse, the second is more than a little presumptuous. The phrase 'Arcades ambo, / Et cantare pares, et respondere parati', from the seventh of Virgil's *Eclogues*, translates as 'Arcadians both, evenly matched in song and ready to respond'. There is also the more lightly phrased translation, given by Patrick Crotty, which inflects 'Arcades ambo' as 'rascals both' or 'two rascals'.[19] With this allusion, and between these translations, Dermody wills a poetic parity, and a cheeky camaraderie, between himself and Burns and anticipates a happy meeting of minds and talents:

> Yet, would I glad, gang out with thee,
> To strew my barley on the lea;
> Wow! We would gloriously agree,
>   Poetics gabbling,
> Ne, ever, o'er the dram, would we,
>   Be squabbling.

What is remarkable about this poem is that it draws not just upon Burns but upon those poets who influenced Burns, chiefly Allan Ramsay and Robert Fergusson, themselves exponents of the traditional 'Standard Habbie' form in which Dermody is gaily expressing his sense of poetic affinity. Not merely latching onto the Burnsian moment, therefore, Dermody, deeply and widely read in spite of his foibles, was led, through Burns, to read in the eighteenth-century Scottish literary heritage. The exclamatory 'Wow!' is uniquely and originally Scottish, first appearing in Gavin Douglas's *Eneados*, a 1513 translation of Virgil's *Aeneid* into Scots. In a suggestive article on Fergusson's vernacular, Janet Sorenson has argued that the word subverted 'eighteenth-century British linguistic propriety'. Excluded from Johnson's *Dictionary of the English Language* (1755), Sorenson theorises as to the word's status as a sonic 'blurring of animal and human . . . where the line between animal cry and human language dissolves in onomatopoeic sound'. Against the disembodied, rationalistic strictures of public discourse and metropolitan modernity, this word could invoke, and perform, 'the affective body'. Fergusson's vernacular thus challenged, in Sorenson's reading, the Edinburgh literati and their anaemic concessions to cultural assimilation.[20]

By Burns's time, of course, the vernacular was, in Edinburgh and beyond, admitted – domesticated, even – by a new sensibility. Burns would deploy a 'wow' in his poem 'On the Late Captain Grose's Peregrinations thro' Scotland, collecting the Antiquities of that Kingdom', though this usage appeared a year too late to have prompted Dermody's inflection. Dermody's use of the word recalls earlier soundings in Fergusson's Habbie-style 'The King's Birth-Day in Edinburgh' or his poems in the festive 'Christ's Kirk on the Green' genre such as 'Hallow-Fair' and 'Leith Races'. (Dermody would demonstrate his breadth of generic reference when he penned his own roisterous 'Christ's Kirk' style poem entitled 'Lory's of the Lane').[21]

Perhaps more influential again in 'Tam to Rab' is Allan Ramsay. Dermody's 'wow' recalls Ramsay's *Elegies*, such as that on Maggy Johnson, in which the exclamation appears, as in Dermody, at the beginning of the second line of a Standard Habbie stanza. Similar usages occur in the post-script to the 'Elegy on John Cowper' and the 'Elegy on Lucky Wood'. The fraternal, jovial 'wow' is sounded too in the 'Familiar Epistles' between Ramsay and William Hamilton of Gilbertfield, collected, with the afore-mentioned, in the Edinburgh *Poems* of 1720, a collection with which Dermody seems to have been familiar. Ramsay's work was widely read and published throughout the eighteenth century in Dublin. Thus, in the fourth stanza, Dermody invokes Ramsay to demonstrate his broader knowl-edge. Ramsay appears as a talisman of poetic energy, whose influence will be both trimmed by Reason and augmented by Imagination:

> Allan's bra' lilts we wou'd rehearse,
> And laugh, and weep, and talk in verse;
> While grey-ey'd Judgment, sapient nurse,
>   Our thoughts would prune,
> And Fancy, roseate bands disperse,
>   Our brows to crown.

In the stanza following, Dermody confesses his ardent admiration by play-ing upon the then credible image of Burns as a poet who had received little education and whose work was thus untainted by intellectual trickery. He confides in his counterpart the sense of certainty that they will, as poets of a piece, meet: 'And, sure, I am, / 'Ere from this wicked world we part, / You'll jostle Tam'. And when they do, they will 'quaff stout whiskey, at our ease'; they will 'clink the can', and together rise above 'reptile man'.[22] As a concluding note, this understanding of an elite poetic equivalence sits somewhat oddly with Burns's own social and poetic self-stylings, and signals, perhaps, why Dermody would never quite manage to cultivate the talent, or indeed the appeal, of Burns. For Dermody was often concerned, even when deploying Scottish vernacular modes and forms, to establish superiority in intellect above the common man; and using those modes in this context was itself a measure of his elite poetic abilities. Both poets were capacious drinkers and carousers; but whereas Burns's poetry of sociabil-ity was successful in its coming convincingly 'from below', Dermody was, comparatively, more inclined to make the social world of his poetry second-ary to displays of technical virtuosity and practised sensibility. The Killeigh poems demonstrate a clear desire to evoke the bonhomie of everyday life in the Irish midlands; it is interesting, though, that they should be written, not in Irish amhrán metre or in the macaronic modes of some lower-class Irish poets writing in English. Dermody is instead concerned to flex his formal muscle in ways which will facilitate his rise in literary constituencies outside Ireland, constituencies to which he would ultimately migrate later in the 1790s, self-justifyingly deciding that the Irish poetic scene was an incubator of mediocrity.

But Dermody's churlishness was only one side of the story. His patrons were no longer willing to support him and, on the rare occasions when they were, he believed that they were smothering him. Several of Dermody's patrons had sought, at various times, to have him more formally educated at Trinity College in Dublin. On all occasions, however, he wriggled free – a sort of eighteenth-century Irish Huck Finn – of attempts to 'civilise' him. There was a certain appropriateness to such an untameable character using the Burnsian mode, as Dermody did in his good-humoured 'Ode to the Collegians', in which the boisterous humours of Trinity students would wrestle against the controlling tendencies of college authorities:

> Squarecaps, and round, all honest boys,
> May Tutors ne'er cry down your joys,
> Or study, which bright Jest destroys,
>   Teaze ye, when mellow!
> Ne Satan, come, with sawcer eyes,
>   In shape of Fellow!
>
> No Porter, with obstrep'rous summons,
> Startle your nap, with early drummings;
> Be yours, short lectures, and long Commons,
>   To gar you cheary!
> For, in this life, whatever come on's,
>   Let's e'en be merry,
>
> Let all your chamber-girls be pretty,
> Your chums, facete, and free, and witty;
> Your Matters, not inclin'd to fret ye,
>   Wi' too much knowledge;
> And then, mon dieu! old Dublin City,
>   May boast her College! (55)

This is a kindlier, more positive version of college life than that found in Burns's 'Epistle to J. Lapraik' – in which, famously, collegians '*come out* Asses' from their education, addled with jargon and dispossessed of 'Nature's fire' – though it is clearly influenced by that poem in being self-consciously the work of a poet writing on college life from the outside.[23] In Burns's epistle the learning peddled in universities is disparaged as unproductive in the cultivation of poetical ability, whereas in Dermody's more benign view college life is no more than an idle diversion for the well-to-do, not as corrupting as in Burns's poem but considered, perhaps, to be just as unnecessary.

Equally unimpressed by such learning, then, Dermody continues through much of the 1792 collection to exercise his 'natural' touch, always mediated through Scots dialect. In two songs, and in 'A Scotch Serenade', he partakes of Burns's amatory reputation, but localises it. In having the object of his affections in one song come from further to the north within Ireland, he makes the dialect a little more geographically appropriate:

> Some folks, there are, gang trig, and fine,
> In silks, and sattins, idly flaming;
> But She I love, is all divine,
> Their artfu' toil, and dresses shaming,
> Gin, She were but a cottage-Lass,
> And I, a Shepherd boy;
> I'd let those tempting Damsels, pass,
> Sweet Ann of Aughnacloy.
>
> My Annie's locks, as sunbeams, bright,
> Her e'en, sa' mild, Love's starry seat,
> Her cheeks, like Morning's purple light;
> Without the aid of art, compleat,
> Gin she were, dost in russet weed,
> And I, a Shepherd boy,
> I'd take thee, as Heav'n's choicest meed,
> Dear Ann of Aughnacloy. (60)

This piece is closer in form, and indeed in content, to the easy love songs contained in the *Scots Musical Museum*, published in the years between the appearance of Burns's first volume and Dermody's, and which the latter seems to have known. Accordingly, the refrain of 'A Scotch Serenade' demonstrates the broader influence of Scottish vernacular song culture over Dermody during this period:

> Will you na' ope the door, my love,
> Will you na' let me in,
> Who, weeping, wait, the glance of fate,
> From your twa' een.

There is in this poem a reference to the thistle, which 'trembling to the gale, / Hath nai sic thorns as love?', while Love itself – and in this image Dermody anticipates the simplicity, if not the sentiment, of Burns's later, famous, poem – 'like a rose-bud, sweetly blooms, / But oft doth canker prove' (68).

The 1792 collection was a promising venture, and this was largely due to Scottish influences which seemed tonally and temperamentally to suit Dermody. Why, then, were several of Dermody's Standard Habbie verse epistles and mock-elegies – those describing the very real characters of Killeigh – not included in the 1792 Dublin *Poems*? It may have been to avoid overloading the collection with Scottish modes; or it may have been decided by his patrons and publisher – the decidedly middle-of-the-road John Jones of Grafton Street – that the characters of these other poems were too coarse, too rural and too local, and therefore uninteresting to a polite Dublin readership. Whereas Burns had come, seemingly from nowhere, to impress the Edinburgh literati with his supposedly unstudied yet already disciplined poetic exuberance, Dermody had arrived in Dublin a prodigious child-classicist whose poetic talents could yet be fashioned, theoretically at least, to suit his patrons' tastes and temperaments. Thus, some of his most colourful poetic work was sidelined until after his death, when Raymond would republish a fuller set of Burnsian poems in *The Harp of Erin* (1807).

In his verse epistles, Burns had fashioned a persona who participates in a kind of fond and informal fraternity. Liam McIlvanney comments upon Burns's attempt to cultivate a sense of himself as a bardic figure and not as an official poet: 'From the beginning', writes Liam McIlvanney, 'Burns had a very clear-sighted awareness of what publication would mean to him, of the humiliating relationships of patronage and condescension in which it would involve him.'[24] Dermody commented upon such compromises, but he could never escape them; and while in the 1792 collection the poetic 'gabbling' is to be with Burns the literary celebrity, the pieces in the posthumous publications eulogise lowlier fellows, such as John Baynham, the Killeigh parish clerk, 'A penman fine by critics reckon'd'. Dermody laments that 'no more shall younkers crowd, / About thy hearth, and gabble loud', but with a Swiftian lash concedes that no one thought well of Baynham, 'Till thou wast dead'. Burns's 'Tam Samson's Elegy' is an obvious forerunner here, providing a template for what we might call Dermody's 'proleptic' elegies. Baynham's death and epitaph demand anointment 'With gills of noblest usquebaugh' but all of this is contradicted in a postscript – a longer version of Burns's 'Per Contra', in which Tam Samson turns out to be 'unskaith'd by Death's gleg gullie'.[25] In Dermody's poem, news of Baynham's death is contradicted by the jovially argumentative re-appearance of the 'deceased':

> After inditing these sad stories,
> I hap'd to hear some brother tories
> Ranting and roaring loud at Lory's,
>   Not quite well bred;
> I enter'd, and exclaim'd, 'Ye glories,
>   John Baynham's dead.'

> Scarce had I spoke, when 'neath the table
> Something sigh'd out most lamentable:
> Anon, to make my song a fable,
>   Starts out brave John;
> Sitting by Jove above! most stable:
>   On wicked throne.

> They press'd my sitting: marv'lous dull,
> I gap'd at Banquo like a fool,

And cried 'Good sirs, the table's full,
                And there's a spirit,'
'Come reach,' quoth sprite, 'an easy stool:'
                And lent a wherret.

'You rogue,' said he, 'how dare you write
Such stuff on me, as dead outright;
I think, by this good candle-light,
                You've earn'd a drubbing.
'Pho! Peace,' said I, 'I'll blot it quite;
                Aye, by St. Dobbin.'

Witness therefore, by my small finger,
John chooses still on earth to linger,
As penman, poet, toper, singer,
                In trade full thriving;
Know then, old bellman, barber, tinker,
                John Baynham's living.[26]

The same model is used to lament the passing of gabbling 'Will Gorman, The Killeigh Weaver', a deviser of merry tales who would 'pen songs on the corner-cross / Or lay them on the pump across, / With cautious look', and who, while weaving, would 'verses make on this or that' –

On Norah's stockings, Nelly's hat,
                Or Nancy's garters
Or satires pen black as my hat,
                And cut in quarters. (I, 212)

In 'A Lamentable Elegy on Nicholas, The Killeigh Taylor' (I, 213–16), the figure of Old Nick is invoked, as it was in several of Burns's poems, to show how such low company tended to carnivalesque floutings of religious authority, and to comment upon his fraternity's too-ready availability to the temptations of drink and love. And in 'The Death of Poor Davie, the Killeigh Piper' (217–21), Dermody, returning to the narrative of Tam Samson, sets out on a 'Come all ye' (in Habbie form) in which Davie, purveyor of a 'windy music' which could make both player and listener sick, is thought to have been taken by 'Death, the gilligapus' – an entity defined in Ramsay's 'Glossary' as 'a staring, gaping Fool'.[27] He will be commemorated in verse epitaph to inform the curious that '*Hic jacet davie*' – a nod to the '*Hic jacet*' of Burns's 'On Wee Johnie' – or at least, it would if he were indeed dead; once again, a 'Recantatory Postscript' clarifies that Davie is in fact alive and well.

Crowning the Burnsian sequence is a pair of Standard Habbie poems on the poet's own self which were clearly influenced by 'The Bard's Epitaph', the last of Burns's 1786 *Poems*. In Burns's poem self-aggrandisement is

subtly mixed with an implicit acknowledgement of the dangers abiding
in the very excesses of emotion and sentiment which made the poet great.
As Dermody would do, Burns appeals to brotherly conspirators, who are
invited to shed a tear over the grave of the Bard. An underlying echo of
Gray's 'Elegy' thus frames a survey of those whose lives have been obscured
by a lack of application: the 'whim-inspir'd fool', 'the Bard of rustic song'
who is encouraged to sigh 'with a frater-feeling strong', and the man of
'judgment clear', whose own wildness prevents him from doing as he himself instructs. The 'Poor Inhabitant' described in the second from last stanza
is perhaps Burns as he imagined himself, 'quick to learn and wise to know'
until 'thoughtless follies laid him low, / And stain'd his name'. Putting
his imagined dead self forward as a cautionary tale, Burns addresses, at
the poem's close, his ostensibly impressionable reader, advising 'prudent,
cautious, *self-controul*' as the key to wisdom.[28]

As an exploration of the conflict between anarchic talent and the need
for discipline, 'The Bard's Epitaph' had a lot to offer Dermody, who, in
spite of his egotism, demonstrated a comic awareness of his own limitations. The first of his self-addressing poems, 'My Own Elegy' (1, 221–5),
follows on from earlier poems in the mock-elegiac vein, while the second,
'An Ode to Myself', is an intriguing exploration of the poet's complex existence: as drinker and poet, as teenage womaniser, as well-read classicist
and frequenter of taverns. He declares himself a 'prince of jovial fellows
/ Tuning so blithe' his 'lyric bellows'. In the interests of seeming like a
good sport, Dermody proclaims himself, a little dishonestly, to be 'Of no
one's brighter genius jealous'.[29] Making no grand claims, he uses a diminutive voice, describing himself as a poet 'Whose little span / Is spent 'twixt
poetry and alehouse, / 'Twixt quill and cann!' (1, 225).

In these lines, and in the biographical contradictions they express
and suggest, is encapsulated much of the frustrating duality of Thomas
Dermody. His was a generally democratic spirit which sought to cultivate
fellowship, between himself and his Killeigh friends, or between himself
and Robert Burns. However, caught between the boozy world of the 'cann'
and the more genteel world of the 'quill', his artistry could also tend to jeal-
ousy and elitism. He would, like Burns, move between writing a poetry of
lower-class sociability and a poetry of sensibility in the fashionable English
mode. A minor poet emerging from a regional periphery in linguistic transition, Dermody, obsessed with Anglophone literary fame from an early age,
and encouraged in that obsession by patrons and admirers of his youthful
prowess, had left a bilingual world behind him in Clare to learn his poetic
craft largely in imitation of English (and Anglo-Irish) models. He would
draw upon Milton, Spenser, Shakespeare, Pope, Gray and Goldsmith, and
would allude throughout to the classics in which he was so prodigiously
versed. But it was with Burns that he shared the most organic and successful affinity. The impact of Burns's work was immediate in Ireland, and

chimed with the new spirit of regional and radical possibility in the early 1790s. Burns's influence offered Dermody a productive 'third way' in his most successful and promising years. The fact that an Anglophone Munster poet was able to imitate Burns's dialect work demonstrates that, between Ayr and Clare, the latter's energetic forms and modes of expression had a wider cultural availability and communicability. Alan Bold, in *A Burns Companion*, argues that when Burns 'was most honest as a poet, he was most Scottish'.[30] Paradoxically for a poet from the Irish mid-west, the same might be said of Tom Dermody.

Notes

1. James Grant Raymond, *The Life of Thomas Dermody, interspersed with Pieces of Original Poetry*, 2 vols (London, 1806), vol. II, p. 331.

2. *The Rights of Justice, or Rational Liberty; A Letter to an Acquaintance in the Country. From Thomas Dermody* (Dublin, 1793), pp. 22–3.

3. Kenneth Simpson, 'The vernacular Enlightenment', in Johnny Rodger and Gerard Carruthers (eds), *Fickle Man: Robert Burns in the 21st Century* (Dingwall: Sandstone Press, 2009), pp. 91–103, 102.

4. Francis Jeffrey, 'Review of R. H. Cromek's *Reliques of Robert Burns*', in Donald A. Low (ed.), *Robert Burns: The Critical Heritage* (London: Routledge and Kegan Paul, 1996), pp. 178–95, 178.

5. Andrew Noble, 'Wordsworth and Burns: the anxiety of being under the influence', in Carol McGuirk (ed.), *Critical Essays on Robert Burns* (New York: Twayne, 1998), p. 53.

6. Alan Richardson, *Literature, Education and Romanticism: Reading as Social Practice* (Cambridge: Cambridge University Press, 1994), pp. 249–50.

7. Michael Scrivener, *Seditious Allegories: John Thelwall and Jacobin Writing* (University Park, PA: The Pennsylvania State University Press, 2001), p. 284.

8. Robert Southey, *The Life and Correspondence of Robert Southey*, ed. Charles Cuthbert Southey, 6 vols (London, 1849–50), vol. II, p. 153; Thomas Dermody, 'My Own Character, To a Lady', in Thomas Dermody, *Poems on Various Subjects* (London, 1802), p. 149.

9. See R. B. McDowell (ed.), *Analecta Hibernica* 17 (1949), p. 90.

10. Liam McIlvanney, *Burns the Radical: Poetry and Politics in Late Eighteenth-century Scotland* (East Linton: Tuckwell Press, 2002), p. 67.

11. Raymond, *Life of Thomas Dermody*, vol. I, p. 115.

12. Henry Boyd, *The Woodman's Tale, After the Manner of Spenser. To Which are Added, Other Poems, Chiefly Narrative and Lyric, and the Royal Message, A Drama* (London, 1805), p. 110.

13. Anya Taylor, *Bacchus in Romantic England: Writers and Drink, 1780–1830* (New York: St Martin's Press, 1999), p. 59.

14. *Monthly Review* 52 (January 1807), pp. 54–5.

15. Robert Crawford, *The Bard: Robert Burns, a Biography* (Princeton: Princeton University Press, 2009), pp. 202, 202, 203.

16. Stephen Dornan, 'Thomas Dermody, Robert Burns and the Killeigh Cycle', *Scottish Studies Review* 6 (2005), p. 14.

17. Bryan Coleborne, 'Anglo-Irish Verse 1675–1825', in *The Field Day Anthology of Irish Writing*, 3 vols (Derry: Field Day, 1991), vol. I, p. 417.

18. Dornan, 'Thomas Dermody', p. 18. See also Stephan Dornan, 'Beyond the Milesian Pale: The Poetry of James Orr', *Eighteenth-Century Ireland: Iris an Dá chultúr* 20 (2005), pp. 146–8.

19. Thomas Dermody, 'Tam to Rab', in *The Penguin Book of Irish Poetry*, ed. Patrick Crotty (London: Penguin, 2010), p. 357.

20. Janet Sorenson, 'Wow and other cries in the night: Fergusson's vernacular, Scots talking heads, and unruly bodies', in Robert Crawford (ed.), *Heaven-Taught Fergusson: Robert Burns's Favourite Scottish Poet* (East Linton: Tuckwell Press, 2003), pp. 117, 117, 122.

21. See Raymond, *Life of Thomas Dermody*, vol. I, pp. 202–6.

22. Thomas Dermody, 'Tam to Rab. An Odaic Epistle', in Thomas Dermody, *Poems, Consisting of Essays, Lyric, Elegiac, &c. Written between the 13th and 16th years of his Age* (Dublin, 1792), pp. 53–4. Hereafter all page references to the 1792 *Poems* will be included in the text.

23. Robert Burns, 'Epistle to J. L*****K, An Old Scotch Bard', in Robert Burns, *Poems, Chiefly in the Scottish Dialect* (Dublin, 1787), p. 203. See also K 57, I, 87, 69, 73.

24. McIlvanney, *Burns the Radical*, p. 100.

25. Robert Burns, 'Tam Samson's Elegy', in Burns, *Poems, Chiefly in the Scottish Dialect*, p. 107. See K 117, I, 276, 99.

26. Thomas Dermody, 'John Baynham's Epitaph', in Thomas Dermody, *The Harp of Erin, Containing the Poetical Works of the Late Thomas Dermody*, 2 vols (London, 1807), vol. I, pp. 206–10. Hereafter all page references from *The Harp of Erin* will be included in the text.

27. Allan Ramsay, *Poems* (Edinburgh, 1720), p. 372.

28. Robert Burns, 'A Bard's Epitaph', in Burns, *Poems, Chiefly in the Scottish Dialect*, pp. 251–2. See K 104, I, 247, 29.

29. This self-proclaimed lack of ego may have been true of happier days spent in Killeigh, but not of his disillusioned final years in London, when and where he could be petulantly jealous of the success of others. On 17 April 1801, he would write to Robert Owenson: 'Who is the *Mr. Moore* Sydney mentions? He is nobody here, I assure you, of eminence' (Sydney Owenson, *Lady Morgan's Memoirs: Autobiography, Diaries and Correspondence*, 2 vols (1863, London, 1868), vol. I, pp. 203–4). He retracted his surliness in a letter to Sydney Owenson on 14 September 1801: 'You are mistaken if you imagine I have not the highest respect for your friend Moore . . . I am told he is a most worthy young man, and I am certain myself of his genius and erudition' (vol. I, p. 218).

30. Alan Bold, *A Burns Companion* (Basingstoke: Macmillan, 1991), p. 81; cited, in a discussion of the critical debate surrounding the authenticity of Burns's dialect, in David Fairer, *English Poetry of the Eighteenth Century, 1700–1789* (London: Longman, 2003), p. 181.

CHAPTER 11

'Simple Bards, unbroke by rules of Art': The Poetic Self-Fashioning of Burns and Hogg

Meiko O'Halloran

As James Hogg sought to create a place for himself in both the early nineteenth-century marketplace and British literary history, he drew on a specifically Scottish lineage to fashion his identity as a poet. His marketing of himself as an untutored bard was clearly a direct response to Robert Burns's carefully constructed image as a natural genius or poetic prodigy who lacked formal learning – but in the wake of Burns's monumental success, Hogg also felt the need to be more ambitious about presenting himself as a poet who could speak to and for the Scottish nation if he was to be recognised in his own right. As I will demonstrate in this essay, Hogg's desire both to follow and supersede Burns shaped his conception of his most successful collection of poems, *The Queen's Wake* (1813). Burns had not only provided a model of how Hogg could prosper in the literary marketplace but also how he could help to promote the long-term survival of his local and national literary communities.

Hogg's biographical self-fashioning captures his emulative and competitive relationship to his most important Scottish literary ancestor. When Hogg revised his autobiography at the age of sixty-two, Burns's meteoric model of natural genius was still on his mind. In keeping with the earlier versions of his memoir which had appeared alongside his poems in *The Mountain Bard* (1807, 1821), Hogg recounted his origins as the son of Ettrick tenant farmers, descended from a line of shepherds – but this time, he added that he was born on 25 January 1772 (exactly thirteen years after Burns). His family's sudden financial ruin had made it necessary for him to begin work as a cowherd at the age of seven, he explained, ending his schooling after only a few months. Playing up to the image of a Rousseauvian noble savage, he gives an engaging account of his laborious efforts to read his master's books in his late teens – including two works which his readers would have recognised as Burnsian favourites, William Hamilton's version of Blind Harry's *Wallace* (1722) and Allan Ramsay's *The Gentle Shepherd* (1725). At this point in his earlier memoirs, Hogg recalls his first attempts to compose songs and plays in the mid-to-late 1790s, followed by the untimely dispatch of *Scottish Pastorals* (1801), comprising poems which he transcribed from memory on a whim, while waiting between sheep markets, and had printed at his own expense. Although he regrets pushing his early poems 'headlong into the world . . . without either patron or preface', there is also a playful Burnsian paradox in the autodidact retrospectively characterising his work with a quotation from his favourite Shakespeare play, *Hamlet*, ' "unhoussell'd, unanointed, unaneled; with all their imperfections on their heads" '.[1] Here, Hogg echoes Burns's paradoxically erudite expression of his fears of being 'dragged forth, with all my imperfections on my head, to the full glare of learned and polite conversation' as he prepared to enter the drawing rooms of the Edinburgh literati after the success of his Kilmarnock volume.[2] Like Burns, Hogg was consciously constructing a public image as he moved from the privacy of composing poetry to appearing publicly as a poet. His allusion serves to consolidate his affinity with Burns, showing off his knowledge of Shakespeare even as he mocks himself for being ill-prepared to cross the threshold as a published author.

As Hogg revised his memoir for the last time, he gave a more flamboyant performance, boldly claiming his literary kinship to Burns by introducing a pivotal new part of his story: he had been inspired to become a poet after hearing 'Tam o' Shanter' recited for the first time by 'a half daft man' who also told him Burns's life story while he was shepherding on a hillside in 1797, in his mid-twenties.[3] Appropriating the conventions of Puritan spiritual autobiography, Hogg implied that a providential hand had invited him to take up Burns's mantle and seek public recognition for his poetic gift. While Burns's poetry 'delighted' him, hearing of the author's extraordinary achievements and his recent death made him weep. In his romanticised recollection, this experience formed 'a new epoch' in his life, giving rise to a hope that he might one day succeed Burns as Scotland's national poet:

> Every day I pondered on the genius and fate of Burns. I wept, and always thought with myself – what is to hinder me from succeeding Burns? I too was born on the 25th of January, and I have much more time to read and compose than any ploughman could have, and can sing more old songs than ever ploughman could in the world . . . I resolved to be a poet, and to follow in the steps of Burns.[4]

Crucially, Hogg wanted to compete with Burns, not just tread in his footsteps – a point which he acknowledges as he leaps forward to a moment in 1812, when he confided to a friend his 'inward consciousness that I should yet live to be compared with Burns; and though I might never equal him in some things, I thought I might excel him in others'.[5] It was apt that Hogg's revised memoir was published in his penultimate collection of stories, *Altrive Tales* (1832), for his account of 'the first time I ever heard of Burns' may have been his tallest tale yet.[6] After its publication, Hogg discovered that he was not, in fact, born on the same day as Burns; his baptism was recorded in a parish register for 9 December 1770.[7] And yet, as a portrait which captures Hogg's self-dramatisation as a fellow 'rustic Bard' and 'lab'ring Hind' (to borrow terms from Burns's narrative of his own poetic election, 'The Vision', K 62, I, 110), his account has integrity. For most of Hogg's life, his imagined affinity with Burns, and the supposed coincidence of their birthdays, shaped his identity and gave him a sense of validation as an uneducated labouring-class poet, and a bold adventurer in a host of other genres. More immediately, Hogg's vivid self-portrait serves to highlight his significant debt to Burns's strategic self-dramatising.

Hogg's fascination with Burns was bound up with their mutual flair for authorial performance. His wily turn as a weeping autodidact who answers the call of a Burnsian apostle was an especially apposite form of homage to the ploughman poet who had negotiated the hazardous dual worlds of polite patronage and a rising literary marketplace through his virtuoso role-playing and his strategic deployment of myriad personae. By the early nineteenth century, as aspiring writers faced an increasingly savage review culture, dominated by powerful Scottish critics and magazine editors such as Francis Jeffrey, John Wilson and John Gibson Lockhart, it was small wonder that Hogg should take his cue from the survival strategies of a poet whose quick-witted shape-shifting had enabled him to attract and sustain the adulation of readers of all walks of life, from all across Britain. Drawing on recent critical re-evaluations of Burns by Fiona Stafford, Nigel Leask, Liam McIlvanney and Robert Crawford,[8] and building on discussions of Burns's importance for Hogg by Douglas Mack, Gillian Hughes, Karl Miller, Valentina Bold, Kirsteen McCue and Patrick Scott,[9] this essay aims to shed new light on Hogg's debt to Burns by examining his poetic self-fashioning as a 'Naturae Donum' or 'Gift of Nature' in his first major collection of poems, *The Queen's Wake* (1813), in response to Burns's performance as a 'Simple Bard, unbroke by rules of Art' in his debut collection, *Poems, Chiefly in the Scottish Dialect* (1786).

The need to craft and promote an appealing and distinctive literary persona had special resonance for late eighteenth-century and Romantic 'peasant poets' in the polite literary culture of their times, but adopting the naïve persona of an untutored poet was not enough in itself to impress the critics. Reviewers of Hogg's *The Mountain Bard* (1807) and *The Forest Minstrel* (1810) routinely noted that the shepherd poet had modelled himself on the 'Heaven-taught ploughman', but the critical reception of his early works remained subdued.[10] By contrast, *The Queen's Wake* excited the admiration of reviewers, general readers and leading poets such as Southey and Byron. Its rapid circulation in a further five editions helped to realise the personal advent which Hogg had imaginatively figured in the poem – his emergence from local obscurity to win acclaim as a national competitor. Just as the Kilmarnock and Edinburgh editions of *Poems, Chiefly in the Scottish Dialect* had transformed Burns from a local to a national bard, so *The Queen's Wake* established Hogg's literary fame in his lifetime and for the

rest of the nineteenth century. Here, I suggest that Burns's intricate root-
ing of his ploughman persona within a portrait of the people, poets, manners, language, customs and superstitions of his native Ayrshire – with the
express intention of putting his beloved home region on the map of literary
history[11] – was formative to Hogg's fashioning of his local and national
bardic identity in *The Queen's Wake*. He not only appears as the sixteenth-
century Ettrick bard who travels to Edinburgh to compete in a national
poetry contest hosted by Mary, Queen of Scots, but also as his modern
descendent, the Ettrick Shepherd narrator, who presents a vibrant portrait
of Scotland through her competing bards and their ballads. Recognising
the marketable appeal of Burns's image as a natural genius, and aiming to
attract support for his own quest as a Scottish poet in the literary marketplace, Hogg shrewdly harnessed his personal aspirations to an ambitious,
epic national vision. He embedded his Ettrick Shepherd persona in a narrative which promoted Scotland's claims as the birthplace of great literature –
putting forward an imagined Scottish Marian tradition to rival the English
Elizabethan Golden Age.

Burns's multi-layered performance began on the title-page of *Poems,
Chiefly in the Scottish Dialect* – introduced to the world in July 1786, with
the title and his name in large letters, and the following epigraph:

> THE Simple Bard, unbroke by rules of Art,
> He pours the wild effusions of the heart:
> And if inspir'd, 'tis Nature's pow'rs inspire;
> Her's all the melting thrill, and her's the kindling fire. ANONYMOUS[12]

The epigraph is integral to Burns's projected narrative as an author;[13] it
brings forward a bard who has long existed outside the boards of print
culture, and who now steps out of the shadows to occupy a central position
on the title-page of a young poet's first work. Despite the striking contrast
between the large typography of 'ROBERT BURNS' above and the anonymity
of the poet whose verses appear beneath, there was, perhaps, an implied
fraternity between them. As he made his first appearance 'in guid, black
prent' (K 79, I, 179, 38), Burns had no idea how astonishingly successful he
would be in achieving 'that dearest wish of every poetic bosom – to be distinguished' (K, III, 972). But his use of this epigraph to construct his authorial identity seems to signpost his aspirations to move from unpublished
provincial obscurity to a position in which he and his fellow Ayshire bards
could command public attention. The epigraph is pertinent to many of his
poetic preoccupations. Even as he mapped himself onto and developed the
persona of the 'Simple Bard', Burns took the author of the epigraph – an
anonymous brother bard – with him, into his book of poems. He was also
implicitly taking into print the vitality of spoken poetry and the importance
of an oral tradition in fostering strong bonds of community – between bards
and their audiences, but also between bards themselves.

A sense of brotherhood with unpretentious and often local, obscure and impoverished bards infuses Burns's collection from beginning to end.[14] It emerges not only in the author's many verse epistles to his friends, 'To J. S****', 'Epistle to Davie, a brother Poet', 'Epistle to J. L*****k, an Old Scotch Bard' and 'Epistle to W. S*****n, Ochiltree', but also, poignantly, in his appeal for 'frater-feeling' with any 'whim-inspir'd fool' and 'Bard of rustic song', whom he invites to commune with him at his graveside, in the closing poem, 'A Bard's Epitaph' (K 104, I, 247). Burns's poetic fellowship not only transcends the limits of mortality but also boundaries of class, education, language, location and nationality. As his masterly use of quotations and allusions amply demonstrates, he enters into dialogues with dead as well as living poets – including cherished Scottish favourites, Ramsay, Fergusson, Beattie and Thomson, but also great English poets such as Milton, Pope and Gray. His tone in many of the poems is startlingly familiar, frank and confident, casually placing him on an equal footing with eminent authors who had created major literary landmarks, as well as those who were socially dispossessed and little known. For all his self-mocking humour about poetic ambition ('Then farewell hopes of Laurel-boughs / To garland my poetic brows!', K 79, I, 180, 49–50), this collection expresses real hopes and fears about the immediate survival of poets and their longevity in print.

Burns's bardic performance was all the more important if he was to secure his readers' support beyond their subscription to his first volume of poems. From the beginning, he emphasises his emotional integrity. His chosen epigraph foregrounds a strong, dignified and authoritative Bard who exemplifies genuine feeling over affectation, simplicity over sophistication, wildness over cultivation, natural talent over scholarly learning and spontaneity over 'rules of Art'. 'Unbroke' carries connotations of raw energy and untamed talent – of being not only rough and unconventional but also original, distinctive and, perhaps, unbreakable. Being imperfect and untrained in literary conventions also suggests the poet's rugged sincerity. His articulation of 'the wild effusions of the heart' anticipates the 'spontaneous overflow of powerful feelings' with which Wordsworth began to define good poetry in his Preface to *Lyrical Ballads*.[15] Burns's 'Simple Bard' is not a polished or refined product, then, but a gift of Nature who feels intensely and is invigorated and inspired by *her* power and authority – ignited by her 'kindling fire'. This bardic character invites the sympathetic interest and admiration of readers.

By contrast, the poet of the Preface gives a complex rhetorical performance in which he apologises for the lack of education which the epigraph celebrates, while making casual references to Theocritus and Virgil, and placing himself in relation to Ramsay and Fergusson. The cool formality and finesse of Burns's prose emphasises his self-awareness and guardedness, complicating his claims of unselfconscious simplicity and spontaneity:

that he addresses a multifarious general public, as well as a select group of known readers, heightens the feeling of a performance. There are tensions between the private and public as the author brings forward for commercial consumption 'the little creations of his own fancy' – those private distractions from 'the toil and fatigues of a laborious life' in which he explores a tumultuous mass of personal thoughts and feelings ('the loves, the griefs, the hopes, the fears in his own breast') and yearns to find solace ('some kind of counterpoise to the struggles of the world', K, III, 971). Whereas the poems emphasise friendship, sympathy and understanding between the poet and his fellow creatures and brother bards, a critical audience is projected in the Preface, in the hostile voices which the author anticipates will 'brand' him 'An impertinent blockhead, obtruding his nonsense on the world', the 'Critic [who] catches at the word *genius*', and those who may charge him with 'Dulness and Nonsense' (K, III, 971–2). Thus, the many voices of Burns begin to emerge before readers have even reached his poems.

Burns dramatises all of these elements in the sequence of poems which follow – the spontaneous bard, his antagonistic critics, his relationships to other poets, and the friendships which sustain him in his fight for survival. The bard, an unpolished product of Nature, faces with 'tentless heed' a hostile world of socio-political injustice, hypocrisy, corruption, financial insecurity, freezing weather, disparaging criticism, self-doubts and dark uncertainty about the future (K 79, I, 180). Despite Burns's bold and versatile use of voice and literary form, readers repeatedly encounter his anxieties about his possible destitution and the collective lot of many struggling poets and socially marginalised figures. When Poor Mailie the sheep expires in a ditch as a result of being tethered, the bard deplores 'that vile, wanchancie thing – *a raep*!' which even fills men 'wi' chokin dread' (K 25, I, 36). But the epistle to James Smith, which immediately follows, suggests that a bard who remains 'unbroke by rules of Art' may have an equally, if not more, devastating end. Although Mailie dies because of the rope her master has placed around her neck, she remains a faithful servant until her last breath. By contrast, Burns claims to be bound only by ties of friendship. Celebrating his poetic freedom in a 'fit o' rhyme' addressed to James Smith, the young friend and poet with whom he planned to emigrate, he claims to 'rhyme for *fun*' rather than money or accolades, but he is no less a prey to misfortune and chance:

> The star that rules my luckless lot,
> Has fated me the russet coat,
> An' damn'd my fortune to the groat;
>   But, in requit,
> Has blest me with a *random-shot*
>   O' countra wit. (K 79, I, 179, 31–6)

Despite his 'luckless' fate, he receives an arbitrary gift which gives him a measure of autonomy; the same star that damns him to a life of poverty compensates him with the mental reflexes of 'wit' – implying humour, perspicacity and mental agility – which enable him to weather the vicissitudes of life. Soberingly, he goes on to predict for himself and other '*Poor wights*' who observe 'nae rules nor roads' an aimless life of 'eternal swervin', in which they 'zig-zag on; / Till curst with Age, obscure an' starvin, / They aften groan' (K 79, I, 182, 112–14). Mailie, whose loyal service and virtue are irreproachable, may justly curse the rope which kills her, but her modest request that sheep be allowed to 'wander at their will' is ominously juxtaposed with the bard's assertion that those who truly wander wilfully in fact run the risk of starving to death (K 24, I, 32). Mailie's dignified, eloquent and orderly dying speech may even seem enviable to those who 'groan' with the hunger, anguish and exhaustion of pursuing their own course.

Since the bard's 'wit' is his only tool of defence against poverty, he celebrates his gift with gusto ('I jouk beneath Misfortune's blows', K 79, I, 183, 147) and revels in the company of similarly energetic and lawless local brother bards, 'the hairum-scairum, ram-stam boys / The rattling squad', who are despised by the slaves of social rules (K 79, I, 183, 165–6). Though the risks are high for a bard who strikes out on his own path, he is impelled to compose poetry in his own style and for his own satisfaction, whatever the personal cost. As a farmer, Burns ploughed the earth steadily, but artistically and materially he saw his life as an erratic zig-zag. Hogg could keenly relate to Burns's sense of being at the mercy of external forces and his restless desire for poetic liberty. As a shepherd, he imposed a protective order over sheep like Mailie, but he sought to exert control over his own life by composing poetry which would win him fame and enough money to live on. Both poets needed to secure an audience which included wealthy and well-educated readers if they were to survive through their art.

The tension between the bard's vulnerability to misfortune and the autonomy and control of his writing is a prominent feature of *Poems*; the confidence with which Burns shaped his poetry was clearly at odds with his vulnerable existence outside the printed page. For Hogg and other readers who shared Burns's precarious material circumstances, this dramatic tension must have had the effect of heightening his valiant resilience and making his defiant humour all the more appealing. Knowing that *Poems* had subsequently catapulted Burns into the position of chief Scottish bard, Hogg could see the collection as part of a heroic narrative in which the ploughman poet from Kyle overcomes intense physical hardships as well as social prejudices against his poverty and lack of formal education, writing himself into the national arena against the odds. He recognised the hostile world that Burns described. At the heart of the collection, adversity is frequently figured through the harsh winter landscapes and overpowering natural elements to which individuals are perilously exposed. In 'The Cotter's

Saturday Night', the warmth and joy of pious family life are a precious nightly refuge from the daily hardships of manual labour outside the cottage, where 'November chill blaws loud wi' angry sugh' (K 72, I, 146, 10). This makes the destruction of the nest in 'To a Mouse' all the more disturbing. The helpless plight of the mouse who must face 'Winter's *sleety dribble*' with no home prompts the poet to confront the fearful uncertainty of his own future (K 69, I, 128, 35). The next poem, 'Epistle to Davie, a brother Poet', finds him sheltering from and composing homely jingles to survive the onslaught of winter, as 'winds frae off Ben-Lomond blaw / And bar the doors wi' driving snaw' (K 51, I, 65, 1–2), but the bleak weather and barren landscapes of 'Man was made to mourn, a Dirge' and 'Winter, a Dirge' seem to express an internal desolation. The shepherd poet who faced the same fears of financial destitution, and who strove to withstand whatever the elements threw at him, could fully appreciate the mental and physical resilience with which Burns defined himself. He also saw the advantages of staging an authorial performance to gain public acceptance.

By presenting himself as a 'Simple Bard' whose poetry is spontaneous and inspired and whose integrity is unshakeable, however rough and unsteady his life, Burns had made a radically different kind of poetic hero attractive to polite readers. Despite the mighty tempests which threaten to engulf the bard of *Poems, Chiefly in the Scottish Dialect*, poetry and poetic fraternity are repeatedly represented as powerful stays against hardship. In the face of adversity, Burns pours the full force of his wit and the fire and energy of his passions – his ability to rage, to love, to hope, to despair, to laugh, to mock and to lament – creating an extraordinarily strong and invigorating sense of community, even in his fleeting relationships, with men, women, beasts, flora and even with the Deil himself. Collectively, the poems demonstrate that, for Burns, poetry is a connective life-giving force, a source of solace, a stimulus to independent thought, a means of voicing political protest and a form of emotional exploration which is vital to his existence. Composing poetry enables him to relate to others and understand himself better, as he grapples with the joys and griefs of this world and considers the supernatural possibilities of the next. Above all, Burns had made himself admirable as both a local and a national bard; moving from outspoken socio-political critique to intensely personal concerns, and back again, he championed the value of local poetry, while also promoting Scottish poetry and the Scottish vernacular to a non-Scottish audience.

Hogg's narrative performance as a bard whose 'wareless heart, and houseless head' defy the 'cold winds of adversity' makes clear that he was deeply impressed by Burns's bardic persona.[16] He responds to Burns's achievement by dramatising his quest to succeed him in the marketplace, hoping to follow him into the chronicles of literary history. Marketed as an elegant bourgeois product, 'THE QUEEN'S WAKE' was proclaimed on the title-page, with the subtitle, *A Legendary Poem*, in an antique Gothic style of script –

the word 'legendary' not only emphasising Hogg's use of old legends but also suggesting the fame to which he aspired. Beneath his name, the epigraph from Collins's 'Ode to Fear' introduces Hogg as a reader of Collins, his poem a response to the Bards created by eminent mid-eighteenth century poets who also included Gray and Macpherson. While Hogg lays claim to his native oral bardic tradition, he participates in the textual transformation of bardic figures. Whereas Collins addresses fear as a 'Dark Pow'r' whose withering impact blasts his view,[17] Hogg removes fear and strengthens the poet's authority as he addresses his readers:

> Be mine to read the visions old,
> Which thy awakening Bards have told;
> And whilst they meet thy tranced view,
> Hold each strange tale devoutly true.   COLLINS[18]

Rewriting 'blasted' as 'tranced', Hogg emphasises possession – the poet's inheritance of old visions from ancient Bards ('Be mine'), the 'tranced view' of his audience and the way in which they might 'hold' the tales through a willing suspension of disbelief. As part of Hogg's construction of his poetic identity, the epigraph suggests that, like Collins, he is a reader of orally and textually imparted visions but that he is also, like Burns, an inspired poet who seeks to cast a spell over his audience.

Hogg shares Burns's view of his poetic gift as a vital stay to his mental and emotional survival in a harsh world. He even takes up Burns's advice to John Lapraik to 'Come kittle up your *moorland harp* / Wi' gleesome touch!' and 'Ne'er mind how Fortune *waft* an' *warp*; / She's but a b–tch' (K 58, I, 91, 45–8). *The Queen's Wake* accordingly begins with an energetic address to the elements which foregrounds the enduring bond between the Ettrick Shepherd and his harp, striking the keynotes of optimism, survival and resilience in the face of adversity:

> Now burst, ye Winter clouds that lower,
> Fling from your folds the piercing shower;
> Sing to the tower and leafless tree,
> Ye cold winds of adversity;
> Your blights, your chilling influence shed,
> On wareless heart, and houseless head;
> Your ruth or fury I disdain,
> I've found my Mountain Lyre again. (Introduction, ll. 1–8)

Unlike the Aeolian harp, a symbol of the poet passively animated by Nature, Hogg's 'Mountain Lyre' is an emblem of the poet's dynamic gift, which is rooted in the oral culture of his native Ettrick. Responding to the aged Ossian and his harp in Macpherson's Highland epic, Hogg strives, like Burns, to restore the poet's vigour, defying the elements and promoting himself as a strong Lowland bard.

The Ettrick Shepherd is both a local poet and national singer with concerns about the survival of poets and poetic traditions. In keeping with the mixture of defiant jubilation and mournful lament in Burns's *Poems*, *The Queen's Wake* fuses elegy with celebration, as the Shepherd claims to reignite a bygone tradition. While the title announces a narrative of national loss, a Marian poetic tradition which has disappeared, the antiquated term 'wake' yields positive meanings – here referring to a poetry contest which Hogg imagines Mary, Queen of Scots, held, early in her reign. Thirty bards from all over Scotland are said to have competed. In reviving the 'wake', the modern Ettrick Shepherd presents the fifteen ballads which have supposedly survived in oral tradition, together with portraits of the competitors. Thus, *The Queen's Wake* is both a narrative poem about an imagined event in Stuart history (a missing piece of Scotland's epic story) and a collection of poems which allows Hogg to show off his versatility, using a variety of genres, subjects and styles.

In order to provide his credentials for the marketplace, Hogg gives himself a poetic genealogy, embedding an ancestral portrait of himself as a Burnsian prodigy within the contest. Appearing between two possible avatars of Macpherson and Scott, Hogg's imaginary ancestor, the Ettrick Bard, is a comically primitive rural outsider whose poverty highlights his suitability to succeed Burns:

> A clown he was, bred in the wild,
> And late from native moors exiled,
> In hopes his mellow mountain strain
> High favour with the great would gain.
> Poor wight! he never weened how hard
> For poverty to earn regard!
> Dejection o'er his visage ran,
> His coat was bare, his colour wan,
> His forest doublet darned and torn,
> His shepherd plaid all rent and worn;
> Yet dear the symbols to his eye,
> Memorials of a time gone by. (Night the Second, 247–58)

Like the '*Poor wights*' among whom Burns counted himself in his epistle to James Smith, the Ettrick Bard must make his own way in life. With his worn-out shepherd's plaid and impoverished appearance, he is essentially a repackaged version of Burns's untutored genius. But this time, Hogg strategically deploys his clownish persona to situate himself, playfully, in literary history. The Ettrick Bard's harp affirms that he is a 'Gift of Nature', with Burns's 'spark o' Nature's fire' in his eye (K 57, I, 87):

> Instead of arms or golden crest,
> His harp with mimic flowers was drest:

Around, in graceful streamers, fell
The briar-rose and the heather bell;
And there his learning deep to prove,
Naturæ Donum graved above.
When o'er her mellow notes he ran,
And his wild mountain chaunt began;
Then first was noted in his eye,
A gleam of native energy. (Night the Second, 297–306)

Substituting a noble family name and lineage with the instrument of his art and wild flowers, Hogg emphasises humble poetic rather than elevated hieratical identity. With Burnsian irony, his uncultivated talent is expressed in an elegant Latin motto, '*Naturæ Donum*', to impress educated readers. The motto was most likely concocted for Hogg by his friend, James Gray, an Edinburgh schoolmaster in classics. With his ancestral avatar, the Ettrick Bard, fulfilling the role of a charming rustic clown, Hogg strove to join the ranks of an established community of poets.

Using his Ettrick Bard and Shepherd personae, Hogg rooted himself imaginatively as an untutored genius at the start of a Scottish Marian tradition which is framed to challenge Elizabethan England. Just as Burns had dramatised his poetic election in 'The Vision' by having his homely Muse, Coila, instruct him to 'Strive in thy *humble sphere* to shine' before crowning him with holly (K 62, I, 113), so Hogg has the eighteen-year-old Mary, Queen of Scots, reaffirm his poetic gift. Although the Ossianic warrior bard, Gardyn, wins the Queen's bejewelled harp, Mary gives the Ettrick Bard a plainer harp which turns out to be musically superior and precisely suited to his poetic talent. Even as Burns had sworn, in his poem to James Smith, to 'wander on with tentless heed', roving among busy ploughs 'An' teach[ing] the lanely heights an' howes / My rustic sang' (K 79, I, 180, 51–4), he strove to speak to and for Scotland in *Poems, Chiefly in the Scottish Dialect*. Hogg was even more conscious of using his rustic persona to further his ambitions. When, at the end of *The Queen's Wake*, the Ettrick Shepherd recalls that his harp has 'taught the wandering winds to sing', he puts a seal on his claim to inherit the mantle of Scotland's favourite rustic bard (Conclusion, 394).

Burns's masterly performance as a 'Simple Bard' was directly instrumental to Hogg's reinvention of himself as a national competitor. *The Queen's Wake* became Hogg's most celebrated work in his lifetime, reaching a sixth edition by 1819, and going on to secure his place in British literature for the rest of the century. In the second edition, a prefatory poetic eulogy from Bernard Barton began 'O Heaven-taught Shepherd!'.[19] When the poem went into a third edition in 1814, Francis Jeffrey gave his influential approval in the *Edinburgh Review*. As Mackenzie had done for Burns in his *Lounger* essay, Jeffrey assumed the task of 'recommending obscure merit' and 'doing honour to neglected genius', eventually declaring Hogg 'a poet – in the highest acceptation of the name'.[20] When, two years later, Hogg boldly placed himself in an emerging canon of Romantic poets in his anonymous collection of parodies, *The Poetic Mirror, or the Living Bards of Britain* (1816), reviewers were not surprised to find Hogg included alongside many of the most famous poets of the age – Byron, Scott, Wordsworth, Coleridge and Southey. The first print run sold out within weeks and was soon followed by a second edition. It would seem that Hogg had not only been accepted as a Scottish poet but was also recognised as a 'Living Bard of Britain'.

Notes

1. James Hogg, 'Memoir of the Life of James Hogg', in James Hogg, *The Mountain Bard*, ed. Suzanne Gilbert (Edinburgh: Edinburgh University Press, 2007), pp. 15, 203, 401n. Hogg quotes from Old Hamlet's description of his murder in *Hamlet*, I, v, 77–9.

2. Robert Burns to William Greenfield, December 1786, in Robert Burns, *The Letters of Robert Burns*, ed. J. De Lancey Ferguson and G. Ross Roy, 2nd edn, 2 vols (Oxford: Clarendon Press, 1985), vol. I, pp. 73–4. See Fiona Stafford, *Starting Lines in Scottish, Irish, and English Poetry from Burns to Heaney* (Oxford: Oxford University Press, 2000), pp. 46–7.

3. James Hogg, 'Memoir of the Author's Life', in James Hogg, *Altrive Tales*, ed. Gillian Hughes (Edinburgh: Edinburgh University Press, 2003), p. 17.

4. Ibid., p. 18.

5. Ibid., p. 18.

6. Ibid., p. 17.

7. See Karl Miller, *Electric Shepherd: A Likeness of James Hogg* (London: Faber and Faber, 2003), p. 341.

8. Fiona Stafford, *Local Attachments: The Province of Poetry* (Oxford: Oxford University Press, 2010), pp. 176–223; Nigel Leask, *Robert Burns and Pastoral: Poetry and Improvement in Late Eighteenth-Century Scotland* (Oxford: Oxford University Press, 2010); Liam McIlvanney, *Burns the Radical: Poetry and Politics in Late Eighteenth-Century Scotland* (East Linton: Tuckwell Press, 2002); Robert Crawford, *The Bard: Robert Burns, a Biography* (London: Jonathan Cape, 2009).

9. Douglas Mack, 'Hogg as poet: a successor to Burns?', in K. G. Simpson (ed.), *Love and Liberty: Robert Burns a Bicentenary Celebration* (East Linton: Tuckwell Press, 1997), pp. 119–27; Gillian Hughes, *James Hogg: A Life* (Edinburgh: Edinburgh University Press, 2007); Miller, *Electric Shepherd*; Valentina Bold, *James Hogg: A Bard of Nature's Making* (Oxford: Peter Lang, 2007); Kirsteen McCue, 'Singing "more old songs than ever ploughman could": the songs of James Hogg and Robert Burns in the musical marketplace', in Sharon Alker and Holly Faith Nelson (eds), *James Hogg and the Literary Marketplace* (Aldershot: Ashgate, 2009), pp. 123–38; Patrick Scott, 'Introduction', in James Hogg, *Memoir of Robert Burns* (Edinburgh: Edinburgh University Press, 2009).

10. Henry Mackenzie, unsigned essay in *The Lounger* 97 (9 December 1786), repro-

duced in Donald Low (ed.), *Robert Burns: The Critical Heritage* (London: Routledge & Kegan Paul, 1974), pp. 67–70, 70.

11. See August 1785, in Robert Burns, *Robert Burns's Commonplace Book, 1783–1785*, ed. J. C. Ewing and D. Cook (Carbondale: Southern Illinois University Press, 1965), p. 36.

12. Robert Burns, *Poems, Chiefly in the Scottish Dialect* (Kilmarnock: John Wilson, 1786), title-page.

13. For critical readings of many of Burns's epigraphs, see Stafford, *Starting Lines*. Jeffrey Skoblow helpfully suggests a form of performance and a biographical narrative in the arrangement of poems in the Kilmarnock volume, but he does not treat the epigraph as part of this, in *Dooble Tongue: Scots, Burns, Contradiction* (London: Rosemont Publishing, 2001), pp. 174–5.

14. See McIlvanney on 'Bardic fraternity in the Kilmarnock verse epistles', in McIlvanney, *Burns the Radical*, pp. 97–119.

15. William Wordsworth, Preface to *Lyrical Ballads* (1802), in *William Wordsworth: The Major Works*, ed. Stephen Gill (Oxford: Oxford University Press, 2000), p. 598.

16. James Hogg, *The Queen's Wake*, ed. Douglas Mack (Edinburgh: Edinburgh University Press, 2004), Introduction, ll. 6, 4. All subsequent quotations from *The Queen's Wake* are taken from this edition and references are given in parentheses.

17. William Collins, 'Ode to Fear', in William Collins, *Odes on Several Descriptive and Allegoric Subjects* (London: A. Millar, 1747), l. 8.

18. James Hogg, *The Queen's Wake* (Edinburgh: George Goldie, 1813), title-page, reproduced in Mack's edition. Adapted from the antistrophe of Collins's 'Ode to Fear', ll. 8–12.

19. See Hogg, *Queen's Wake*, ll. 391–3.

20. Francis Jeffrey, Review of *The Queen's Wake*, 3rd edn, *Edinburgh Review* XXIV (1814), pp. 157–74, 158, 168.

CHAPTER 12

Wordsworth and Burns

Stephen Gill

(I)

In 1844 Wordsworth summoned Burns to his aid. Campaigning against the extension of a railway line into the heart of the Lake District, the elderly Poet Laureate turned to him to strengthen an argument he was making about the importance of local attachments to the 'feeling, pensive heart'.[1] In the first of his *Kendal and Windermere Railway* letters to the *Morning Post* Wordsworth wrote at some length about Burns and quoted from 'To a Mountain-Daisy' and the epistle 'To W . . . S.'[2] This was very nearly Wordsworth's last original publication and it was fitting that Burns should figure so largely in it, for the intertwining of the two had been going on for a long time.

To track backwards from this moment in a survey of Wordsworth's writing life reveals that there is not a decade of it in which Burns is not a substantial presence.[3] Ten years before *Kendal and Windermere Railway*, that is, in the early 1830s, a late tour of Scotland had prompted a cluster of poems about Burns. A little over ten years before that, in 1820, Wordsworth had appended a Postscript to his *River Duddon* sonnet sequence. It concludes with a peroration about 'The power of waters over the minds of Poets', which segues from Virgil to Burns and ends with a four-line quotation from 'To W . . . S.' 1816 saw the publication of his *Letter to a Friend of Robert Burns*, a substantial prose work at thirty-seven printed pages in its original form. In 1815 in the *Essay, Supplementary to the Preface* to the collected poems volumes, Wordsworth had cited Burns in a roll-call of great Scottish poets stretching back to Dunbar. The presence of Burns in Wordsworth's most important and innovative collection after *Lyrical Ballads*, the *Poems, in Two Volumes* of 1807, hardly needs to be stressed. One subsection consists of poems emanating from the Wordsworths' tour of Scotland in 1803 and includes the 'Address to the Sons of Burns'. Other poems in the collection echo Burns in form and subject matter and in one or two cases allude to him by direct, signalled quotation.[4]

Work from this period, which Wordsworth did not publish and so which is little known, also involves Burns. In one of the earliest manuscripts of *The Ruined Cottage* the poem is preceded by an epigraph from the 'Epistle to

J. Lapraik', and as soon as the Pedlar, the wisdom figure, is introduced, Burns comes with him:

> His eye
> Flashing poetic fire, he would repeat
> The songs of Burns, and as we trudged along
> Together did we make the hollow grove
> Ring with our transports.

When he returned to this unfinished poem a few years later, Wordsworth developed the figure much more fully as Scottish – from a Covenanting household and steeped in 'Scotch songs ... Scotch poetry, old ballads, & old tales / Love-Gregory, William Wallace & Rob Roy.'[5] The point should be emphasised: at the very moment that the old Leech Gatherer in 'Resolution and Independence' is opening his heart to the poet with 'a stately speech! / Such as grave Livers do in Scotland use, / Religious men, who give to God and Man their dues' (103–5), at this moment in another poem Wordsworth is trying to create a character who has all the gravitas of the Leech Gatherer but much more joy.

The work on *The Ruined Cottage* and *The Pedlar* belongs to 1802/3. A year or two earlier Burns had been crucial in the formation of Wordsworth's poetics. In the summer of 1798 Coleridge had urged Wordsworth to recognise that he had it in him to compose the first ever truly philosophical poem in the language, to be called *The Recluse*. To do so would mean confronting Milton on his own ground – a lofty height. In the 'Preface' to the 1800 *Lyrical Ballads*, however, Wordsworth spells out reasons for hoping that the poems in the collection might interest mankind permanently and they have nothing to do with reconsiderations of Jehovah and his choir of shouting angels and everything to do with what Wordsworth had found on rereading Burns over the winter of 1799 – 'every where you have the presence of human life'.[6] Burns's poems and the Prefaces to the Kilmarnock and Edinburgh editions were instrumental in enormously productive ways – they helped shape the enlarged editions of *Lyrical Ballads* in 1800 and 1802; they contributed to Wordsworth's developing conception of the Poet; most important of all perhaps, they offered possibilities for creative admiration and emulation, in such contrast to the inhibiting majesty of the project for *The Recluse*.[7]

The *Lyrical Ballads* of 1798 and 1800 are, of course, the foundation volumes of Wordsworth's career, but Burns was a presence from its very beginnings. In its evocation of the sights and sounds of twilight, *An Evening Walk* (1793) – Wordsworth's first discrete publication – touches on, 'The *sugh of swallow flocks that twittering sweep.' The asterisk takes the reader to a footnote that explains the meaning of the 'Scotch word' and identifies its source in 'Burns's Cotter's Saturday Night', some stanzas of which were reprinted in William Gilpin's *Observations, Relative to Picturesque Beauty*, *on Several Parts of Great Britain; Particularly the Highlands of Scotland* (1789).[8]

But Wordsworth did not need Gilpin to take him to Burns. When he was just seventeen, his schoolmaster, Thomas Bowman, lent him the Kilmarnock *Poems* in the year of its publication.[9] In October 1787 Wordsworth got a copy for his sister from the Penrith bookclub. Dorothy had asked him to look for it, having had Burns's poems recommended by her friend Jane Pollard, daughter of a Halifax mill owner. These facts are testimony to something very remarkable. Burns's *Poems, Chiefly in the Scottish Dialect* was published in an edition of a little over 600 copies in July 1786.[10] Within weeks the headmaster of Hawkshead School in the remote Lake District was lending out his copy. Within a few months Burns's collection had made it into a manufacturing family in Halifax and to the circulating library in Penrith.

In Stirling during his 1803 Scottish tour Wordsworth bought another copy of Burns, the 1802 Dundee edition, and the next tour likewise prompted another purchase – the 1813 *Poetical Works* bought in Perth in August 1814.[11]

A brisk survey has outlined the extent of Wordsworth's involvement with Burns and it can be documented until almost the end of his life, when he added a new 'Print of the Head of Burns' to his gallery of illustrious poets. It joined the two others he already possessed, one of which had been presented by Burns's sons. Two years later, in his seventy-ninth year, Wordsworth was still lamenting that he never met Burns, given his early and 'lively sympathy with his extraordinary genius'.[12]

Many of Burns's poems he knew by heart. Allan Cunningham heard Wordsworth recite the epistle to 'J. Lapraik' 'with commendations . . . pointing out as he went the all but inimitable ease and happiness of thought and language' (K, III, 1068). This and other favourites he referred to and quoted from again and again. Burns's quotidian presence is strikingly confirmed by a reminiscence of the poet in 1841 deciding to plant holly berries at Lancrigg, Mrs Fletcher's house in Easedale.

'I made the holes', her daughter recorded, 'and the Poet put in the berries. He was as earnest and eager about it, as if it had been a matter of importance; and as he put the seeds in, he every now and then muttered, in his low solemn tone, that beautiful verse from Burns's Vision:

> And wear thou this, she solemn said,
> And bound the holly round my head.
> The polished leaves and berries red
>   Did rustling play;
> And like a passing thought she fled
>   In light away.'[13]

Wordsworth's more formal tributes to Burns are numerous and not in the least casual or formulaic. Burns, he declared in 1799, is 'energetic solemn and sublime in sentiment, and profound in feeling'. In 1803, standing at Burns's grave, Wordsworth honoured him unequivocally as a 'Spirit fierce and bold'. No monument to Burns is needed, Wordsworth insisted in 1819, because having taken 'permanent root in the affections of his Countrymen . . . he has raised for himself a Monument so conspicuous, and of such imperishable materials, as to render a local fabric of Stone superfluous'. Towards the end of his life it is this appeal of Burns to common humanity that is stressed: he 'interests and affects us' as 'a human being, eminently sensitive and intelligent'.[14] Many more tributes could be adduced.

In *Scottish and Irish Romanticism* Murray Pittock remarks that Wordsworth,with a penchant for not paying 'the debts he owed', was guilty of 'suppressing the extent of Burns's influence on him'. To the contrary, it might be said that Wordsworth missed almost no opportunity of broadcasting his knowledge of and attachment to Burns. It is notable that in Markham L. Peacock's old but invaluable garnering of *The Critical Opinions of William Wordsworth* more pages are devoted to Burns than to any other writer save Coleridge.[15]

(II)

Wordsworth revered Burns as one poet might another – as a technician of language, as a fellow-artist. The poet who introduced Cumbrian dialect words into the 1800 *Lyrical Ballads* and glossed them was obviously following the example of the Kilmarnock *Poems*. But there was something more. There was a sense of kinship, which Wordsworth fostered in imagination right through to old age. Writing to Allan Cunningham in 1825 he exclaimed, 'Do not say I ought to have been a Scotchman. Tear me not from the country of Chaucer, Spencer, Shakespeare and Milton.' What Cunningham had said was perhaps no more than a light-hearted sally, but it prompted Wordsworth to continue with this very important declaration: 'ever since the days of childhood . . . I have been more indebted to the North than I shall ever be able to acknowledge.'[16] He was writing to someone who as a boy had walked in Burns's funeral procession – there was no need to tell him what place Burns held in his heart. In a late recollection of the impact the 1786 poems had on him – 'the simplicity the truth and the vigour of Burns' – he declared that 'Familiarity with the dialect of the border Counties of Cumberland and Westmorland made it easy for me not only to understand but to feel them.'[17] Wordsworth fostered the idea of personal closeness to Burns even further. Ever after he and his sister as travellers in 1803 had discovered that it is just possible to see the Cumberland mountains from near Ellisland, Wordsworth confessed that he had been given to 'indulging . . . in the fancy that we might have been personally known to each other, and he have looked upon those objects with more pleasure for our sakes'.[18]

It is a nice fancy. What we can be sure of, though, is that at various moments of Wordsworth's life this 'fancy', that he and Burns were intertwined, as poets, worked to more creative effect than at any other. The first is the moment when the second enlarged edition of *Lyrical Ballads* was coming into being. In a ground-breaking essay, Daniel Sanjiv Roberts pointed out the importance of Currie's *Burns* in the genesis of the Preface to the 1800 *Lyrical Ballads*.[19] Just as the manifesto element of the Preface was being finalised, with bold assertions taking shape about how low and humble subject matter was to be dealt with in appropriate language, Wordsworth and Coleridge were simultaneously reading Burns's poetry and learning about the culture in which it was fostered.[20] Other scholars have recently discussed the significance of this conjunction. In *Robert Burns and Pastoral*, Nigel Leask devotes a section to 'Burns, Wordsworth, and Romantic Pastoral', in which he explores the ways in which the Preface to *Lyrical Ballads* 'appears to respond quite specifically to Currie's "philosophical" attribution of Burns's genius to the manners of the Scottish peasantry as a class'. Reflecting on 'Wordsworth's Obligations to Burns', Fiona Stafford has argued that for Wordsworth in 1800 'the new edition of Burns's wonderful work, with its editorial endorsement of local truth as the basis for genuinely emotive poetry, could not have been more welcome. Here was a volume that offered corroboration for his own bold decision to move to the Lakes and draw on their largely unplumbed depths.'[21]

The second moment follows almost immediately, in the period around 1802 to 1803. The poet who confessed in February 1799 that he could never read Burns's 'Despondency. An Ode' 'without the deepest agitation'[22] had begun a four-stanza poem in which the first stanza declares, 'The things which I have seen I now can see no more', and the last ends by asking, 'Whither is fled the visionary gleam? / Where is it now, the glory and the dream?' Coleridge responded tentatively to this lament for lost blessedness in the verse letter that was the earliest version of 'Dejection: An Ode', but what his contribution to the poetic dialogue did was to offer neither consolation nor answer but to define the area of questioning with a more painful clarity.[23]

It was a moment of crisis for both poets, which had at its core the stress of profound aesthetic problems being as yet unresolved. But such challenges, fundamental to their artistic identities, were at this moment matched in weight and importunity by others – the demands of maintaining domestic and personal equilbrium in the face of a vexing present and a very uncertain future, of paying the bills and feeding one's family. At a time of gathering national emergency, Wordsworth was compounding the obligations he already had, primarily but not exclusively to his French family, by getting married. It was imperative that he should get an income. His relationship with Coleridge was under strain. And every strand in this web of apparently domestic tensions had a bearing on his choice of life and future as a poet.

But Wordsworth did survive. His most creative years were about to begin. His emergence from Despondency and Dejection seems to have come about in part, first, from the imaginative restoration conferred by the composition of 'Resolution and Independence' and, second, from the enormous enlargement of experience gained from the tour of Scotland in 1803. In both of these saving events the figure of Burns plays a crucial part.

Nigel Leask in *Robert Burns and Pastoral* and Fiona Stafford in *Local Attachments* have both explored the Scottish dimension to this troubled period of Wordsworth's life. In 'Resolution and Independence', as Stafford points out, the 'figure of Burns is invoked directly, but his poetry is also echoed at every turn' and he thus becomes a 'presence' whose 'work inspire[s] fresh hope'. Elsewhere, in a penetrating essay, Stafford has also explored the impact on Wordsworth's creative life of the tour of Scotland he undertook with his sister in 1803 and her sympathetic inwardness with how both the Wordsworths imaginatively absorbed this life-changing expedition produces a much more positive assessment than Leith Davis's somewhat reductive take on it in *Acts of Union* (1999). Encounters with different people and customs and engagement with another language ('Will no one tell me what she sings?'), Stafford rightly concludes, 'renewed Wordsworth's faith in visionary possibility by revealing the importance of people living in places at once traditional and extraordinary'.[24]

The third moment in Wordsworth's life that matters in his imaginative relation to Burns is one that is inextricably linked to the past – it is the period from 1833 to 1835.

In the summer of 1833 Wordsworth made a short tour of Western Scotland. The return journey took him through places and across rivers which, he told Allan Cunningham, he was very glad to see for Burns's sake. At one moment a fellow-passenger on the top of the coach gestured to Mossgiel farm and the result was this:

> 'There!' said a Stripling, pointing with meet pride
> Towards a low roof with green trees half concealed,
> 'Is Mossgiel farm; and that's the very field
> Where Burns ploughed up the Daisy.' Far and wide
> A plain below stretched sea-ward, while, descried
> Above sea-clouds, the Peaks of Arran rose;
> And, by that simple notice, the repose
> Of earth, sky, sea, and air, was vivified.
> Beneath 'the random *bield* of clod or stone'
> Myriads of Daisies have shone forth in flower
> Near the lark's nest, and in their natural hour
> Have passed away, less happy than the One
> That by the unwilling ploughshare died to prove
> The tender charm of Poetry and Love.[25]

It is a poem that takes off, as so many of Wordsworth's lyrics do, from an apparently trivial chance event, but this elegantly turned piece, which might look almost like a five-finger exercise for such an accomplished sonneteer, exists within a matrix of memories and present-day emotions that was both enormously painful and yet fertile.

The sonnet plays on and quotes from Burns's 'To a Mountain-Daisy'. This was one of Wordsworth's favourites, something he shared with his sister, Dorothy, who singled the poem out for special commendation in the letter already mentioned to Jane Pollard in 1787. When Wordsworth visited Scotland in 1803 it was in the company of Dorothy. They visited Burns's grave together and together saw Ellisland. But the 'dear, dear Sister' of 'Tintern Abbey', the Dorothy who in 1803 could match William step for step as they walked twenty miles or more a day, was now far into dementia and rarely left her room. Twice already the family at Rydal Mount had thought she was dying and now in 1833 Henry Crabb Robinson, Wordsworth's companion on the Scottish tour, confided to his diary that he did not expect ever to see Dorothy Wordsworth again.[26]

Every new sight must have reminded Wordsworth of the watershed moment of 1803, when he visited what he described as 'the most poetical Country I ever travelled in' – Scotland – in the company of one of the two people to whom he said his intellect was most indebted – Dorothy.[27] But memories of 1803 flooding back in 1833 also brought someone else to mind, someone else very dear to him: Sir Walter Scott.

Wordsworth had first met Scott in September 1803 and their mutual liking seems to have been immediate. Sending the poem 'Yarrow Unvisited' to Scott, Wordsworth told him that it had been written 'not without the hope of pleasing' him. This gesture from one poet to another, what Wordsworth in another context calls 'this offering of my love', was recalled with immense poignancy three decades later, when Wordsworth visited Scott for the last time.[28] The two men went through rituals which they must have been conscious of as goodbyes. They visited the Yarrow together and then, as Scott talked of his impending departure for Italy, in a gesture of exquisite tact, he quoted 'Yarrow Unvisited' back to Wordsworth. That Scott was failing was plain to see and so when Wordsworth bade farewell to 'this wondrous Potentate' in another sonnet, it was with deep foreboding. The result was 'On the Departure of Sir Walter Scott from Abbotsford, for Naples', a wonderful poem, worthy of its subject and the occasion. It is, though, an elegy in all but name.[29] And now Scott too was dead.

What happened next brings Burns back into the picture. Charles Lamb died in 1834 prompting Wordsworth to compose some memorial verses and according to his own account a 'train of melancholy reflexion . . . produced several things in some respects of the same character'.[30] The train of melancholy reflection about Scott and Coleridge and Dorothy led inevitably to the Scottish tour of 1803 and ultimately to a piece written then but which remained unpublished, a three-stanza poem entitled 'Ejaculation at the Grave of Burns.' True to habitual practice, Wordsworth started tinkering with it and soon had not only added eleven stanzas, but composed a companion piece, 'Thoughts Suggested the Day Following on the Banks of the Nith'. As Nigel Leask has observed, the poems '[pay] homage by adopting Burns's trademark "Standard Habbie" stanza'.[31]

The two poems first appeared in the 1842 collection, *Poems, Chiefly of Early and Late Years*, before being gathered into the next edition of Wordsworth's Collected Poems. Thus from 1845 onwards, and of course in all modern editions of the Collected Poetical Works, these two appear at the very beginning of the section 'Tour of Scotland, 1803' and the poem now called 'At the Grave of Burns' is dated '1803' – that is, of course, when the Wordsworths actually visited the grave. But it is *not* a poem of 1803. Three-quarters of 'At the Grave of Burns' was written in 1835 and the *whole* of 'Thoughts Suggested the Day Following' was. The manuscript evidence about the chronology of composition here is incontrovertible – but that mattered not a jot to the author of those manuscripts. In a strong demonstration of a certain kind of high Romantic conception of the poem, Wordsworth insisted that what he wrote in 1835 expressed his feelings of thirty-two years before; that 'At the Grave of Burns's was really a poem of 1803; and that the companion piece recorded what he actually felt when in sight of Burns's residence on the banks of the Nith, at the same period.[32]

Well, yes and no. The opening stanza of 'At the Grave of Burns' undoubtedly captures the intensity of Wordsworth's response in 1803, 'I shiver, Spirit, fierce and bold / At thought of what I now behold.' In her journal of the tour Dorothy Wordsworth records that their overwhelming sense of melancholy was mixed up with anxious thoughts about their own and Coleridge's future.[33] The dejection of her brother's 'Resolution and Independence' written the previous year was not simply a rhetorical feint. The recognition that 'there may come another day to me / Solitude, pain of heart, distress, and poverty' was uttered with intense and justifiable seriousness by a poet whose collected oeuvre by 1802 had barely cleared 500 copies. But what gives these later poems their power is that quickened memory of the past is shaped by one who is very conscious of the present moment. They are poems of 1803 but also poems of 1835. The warm tributes embody both the feelings of the young Wordsworth, who had stood at Burns's grave in 1803 only too aware that at thirty-three he was already within a year or two of the age at which the 'poor Inhabitant below' had died, and the reflections of a poet in his mid-sixties, whose career path was now laid out and who was conscious of how much he owed to the one who had shown him, in youth, 'How Verse may build a princely throne / On humble truth'.

Both poems linger on thoughts about what might have been, had Wordsworth and Burns become friends:

> What treasures would have then been placed
> Within my reach; of knowledge graced
> By fancy, what a rich repast.

By alluding to Burns through choice of stanza form and quoting directly from 'To a Mountain-Daisy', 'A Vision' and 'A Bard's Epitaph', the two poems incorporate in their very texture their creator's acknowledgement of artistic indebtedness. But what is most fine about them, to my mind, is that Wordsworth voices so powerfully not only what he owes to Burns but also what mankind does. Could there be a stronger, more generous tribute than this stanza?

> Through busiest street and loneliest glen
> Are felt the flashes of his pen;
> He rules mid winter snows, and when
>   Bees fill their hives;
> Deep in the general heart of men
>   His power survives.

The lovely conceit of this is that Burns's poetry survives and will survive because it both draws on what concerns human beings most deeply and speaks its own message to them. It takes us straight from 1835 back to 1802 when Wordsworth was thinking continually about Burns and Poetry and Scotland, and to that moment in the Preface to *Lyrical Ballads* where he tries to answer the question, 'What is a Poet?':

> He is a man speaking to men: a man, it is true, endued with more lively sensibility, more enthusiasm and tenderness, who has a greater knowledge of human nature, and a more comprehensive soul, than are supposed to be common among mankind; a man pleased with his own passions and volitions, and who rejoices more than other men in the spirit of life that is in him.[34]

There can be little doubt that in this passage he was looking to Burns – as he was to continue to do for the rest of his life, one great poet acknowledging another.

Notes

1. William Wordsworth and Dorothy Wordsworth, *The Letters of William and Dorothy Wordsworth*, 8 vols (Oxford: Clarendon Press, 1967–93), are referred to throughout this essay. Individual volumes are: *The Early Years 1787–1805*, ed. Chester Shaver (1967); *The Middle Years, pt 1: 1806–1811*, ed. Mary Moorman (1969); *The Middle Years, pt 2: 1812–1820*, ed. Mary Moorman and Alan G. Hill (1970); *The Later Years, pt 1: 1821–1828*, ed. Alan G. Hill (1978); *The Later Years, pt 2: 1829–1834*, ed. Alan G. Hill (1979); *The Later Years, pt 3: 1835–1839*, ed. Alan G. Hill (1982); *The Later Years, pt 4: 1840–1853*, ed. Alan G. Hill (1988); *A Supplement of New*

Letters, ed. Alan G. Hill (1993). Throughout the notes this edition is referred to serially as *WL*, I–VIII.

2. The two letters to the *Morning Post* of 11 and 20 December 1844 were reprinted in 1845 as a pamphlet, *Kendal and Windermere Railway*. See William Wordsworth, *The Prose Works of William Wordsworth*, ed. Jane Worthington Smyser and W. J. B. Owen, 3 vols (Oxford: Clarendon Press, 1974), vol. III, pp. 329–66. The Burns material appears on pp. 344–6. Future citation to *Prose*.

3. Pioneering work was done by Russell Noyes in 'Wordsworth and Burns', *PMLA* LIX (1944), pp. 813–32.

4. For the *River Duddon* Postscript, see William Wordsworth, *Sonnet Series and Itinerary Poems, 1820–1845*, ed. Geoffrey Jackson (Ithaca and London: Cornell University Press, 2004), pp. 76–7. The *Letter to a Friend of Robert Burns* is *Prose*, vol. III, pp. 109–36. For the *Essay Supplementary* reference to Burns, see *Prose*, vol. III, p. 78. For the 1807 collection see William Wordsworth, *Poems, in Two Volumes, and Other Poems, 1800–1807*, ed. Jared Curtis (Ithaca, NY: Cornell University Press, 1983).

5. William Wordsworth, *The Ruined Cottage and The Pedlar*, ed. James Butler (Ithaca, NY: Cornell University Press, 1979), pp. 42, 46, 329.

6. Wordsworth to Samuel Taylor Coleridge, 27 February 1799. *WL*, vol. I, p. 256.

7. Nigel Leask has argued persuasively his 'contention that the Scottish vernacular influence on Wordsworth (largely mediated by Burns) offered a strong ideological counterweight to the literary hegemony of London, assisting him to formulate the poetic theory of the 1800 *Preface*' ('Burns, Wordsworth and the Politics of Vernacular Poetry', in Peter de Bolla, Nigel Leask and David Simpson (eds), *Land, Nation and Culture: Thinking the Republic of Taste* (Houndmills: Palgrave Macmillan, 2005), pp. 202–22, 214).

8. William Wordsworth, *An Evening Walk*, ed. James Averill (Ithaca and London: Cornell University Press, 1984), p. 68.

9. For reminiscence by Bowman's son of his father 'telling how he lent Wordsworth's Cowper's "Task" when it first came out, and Burns's "Poems"', see T. W. Thompson, *Wordsworth's Hawkshead*, ed. Robert Woof (London: Oxford University Press, 1970), p. 344.

10. I draw here on Robert Crawford, *The Bard: Robert Burns, a Biography* (London: Jonathan Cape, 2009), p. 225.

11. The 1803 purchase is now in Cornell University Library; the 1814 purchase is in the Wordsworth Library, Grasmere. For details of the chronology of Wordsworth's reading of Burns, see Duncan Wu, *Wordsworth's Reading 1770–1799* (Cambridge: Cambridge University Press, 1993), and *Wordsworth's Reading 1800–1815* (Cambridge: Cambridge University Press, 1995). Dorothy Wordsworth's copy of Robert Burns, *Poems, Chiefly in the Scottish Dialect* (1793) is in The Hugh Walpole Collection of the library of The King's School, Canterbury.

12. Wordsworth to Unknown Correspondent, 2 January 1847; to Charles Gray, 16 March 1849 (*WL*, vol. VII, pp. 827, 892).

13. Christopher Wordsworth, *Memoirs of William Wordsworth*, 2 vols (London: Edward Moxon, 1851), vol. II, p. 438.

14. References here are to the letter to Coleridge, 27 February 1799; to the first line of 'Ejaculation at the Grave of Burns', in Wordsworth, *Poems, in Two Volumes*; letter

to J. Forbes Mitchell, 21 April 1819 (*WL*, vol. III, p. 534); note to '"There!" said a Stripling', in Wordsworth, *Sonnet Series*, p. 648.

15. Murray Pittock, *Scottish and Irish Romanticism* (Oxford: Oxford University Press, 2008), pp. 146, 155. Markham Peacock, Jr., *The Critical Opinions of William Wordsworth* (Baltimore: The Johns Hopkins University Press, 1950), pp. 194–202.

16. Wordsworth to Allan Cunningham, 23 November 1825 (*WL*, vol. IV, p. 402).

17. Both quotations from a note prepared for the 1842 collection, *Poems. Chiefly of Early and Late Years*, but eventually not published. See William Wordsworth, *Last Poems, 1821–1850*, ed. Jared Curtis (Ithaca and London: Cornell University Press, 1999), p. 475.

18. Note to 'Thoughts Suggested the Day Following', in Wordsworth, *Poems. Chiefly of Early and Late Years*. See Wordsworth, *Last Poems*, p. 473. Wordsworth mentions this fancy also in a letter to D. S. Williamson of 27 July 1844, in which he declares his support for the proposed Burns Festival, 'having always thought as highly of him as a poet as any perhaps of his country men do' (*WL*, vol. VII, pp. 581–2).

19. Daniel Sanjiv Roberts, 'Literature, medical science and politics, 1795–1800: *Lyrical Ballads* and Currie's *Works of Robert Burns*', in C. C. Barfoot (ed.), *'A Natural Delineation of Human Passions': The Historic Moment of Lyrical Ballads* (Amsterdam: Rodopi, 2004), pp. 115–25.

20. It is an indication how deeply he had absorbed the *Works of Robert Burns* that in a letter to Scott Wordsworth should make a passing reference to Burns's commendation of Kenmare Loch. It was six years since it had come to his attention in James Currie (ed.), *The Works of Robert Burns*, 4 vols (1800), vol. I, p. 102 (*WL*, vol. II, p. 41).

21. Nigel Leask, *Robert Burns and Pastoral* (Oxford: Oxford University Press, 2010), p. 293. Fiona Stafford, *Local Attachments: The Province of Poetry* (Oxford: Oxford University Press, 2010), p. 128.

22. Letter of 27 February 1799 (*WL*, vol. I, p. 256).

23. For what became the 'Ode: Intimations of Immortality from Recollections of Early Childhood', see Wordsworth, *Poems, in Two Volumes*, pp. 271–7. For the 'A Letter to—' and 'Dejection: An Ode', see Samuel Taylor Coleridge, *Poetical Works*, ed. J. C. C. Mays, 3 vols (Princeton: Princeton University Press, 2001), vol. I, pp. 677–91, 695–702.

24. Stafford, *Local Attachments*, pp. 120–1. Fiona Stafford, 'Inhabited solitudes: Wordsworth in Scotland in 1803', in David Duff and Catherine Jones (eds), *Scotland, Ireland and the Romantic Aesthetic* (Lewisburg: Bucknell University Press, 2007), pp. 93–113, 108.

25. Wordsworth, *Sonnet Series*, p. 599.

26. Diary entry for 17 September 1833. Henry Crabb Robinson, *Henry Crabb Robinson on Books and Their Writers*, ed. Edith J. Morley, 3 vols (London: J. M. Dent & Sons, 1938), vol. I, p. 434.

27. Letter to Walter Scott, 7 November 1805 (*WL*, vol. I, p. 641). Second reference: '[Coleridge] and my beloved Sister are the two Beings to whom my intellect is most indebted' (Letter to William Rowan Hamilton, 25 June 1832 (*WL*, vol. V, p. 536)).

28. Letter to Walter Scott, 16 January 1805 (*WL*, vol. I, p. 530). Second reference to *The Prelude* (1805), XIII, 427.

29. The last meeting of Scott and Wordsworth is discussed more fully in my *Wordsworth's Revisitings* (Oxford: Oxford University Press, 2011), pp. 150–70.

30. Letter to Edward Moxon, 10 December 1835 (*WL*, vol. VI, p. 135).

31. Leask, 'Burns, Wordsworth', p. 202.

32. Wordsworth, 'At the Grave of Burns', in William Wordsworth, *The Fenwick Notes of William Wordsworth*, ed. Jared Curtis (London: Bristol Classical Press, 1993), p. 63, 1843 note.

33. Dorothy Wordsworth, *Recollections of a Tour in Scotland*, ed. Carol Kyros Walker (New Haven and London: Yale University Press, 1997), p. 44, entry for 18 August 1803.

34. *Prose*, p. 138.

CHAPTER 13

The 'Ethical Turn' in Literary Criticism: Burns and Byron

Brean Hammond

The following essay derives strength from the argument that Byron is most intelligibly read as a Scottish writer rather than as a star of the English poetic galaxy: a contention that in turn is bolstered by perceiving him as part of a Scottish laureate tradition in which he is preceded by Burns and indebted to Burns. Such an argument in respect of the Scottish Byron has recently received attention and, in an essay complementary to this one, I have tried to contribute to it, in part by developing the Burns-Byron analogy.[1] In this essay, I will offer a barebones account of the Burns-Byron nexus – only what is necessary to get the focal discussion off the ground. That focus, in this essay, is on ethics. An enabling dimension of any informative parallelism between Burns and Byron is the similar way in which their poetry was received by influential British readers – very differently, in both cases, from the way in which their reputations developed in Europe. By the apparatuses and apparatchiks of early nineteenth-century British institutional criticism, both were perceived to be unethical because they lived unethical lives and their poetry was regarded as apologetic for those ways of life.

That a writer's creative oeuvre must be a direct reflection of his mode of living has been a central premise in literary theory at various times, but it is an assumption long subjected to sociological and political critique and as a result is outdated in modern-contemporary literary theory. It survives only in odd corners, such as in the various anti-Stratfordian hypotheses about Shakespeare's identity. Nevertheless, there has been in very recent years a return to ethics as a central concern in literary theory. The novel in particular has been regarded as a site for examining ethical dilemmas presented through character and situation and the debate within narrative ethics has largely centred on the question of how this can be so, given the constructed nature of the self: with what, exactly, do we identify when we identify with the dilemmas of a fictional character? In the present essay, however, my intention *is* to return to the older question, now almost a taboo subject, of the ethics of writers and their writing; and to consider whether recent ethical and other criticism has anything to offer to that question. Burns and Byron are deployed here as particularly problematic case-studies, because their lives are the stuff of their art to an unusual extent – a definitive aspect of their cults. Unease on this score is not entirely overcome in recent critical reception; indeed, a critical concept, that of 'performativity', has been devised specifically to combat it. Is the aperçu that in Burns and Byron there is a trademark 'performativity' about the way in which their lives are inscribed in their works an adequate answer to the older ethical questions? I pose the question, rather than finding a definitive answer. I open a debate so old that in some respects it may now appear as new.

Burns and Byron

Rescuing Byron from relative neglect in an essay first published in 1937, T. S. Eliot proposed that we consider Byron 'as a Scottish poet – I say "Scottish", not "Scots", since he wrote in English'.[2] Notorious in Byron criticism for the verdict that Byron 'added nothing to the language', Eliot's essay proposes that Byron's 'diabolism' derives from a Scots Calvinist religious background.[3] Shrewdly, Eliot perceives that Byron's satire on Southey in the dedicatory verses to *Don Juan* is 'not indeed English satire at all; it is really a *flyting*, and closer in feeling and intention to the satire of Dunbar'.[4] Eliot discerns that as a satirist upon English society in *Don Juan*, Byron was unrivalled because he was an outsider. And indeed, whenever Byron spoke of the English, for example, in the conversations that Lady Blessington recorded, it was from an external perspective, commenting on the artificiality of English society, its hypocrisy and cant, its refusal to appreciate the men of genius whom it has bred. 'The Scots', meanwhile, 'are certainly very superior people; with intellects naturally more acute than the English, they are better educated and make better men of business'.[5]

The Scottish dimension of Byron's nationality is fully recognised by the poet in the statements he made on the subject. By his own account, he was 'half a Scot by birth, and bred / A whole one' (*Don Juan* X.17): not factually accurate, but very much what in his later years the poet put about and wished to be thought.[6] At least three elements of Byron's poetic voice are embraced in Murray Pittock's checklist of important elements comprising a cultural nationalism. There *is* found in Byron 'the taxonomy of glory . . . the reading of history as a continuous struggle for liberty, by which the national past is reclaimed'.[7] The Bakhtinian heteroglossic linguistic elements that in Burns take the form of the clashing of dialect and standard English, 'anglopetal' and 'anglofugal' locutions in collision, are differently present in Byron in the juxtaposition of contrasting linguistic registers, the macaronic rhymes and the exploitation of class codes. Finally, Byron shared what Pittock calls the 'fratriot' mentality of Scots who promoted the nationalisms of small proto-nations and his support for the cause of Greek nationalism was strengthened by tapping into a network of Scotsmen who actively encouraged its development.

In Byron can be found a sentimental Scottish exceptionalism: Scotland was an exception to a general principle espoused elsewhere in his writing, that nations behaved badly towards other weaker nations. His great regard for the poetry of Burns takes its place in that exceptionalist rhetoric. Not an admirer, in general, of labouring-class poetry, Byron's response to Burns went beyond perceiving him, as he does in *English Bards and Scotch Reviewers,* as a noble exception to the Popean, *Dunciad*-esque apprehension that most cobbler, thresher, tailor and weaver poets were wasting their own time and the public's: merely part of the scribbling itch, the syphilitic writing-disease maddening half the artisans in the land. Byron saw that Burns's stature as a poet lay not in *transcending* the conditions of his birth – the 'heaven-taught ploughman' orthodoxy – but in *representing* them. As he wrote in his Journal for 13 December 1813:

> Allen . . . has lent me a quantity of Burns's unpublished, and never-to-be-published, Letters. They are full of oaths and obscene songs. What an antithetical mind! – tenderness, roughness – delicacy, coarseness-sentiment, sensuality-soaring and grovelling, dirt and deity – all mixed up in that one compound of inspired clay.[8]

Very shortly after reading Burns in November 1813, indeed the next day, Byron began composing a song dedicated to his Aberdonian cousin Mary Duff, an attempt to manufacture his very own Highland Mary in imitation of Burns's by then legendary love for Margaret Campbell.

There are some grounds for saying that Byron hero-worshipped Burns: that his sense of Burns's selfhood was a layer that he wished to add to the pentimento of his own. Among the collection of letters referred to above, Byron would have encountered Burns's self-characterisation provided for Agnes McLehose in a letter dated 28 December 1787:

> I don't know if you have a just idea of my character, but I wish you to see me *as I am*. – I am . . . a strange will o' wisp being; the victim too frequently of much imprudence and many follies. – My great constituent elements are Pride and Passion: the first I have endeavoured to humanise into integrety and honour; the last makes me a Devotee to the warmest degree of enthusiasm, in Love, Religion, or Friendship; either of them or all together as I happen to be inspired.[9]

This Hamlet-like apprehension of Burns's character may well have conditioned Byron's own. Byron perceived in Burns a 'negative capability' similar to that he cultivated in his own persona. The conversations with Byron reported by Lady Blessington record this self-portrait:

> Now, if I know myself, I should say that I have no character at all . . . what I think of myself is, that I am so changeable, being everything by turns and nothing long. – I am such a strange *mélange* of good and evil, that it would be difficult to describe me.[10]

Byron's posturing claim to uniqueness here, the aristocratic *sprezzatura* with which he lays claim to his Manichaean mixture, is developed through two allusions – to Pope's 'Epistle to a Lady', wherein the poet notoriously says that 'Most women have no characters at all', and to Dryden's *Absalom and Achitophel*, where Zimri is said to be 'Everything by starts and nothing long'.[11] This serves as a reminder that both poets have the roots of their poetical being in the great achievements of eighteenth-century couplet poetry. The more pressing point is, however, that Byron's poetic identity, here and elsewhere, is a chorus of citations, a positive statement about his negative capability made by means of a mosaic of literary allusions. One important aspect of Byron's self-definition is formed, I would argue, by absorption of the writing and cult of Burns.

On the thematic level, Burns and Byron had a shared commitment to the causes of liberty and pacifism – arguably the most important aspect of their poetic legacies. Burns's song 'I murder hate by field or flood' carries the 'message' in little of much of *Childe Harold's Pilgrimage* and of the satire on military glory and the siege of Ismail in Cantos 7 and 8 of *Don Juan*:

> I murder hate by field or flood
>   Tho' glory's name may screen us;
> In wars at home I'll spend my blood,
>   Life-giving wars of Venus:
> The deities that I adore
>   Are social Peace and Plenty;
> I'm better pleased *to make one more*,
>   Than be the death of twenty. (K 534b, II, 822, 1–8)

In cadence, Burns and Byron can be surprisingly alike. Having witnessed the oppression of poor servants, Werner's wife Josephine (in Byron's play *Werner*) utters sentiments that call Burns's most famous song, the 1795 'Is there for honest poverty' to mind:

> Even here, in this remote, unnamed, dull spot,
> The dimmest in the district's map, exist
> The insolence of wealth in poverty
> O'er something poorer still – the pride of rank
> In servitude, o'er something still more servile;
> And vice in misery affecting still
> A tatter'd splendour. (1.1.701–7)

If Burns's defence of liberty is seldom as specifically focused as Byron's, a song such as 'See the smoking bowl before us' that closes the cantata *Love and Liberty*, calling as it does for a life of pleasure lived outside the law and in sexual freedom, finds an equivalence in many passages in *Don Juan*.

Burns and Byron were both represented in their own time as having an almost total disregard for the moral law. Antinomianism is an aspect of the wider, more important commitment that the two writers shared to the cause of liberty. Readers' fascination with the figure of the Byronic hero often bled into the identification of that hero with the poet himself. Like Burns, Byron was at the centre of his own epic. As the *Edinburgh Review* of June 1831 expressed the matter: 'He always described himself as a man of the same kind with his favourite creations.'[12] Burns and Byron, through their principal poems, become synonymous with the cause of freedom and democracy. Their lives are seen to be the living embodiments of their causes. Alcoholic and sexual excess, disregard for conventional morality, in Burns's case an affection for Jacobitism and alleged republicanism and in Byron's his espousing of the causes of the Italian Carbonari and Greek independence, ensure that the two poets walk hand in hand to posterity. In their own time, there was bristling certainty about what it would be to read their work 'ethically'. Ethical reading took the form of protecting the public from their degenerative influence. Francis Jeffrey, by whom Byron supposed he had been wounded in a review of *Hours of Idleness* (actually by Henry Brougham),[13] reviewing R. H. Cromek's *Reliques of Robert Burns* in the *Edinburgh Review* in 1809 coined a telling phrase that he might also have applied to Byron. He speaks of 'the *dispensing power* of genius and social feeling, in all matters of morality and common sense'.[14] Jeffrey was as opposed as was Samuel Johnson to the conception that genius was a defence of those who wilfully flout the moral norms under which most members of a community live. Crudely and notoriously in Burns studies, he juxtaposed Burns's poems with what he learned from James Currie of the poet's life:

> It is a vile prostitution of language, to talk of that man's generosity or good-ness of heart, who sits raving about friendship and philanthropy in a tavern, while his wife's heart is breaking at her cheerless fireside, and his children pining in solitary poverty.[15]

Vigorously repudiated as they were by Wordsworth in his *Letter to a Friend of Robert Burns* ([James Gray], 1816), Jeffrey's strictures have been pilloried but have refused altogether to go away.

Similarly for Byron in his own time, ethical reading took the form of attempted censorship. His intimate circle of readers – Croker, Gifford, his publisher John Murray – considered, as the early cantos of *Don Juan* rolled out, that relatively small changes would have prevented fathers from having to 'forbid it their families'.[16] Querulously, Murray complained that *Don Juan* would be the greatest literary production ever, and Byron one of Britain's three or four greatest men, if only he would alter some twenty stan-zas, 'wch by preventing the book from being shewn at a Ladys work table – have cut up my Sale'.[17] Businessman as he was, Murray knew precisely what the price of Byron's genius was likely to be; and it was forced upon the poet very soon in the most material of ways. The publisher Onwhyn issued a pirated edition at 4s. To protect his copyright, Byron would have to go to law and be named as the poem's author. If, however, the Lord Chancellor considered that the poem had an immoral tendency, he would not offer it the protection of copyright law. (Much to Byron's exultation, this had occurred in the case of the very belated publication of the upright Robert Southey's *Wat Tyler* in 1817.) If, further, it could be established that Byron was an immoralist whose tendency was to deprave and corrupt, the paternity rights to his daughter Ada would be endangered. The barrister Lancelot Shadwell, providing counsel to Murray, performed hermeneutic gymnastics to find a respectably healthy moral in *Don Juan*. He discovered that in Don Juan's character was exemplified 'the ill effect of that injudicious moral education . . . which has operated injuriously upon his mind'.[18] Byron was shrewd enough to appreciate that this moral tendency in *Don Juan* would not be generally discerned, and he did not press the suit at law. Nevertheless his impatience with the set of cowardly minnows by whom he was surrounded found frequent expression: 'You ask me if I mean to continue D[on] J[uan] &c. How should I know? What encouragement do you give me – all of you with your nonsensical prudery?'[19]

What should an ethical reading of Burns and Byron look like today? How should they fare under the contemporary rediscovery of an ethical imperative to the reading of literature? I shall describe that current in recent theorising before turning back to the poets.

The 'Ethical Turn'

If 'textuality' was the great theoretical paradigm of the 1970s and 1980s, and if 'historicism' assumed that mantle for the following decade, it may be said that the term 'ethics' has been the critical mantra of our own period. The turn towards ethics has been a turning away from the perceived failure or exhaustion, both of forms of criticism that are not apparently motivated by politics such as deconstruction, and by those such as 'cultural materialism' that are. The need for 'ethics' to govern the relationship between the natural and the economic environments in which we live has never seemed more pressing and forms of ecocriticism are a direct emanation of such anxiety on the cultural plane. Ethical criticism took a major step forward when Emmanuel Levinas emerged as its guiding spirit and when Michel Foucault's later work placed renewed emphasis on subjectivity and agency.[20] The way was prepared by such prophetic voices for a relegitimation of an older reading procedure that treated literary texts as moral reflection, an approach that had been cast into shadow, if not quite desuetude, by the theory revolution.

One focus for new-wave critics taking ethics up has been the relationship between texts and readers. Reading, it has been emphasised, is itself an ethical practice carrying responsibilities. Readers are not necessarily given carte-blanche, as they were under older 'reader-response' methodologies, to exercise their subjectivities upon the text. Doris Sommer argues, for example, that in the case of 'ethnically marked' writing (writing that post-colonial critics call 'subaltern'), there is an absolute duty to submit the critical intelligence to those textual rhetorical devices precisely designed to prevent it from becoming too powerful. Using D. W. Winnicott's conception of the 'good enough' mother so enabling to generations of parents in the 1970s and 1980s, Sommer contends that just as such mothers left a distance between themselves and their children in which the children could be free to be, so there should be 'good enough' critics able to break the 'universalist habit of thinking that they should know more and interpret better than the particularist authors they target'.[21] In similar vein, when Derek Attridge describes the practice of reading as an ethics, he builds on the Levinasian assumption that the readerly 'I' is a split ego, split from the start by its yielding to the Other which is its primary mode of being and irreducible relationality:

> What I affirm when I respond to the text in a way that does justice to its oth-erness is not simply a particular argument or arrangement of words but the creativity of the author or authors in bringing into existence that argument or those words . . . I may know nothing about the author, not even his or her name, but I read the text on the assumption that it is "authored," that it is the creative work, however mediated, of at least one mind . . . a full response to the otherness of the text includes an awareness of, a respect for, and . . . a taking of responsibility for, the creativity of its author.[22]

Attridge is careful, however, to distinguish the nature of this responsibility from any form of conventional morality: 'there is no necessary connection between a responsible relation to otherness as I . . . read a novel and the obligations I have under the moral codes embodied in social norms, religious institutions [or] the law of my country' (28).

One can understand Attridge's recourse to a nonmoral discourse of ethics. He is anxious to avoid what Lawrence Buell discerns as the danger of being pulled back to 'old-fashioned values thematics: the "pre-modern strategy" of making "aesthetic sensibility ultimately subservient to the goal of moral improvement"'.[23] Attridge here replicates a long-standing distinction in moral philosophy between questions of justice and those of the good life: the right versus the good. The former is aligned in the philosophical tradition with Kantian *Moralität* and the latter with Hegelian *Sittlichkeit*: the former with the rules, the latter with a teleological account of what conduces towards the fulfilment and happiness of human beings. Before Attridge, Adam Zachary Newton's influential *Narrative Ethics* had appeared, in which, again, although he writes of 'hermeneutic responsibility' and considers reading to be an ethical practice, he has no place for moral judgements as such. 'A kind of negative capability of response' is as close as he comes.[24] He claims that 'perhaps the profoundest ethical dilemma which reading fiction poses *is just* the fact of solitude . . . forcing one's own single self against and into the world(s) of fictional others' (23). As he further contends, the thrust of narrative ethics is phenomenological and is not to be conflated with a 'deontological' approach to criticism – one, that is, based on the science of duty, the branch of knowledge dealing with moral obligations.

To what, however, does this formalistic approach to reading as an ethical practice and to relations between readers and texts defined as ethical amount? Attridge has a wobbly moment when he asks, 'What is the ethical ground for attention to and affirmation of otherness, when the result of this effort may be without any humanly recognisable merit or indeed may serve inhuman ends? The other that is brought into being may turn out to be a monstrosity.'[25] Judith Butler's resistance is even more vertebrate. She finds to some extent repugnant the founding assumption of Levinasian ethics as expressed in *Otherwise Than Being or Beyond Essence*: the demand imposed upon the self by the face of the Other. In Levinas's words: 'I am as it were ordered from the outside, traumatically commanded, without interiorising by representation and concepts the authority that commands me, without asking myself: what is then he to me? where does he get his right to command?'[26] Butler asks:

> What would it mean to obey such a demand, to acquiesce to such a demand when no critical evaluation of the demand could be made? Would such an acquiescence be any more or less uncritical and unthinking than an acquiescence to an ungrounded authoritarian law? How would one distinguish between a fascist demand and one which somehow affirms the ethical bonds between humans that Levinas understands as constitutive of the ethical subject?[27]

How indeed?

Reading Burns and Byron Ethically

The case-study presented in the present essay is that of Burns and Byron. How do we, in Attridge's terms, 'take responsibility for' their creativity? What would represent a responsible – ethical – reading of their work? In a lecture delivered at the Glasgow Burns conference in January 2009, considering the question whether Burns was 'a transcendental philosopher' or any kind of philosopher, Susan Manning sought to restore the distance, elided by Francis Jeffrey and all who followed in his moralising wake, between Burns's *beliefs* and his *rhetoric*: to put measurable space between, in Jeffrey's words, 'the leading vice in Burns's character, and the cardinal deformity . . . of all his productions'. She deploys the rare and obsolete term 'aversiveness' (*OED* has only one example, dated 1597) to connote a steering away from all enduring senses of selfhood, a rhetorical attitude, a challenge to settled 'beliefs' of all kinds. It's why he can write Hanoverian poems and Jacobite ones, poems devout and skeptical, sentimental and scurrilous; why he can express convincing outrage at the obscenity of slavery, and think of becoming a slave-driver in Jamaica. It's simultaneously true that Burns has one of the strongest, most instantly recognizable poetic 'signatures,' and that in an almost Keatsian sense, he has *no* poetic self.[28]

If one were to abstract the final sentence, blot out the name, and ask 'of whom is this being said?', the answer is as likely to be 'Byron' as it is to be 'Burns'. Another way of putting this might be to say that both poets *perform* the self and, as Manning goes on to show, aversive whimsicality, a refusal to be pinned down that relegates all assumptions of attitude to the momentary, is a dominant tonality of both performed selves. A similar approach was taken by another contributor to this landmark conference, Ian Brown, who argues as follows:

> I want to suggest here that the varieties of 'Robert Burns' – Burns the Radical, Burns the Volunteer, Burns the Patriot, Burns the potential slave-driver, Burns the Tory, Burns the nationalist – all are possible figurations because of both his implicit performativities and the theatricality of his poetry. Both the performative, often song-saturated, mode within which he developed his art and his actual writing practice which is often clearly dramatic – and even in such pieces as *Holy Willie's Prayer* effectively theatrical – is constantly working not only in poetic but performance modes. To look for Burns in his poems would then be like looking for Shakespeare or Arthur Miller in their dramatic characters.[29]

The performativity of the self is a concept gaining currency and is being deployed, as by Manning and Brown, in defence of Burns's inconsistency and to an extent of his ethics.

In his poetry, Byron is as 'aversive' as we have seen his self-descriptions to be, similarly committed to nonce attitudes and rhetorical postures. In his verse, Byron makes himself his own subject just as much as does Wordsworth in *The Prelude*. That self, though, is exasperatingly protean.

> If people contradict themselves, can I
> Help contradicting them, and every body,
> Even my veracious self? –But that's a lie;
> I never did so, never will – how should I?
> He who doubts all things nothing can deny; (*Don Juan* XV, 88)

The Byron who narrates himself in *Childe Harold* and in *Don Juan* does so without Wordsworth's drive towards the sincere and exacting encapsulation of the stages of poetic development.[30] Sometimes the narrator espouses a firm purpose in writing: 'I mean to show things really as they are, / Not as they ought to be' (XII.40). Much more often, he denies that he has any such purpose, his improvisatory manner resulting in his having no idea what he will say next:

> Some have accused me of a strange design
> Against the creed and morals of the land,
> And trace it in this poem every line:
> I don't pretend that I quite understand
> My own meaning when I would be *very* fine;
> But the fact is that I have nothing plann'd. (IV, 5)

and:

> I ne'er decide what I shall say, and this I call
> Much too poetical. Men should know why
> They write, and for what end; but, note or text,
> I never know the word which will come next. (IX, 41)

The directionless nature of *Don Juan* was repeated in Byron's correspondence with Murray. When Murray asked, in a letter of 23 July 1819, whether Byron had any 'Settled Plan for the continuation of this immortal work?', Byron replied that he '*had* no plan', nor did he '*have*' any plan and that the 'Soul of such writing' was its licence.[31]

Here, however, we start to encounter a paradox. Perhaps Byron's greatest legacy to poetry and drama is the 'Byronic hero' – the entirely possessed, fully self-present ego that requires no vindication of his identity from others: in a word, the independent man. The Burns of 'A man's a man for a' that' is, looked at under another aspect, himself a Byronic hero. The equivalent in the Burns canon to the corpus in which Byron develops his characteristic hero is the group of much-loved songs in which a self-sufficient lyric voice expresses sentiments of such beauty that they have been taken by subsequent generations for pure truth, enacting the Keatsian equivalence between beauty and truth that closes the 'Grecian Urn'. Of the lines from 'Ae Fond Kiss'

> Had we never lov'd sae kindly,
> Had we never lov'd sae blindly!
> Never met – or never parted,
> We had ne'er been broken-hearted. (K 337, II, 592, 13–16)

Scott commented that 'they contain the essence of a thousand love tales'.[32] Byron used them as an epigraph for *The Bride of Abydos* (even if inappropriately, since his Selim and Zuleika never have an opportunity even to try out their love). It is a convention of lyric to assert an absolute sincerity, a full presence in what is said of the voice that speaks. How do we reconcile the notion that Burns and Byron are linked by aversiveness and the performativity of the self with the perception that their greatest achievements are characterised by a sense of the innate trustworthiness and purity of their sentiments, the 'poetic truth' of those? To pose this question, I will focus on two lyric poems, 'Ae Fond Kiss' and 'So We'll Go No More a-Roving', pieces in which the equivalent lyrical giftedness of Burns and Byron are triumphantly on display.

Their poetic effect is very different. Burns's song of parting is one that any bereft lover would take in part-exchange. Appropriately lachrymose, eschewing comfort but also bitterness, refusing of course any *analysis* of the meeting and parting, offering the palliative of superlative singularity in the singer's affections – 'But to see her, was to love her; / Love but her, and love for ever' – 'first and fairest', 'best and dearest' – this song contains the essence of the love affair. Byron's is by contrast a fatigued, world-weary performance. The stanzas seem to conclude a longer, unsupplied preamble. The sheer practicalities of love have defeated romance. The body's limitations are expressed in somewhat mystified neoplatonic imagery: 'For the sword outwears its sheath, / And the soul wears out the breast' (5–6). Where Burns's song expresses a pain and darkness that is nevertheless evidence of rich living, Byron's lyric seems to be an early expression of decadence in its substitution of life by exhaustion and death. It is an ancestor of such later lyrics as Ernest Dowson's 'I have been true to thee, Cynara, in my fashion'. Love is not eternal: it needs a break. It is almost a sophisticated pun on love and *lovemaking*, its physical manifestation. Burns's poem is great because it performs sincerity so well; Byron's because it performs worldliness.

What we might call the 'back stories' of the two poems are somewhat shocking, chilling even. The story of Burns's romantic, pastoral and probably Platonic courtship of his 'Clarinda', Agnes McLehose, the estranged wife of a wastrel lawyer, is popular and well known. While Burns was writing the perfervid letters to 'Clarinda', he was impregnating the postwoman: Agnes's maid Jenny Clow, who carried her mistress's letters to 'Sylvander' and who bore Burns's illegitimate son Robert. In 1791, three years after the affair with her and her mistress had ended, Burns was persuaded to visit Jenny, who was by then dying of tuberculosis leaving behind 3-year old Robert. Burns took the opportunity to visit once more his 'Clarinda', and it was for parting with *her*, not the mother of his son, that he wrote 'Ae Fond Kiss'. Agnes McLehose expressed in her journal forty years later the desire to meet Burns in Heaven, but Jenny Clow was more likely to wish to see him in hell first. Within three months of writing 'Ae Fond Kiss', furthermore, Burns had made his connection with Jean Armour into a marriage. Robert Crawford's recent biography of Burns records some of the facts, but beyond referring to the 'strained domestic atmosphere' that his renewed intercourse with Nancy McLehose may have created between the poet and Jean Armour, he does not educe the dark ironies behind a song that allowed Burns, in Crawford's words, 'to perform his intense, private erotic sadness before a public audience'.[33]

The circumstances of 'So We'll Go No More a-Roving' demonstrate some uncomfortable parallels. Byron was in his first winter of residence in Venice, a city he loved for its literary associations as much as for its living inhabitants. He had taken up with a tradesman's wife, Marianna Segeti, but had put distance between her and himself for the duration of the 1817 New Year carnival, so that he could enjoy its recreations. In a state of carnal exhaustion after the delights of carnival, Byron wrote the poem. At exactly this time, his daughter by Claire Clairmont, Allegra, was being born (on 12 January 1817), but, as seems to have been the case with Burns and his son Robert, Byron appeared indifferent and simply would not send for the child. Fiona MacCarthy's coverage of this phase of Byron's life in her recent popular biography emphasises Claire Clairmont's impassioned letters to him, the concern of the Shelleys for the infant and Byron's dilatory indolence.[34]

If the poems are, in Swift's words, 'gaudy tulips sprung from dung', what difference, in the last analysis, does that make?[35] It can be objected that what I have offered as the stories behind the poems is not the 'truth' about the lives but rather a narrativisation of it. So is Robert Crawford's, however, or Fiona MacCarthy's life of Byron, but they do not advertise the fact nor are they sold on that ticket. The part played by any reconstruction of the biographical 'facts' in which the selves that emerge from the poems are rooted remains to be adequately theorised. Susan Manning's separation of beliefs and rhetoric, of life and art – her desire for measurable space between the writer's biography and his poetry – is understandable. I am as averse to letting Francis Jeffrey in by the back door as are other readers; and maybe to say that moral judgement is not our concern is enough to keep him out. Ethical criticism, as we have seen it operating in the present time, concerns itself mainly with texts, readers and the practice of reading. It does not, in the main, concern itself with the ethics of authors, neither does it stray far into non-narrative genres. It eschews deontology. We can, perhaps, draw a distinction between the trustworthiness of the poet, on the one hand, and of the poems, on the other. Josef Stalin might have in a private moment written a 'Hymn to Liberty' and, on one theory of art, its beauty could not be compromised by anything that might come to light about how he spent the remainder of his time.

But can the ethical coupure between authors and their productions really be made so absolute? Are we not in danger of restoring the 'well-wrought urn'? Does knowledge about works of art, the kind of knowledge that we are all engaged in producing, remain hermetically sealed off from the 'well-wrought urn' that is the poem? Or when we once let that genie out of the bottle, do we have any way of squeezing him back inside? 'Self-performativity' is all very well, but how do we distinguish between legitimate and illegitimate self-projections? To say that a creative writer 'performs the self' is surely not to license whatever 'self' s/he deems it expedient to perform. Burns and Byron are alike in being celebrated by the critical tradition as simultaneously the poets of negative capability, of 'aversiveness' and performativity, and of transcendent self-presence. They have somehow managed to have it both ways.

Notes

1. See Murray Pittock, 'Byron's Networks and Scottish Romanticism', *The Byron Journal* 37.2 (2009), pp. 5–14, for discussion and recent bibliography on p. 5. My own contribution to this scholarship is made in 'Byron', in Murray Pittock (ed.), *The Edinburgh Companion to Scottish Romanticism* (Edinburgh: Edinburgh University Press, 2011), pp. 150–65. The argument made there is in many respects supplementary to this one.

2. T. S. Eliot, 'Byron', in Bonamy Dobrée (ed.), *From Anne to Victoria* (London: Cassell, 1937), reproduced in T. S. Eliot, *On Poetry and Poets* (London: Faber, 1957, reprinted 1969), p. 194.

3. Eliot, 'Byron', p. 201.

4. Ibid., p. 201.

5. Lady Marguerite Blessington, *Conversations of Lord Byron*, ed. Ernest J. Lovell Jr. (Princeton: Princeton University Press, 1969), pp. 129–30. See also the sustained passage of attack on the English, pp. 131–2.

6. All references to Byron's poetry are to *Lord Byron: The Complete Poetical Works*, ed. Jerome J. McGann, 7 vols (Oxford: Clarendon Press, 1980–93), except where explicitly stated otherwise.

7. Murray Pittock, *Scottish and Irish Romanticism* (Oxford: Oxford University Press, 2008), p. 7.

8. Lord Byron, *Selected Letters and Journals*, ed. Leslie A. Marchand (London: Pimlico, 1993), p. 346.

9. Robert Burns to Agnes McLehose, 28 December 1787 (Robert Burns, *The Letters of Robert Burns*, ed. J. De Lancey Ferguson and G. Ross Roy, 2 vols (Oxford: Clarendon Press, 1985), vol. I, pp. 189–90).

10. Blessington, *Conversations*, p. 220.

11. Alexander Pope, 'Epistle to a Lady', 2, quoted from Alexander Pope, *The Poems of Alexander Pope*, ed. John Butt (London: Methuen, 1963, repr. 1970), p. 560; and John Dryden, *Absalom and Achitophel*, 548, quoted from John Dryden, *The Poems and Fables of John Dryden*, ed. James Kinsley (Oxford: Oxford University Press, 1958, repr. 1962), p. 204.

12. Thomas Moore, Review of *Letters and Journals of Lord Byron: with Notes of his Life*, *Edinburgh Review* (June 1831), Article XI, p. 570.

13. See Caroline Franklin, *Byron: A Literary Life* (London and New York: Macmillan and St. Martin's Press, 2000), pp. 21–2.

14. Francis Jeffrey, rev. *Reliques of Robert Burns, consisting chiefly of Original Letters, Poems, and Critical Observations on Scotish Songs*, *Edinburgh Review* 13.26 (January 1809), pp. 249–76, 253.

15. Ibid., p. 254.

16. John Murray, *The Letters of John Murray to Lord Byron*, ed. Andrew Nicholson (Liverpool: Liverpool University Press, 2007), Letter 118, 16 July 1819, p. 275.

17. Murray, Letter 122 (14 September 1819), in Murray, *Letters*, p. 289.

18. Murray (14 November 1819), in Murray, *Letters*, pp. 297 and 299 n. 1.

19. Murray (28 May 1819), in Murray, *Letters*, p. 274 n. 5.

20. Lawrence Buell, 'Introduction: in pursuit of ethics', *PMLA* 114.1, *Special Topic: Ethics and Literary Study* (January 1999), pp. 7–19.

21. Doris Sommer, 'Attitude, its rhetoric', in Marjorie Garber, Beatrice Hanssen and Rebecca L. Walkowitz (eds), *The Turn to Ethics* (New York and London: Routledge, 2000), pp. 201–20, 214. Winnicott's ideas were expressed in *Playing and Reality* (London: Tavistock, 1971).

22. Derek Attridge, 'Innovation, literature, ethics: relating to the Other', *PMLA* 114.1 (1999), pp. 20–31, 25.

23. Lawrence Buell, 'What we talk about when we talk about ethics', in Garber et al., *Turn to Ethics*, pp. 1–14, 6 n. 12. Buell is at this point citing an article by Herbert Grabes entitled 'Ethics, aesthetics, and alterity', in Gerhard Hoffman and Alfred Hornung (eds), *Ethics and Aesthetics: The Moral Turn of Postmodernism* (Heidelberg: Universitätsverlag, 1996), p. 17.

24. Adam Zachary Newton, *Narrative Ethics* (Cambridge, MA: Harvard University Press, 1995; 2nd edn 1997), p. 21.

25. Attridge, 'Innovation, literature, ethics', p. 28.

26. Quoted by Judith Butler, 'Ethical Ambivalence', in Garber et al., *The Turn to Ethics*, pp. 15–28, 18.

27. Ibid., p. 18.

28. Susan Manning, unpublished lecture entitled '"Ae spark o' Nature's Fire": was Robert Burns a transcendental philosopher?' delivered at the Glasgow Burns Conference, 15–17 January 2009, p. 12 (reproduced by kind permission of the author).

29. Ian Brown, 'The framing of "Robert Burns" in the Soviet State – a case-study from Armenia' (Unpublished conference paper, Glasgow Burns Conference, January 2009), p. 4.

30. On sincerity in Romantic writing, see further Jerome J. McGann, *Towards a Literature of Knowledge* (Oxford: Clarendon Press, 1989), pp. 1–64. 'The poetry of sincerity – Romantic poetry, in its paradigm mode . . . typically avoids the procedures of satirical and polemical verse. Those latter forms – by their protocols – develop through publicly installed dialogical operations. When Romantic poetry opens itself to those genres it opens itself to the horizon of its antithesis, to the horizon of hypocrisy' (quoted from Jane Stabler (ed.), *Byron*, Longman Critical Readers (London and New York: Longman, 1998), p. 29).

31. Murray, *Letters of Murray to Byron*, pp. 282, 283 n. 6.

32. Robert Burns, *The Songs of Robert Burns*, ed. Donald A. Low (London: Routledge, 1993), p. 453. The lyrics are quoted from this edition.

33. Robert Crawford, *The Bard: Robert Burns, a Biography* (London: Jonathan Cape, 2009), pp. 342, 344.

34. Fiona MacCarthy, *Byron: Life and Legend* (London: Faber, 2002), pp. 324–5.

35. Jonathan Swift, 'The Lady's Dressing Room', 142, in Jonathan Swift, *Poetical Works*, ed. Herbert Davis (Oxford: Oxford University Press, 1967), p. 480.

CHAPTER 14

MacDiarmid, Burnsians, and Burns's Legacy

Robert Crawford

Sometimes Christopher Murray Grieve may have championed William Dunbar rather than Robert Burns, but without Burns and Burns Clubs to duel with Grieve would not have produced the Scots poetry he wrote under the pen name Hugh MacDiarmid. To put it more positively, it was the Burns Federation which, albeit unintentionally, fuelled the greatest Scots-language poetry of the twentieth century. It did so because some of its members were willing to engage with contemporary poetry. If the present essay has a polemical point, it is to suggest that today's Burns Clubs must do so again. The Burns Clubs of MacDiarmid's youth were heirs to the great traditions of earlier Burns celebrations such as that of the Paisley Burns's Birthday Centenary of 1859 where toasts were proposed not just to Burns but also to Shakespeare, Scott, Tennyson, Tannahill, Irish Poetry and Moore, American Poetry and Longfellow, to the Poets of Scotland, and to others.[1] Tennyson was aged forty-nine at the time, Longfellow fifty-one, and the poets of Scotland were of all ages. It was clearly taken for granted that Burns Supperers should have an interest in both older and contemporary poetry internationally. Though this was waning in the early twentieth century, some, including, in their very different ways, Grieve and the Vernacular Circle of the London Burns Club, sought to keep this engagement alive.

Alan Riach has provided an impressive overview of 'MacDiarmid's Burns' in his essay of that title, and I have written elsewhere of MacDiarmid's engagement with Burns in Montrose.[2] What follows has a close focus on the way in which Grieve's engagement with Burnsians' arguments about modern literature helped produce MacDiarmid's Scots poetry. Though Grieve recalled 'Burns . . . was taboo in my father's house and quite unknown to me as a boy', he read some Burns poems at school; but only after 1919 did he accomplish 'a thorough course of reading in Burns, Dunbar, and the other Scots poets'.[3] Nevertheless, he had written from Macedonia in February 1918 about 'a champion Burns's Night, the "Immortal Memory" devolving upon me', while his 1922 recollection of having responded to Burns Supper toasts to 'Scottish Literature' in 'Greece, Italy, and France' indicates that he took part in several World War I Burns Suppers.[4] Grieve's 1919 reading of Burns, Dunbar and others was most probably spurred by the publication that year of G. Gregory Smith's *Scottish Literature: Character and Influence,* which he came to regard as a handbook for a Scottish Renaissance. It gave him the title for his own first published book, *Annals of the Five Senses,* substantially written by 1919 though not published until 1923. Smith saw Burns as 'the end of a process' and a 'barrier to emancipation' rather than as a beginning. Mocking modern perpetrators of 'the surprising travesty called "Braid Scots"', Smith made fun of how 'our poeticule waddles in good duck fashion through his Jamieson [John Jamieson's 1808–9 *Etymological Dictionary of the Scottish Language*], snapping up fat expressive words' to produce something fit only for 'St Andrew festivals in Massachusetts'.[5]

Taking from Smith the idea of the 'Caledonian antisyzygy' and much else, Grieve also absorbed the view that Burns was an end, not a beginning: 'Braid Scots' taken from dictionaries was backward-looking, pointlessly artificial. In *Northern Numbers,* Grieve's November 1920 anthology of 'certain Scottish poets of to-day', only two of the eleven poets (Violet Jacob and Joseph Lee) are represented by work in Scots. Lee's pallidly sub-Burnsian Standard Habbie poem 'The White-Washin' o' Robbie Burns' may carry some very faint anticipations of Grieve's later polemic, but lacks any real energy. Still, in the second volume of *Northern Numbers,* published in October 1921, five out of the nineteen poets use Scots, while several others represented only through English-language work (including John Buchan and Lewis Spence) were associated with advocating the use of Scots in verse. Grieve, the editor, remained commited exclusively to English in his own poetry. He would never use Standard Habbie.

His thinking about such issues was also conditioned by wider debates about Burns and the use of the Scots tongue in poetry. By August 1921 *The Scotsman* was carrying an extended report on the Burns Club of London's campaigning for 'The More Extended Use of Scottish Vernacular Language'. In 1920 this Burns Club had formed a Vernacular Circle which heard distinguished Scottish speakers including John Buchan and the lexicographer W. A. Craigie, Professor of Anglo-Saxon at Oxford, championing the use of vernacular Scots. *The Scotsman* reported that Craigie's 'knowledge of the renaissance of other languages similarly placed to our own gave great heartening'. Prizes in schools and in universities were to be set up; outside schools there were to be 'singing contests' (the Scots word for these was 'Sangschaws', coined by the first President of the Scottish National Song Society by analogy with the older Scots word 'wapinschaw' – a review of men under arms); also proposed were international prizes for compositions in prose and verse.[6]

All this activity of the Burns Club of London was commended in *The Scotsman,* but days later the paper published a long letter from 'C. M. Grieve, Editor of "Northern Numbers"': 'There is no one more keenly interested in the contemporary tendencies and in the future of Scottish literature than I am'. Grieve makes clear that extensive correspondence and consideration of the matter has led him 'to deplore the "manifesto" of the Vernacular Circle Committee of the London Burns Club (*Scotsman*, 22nd inst.) as a terrible example of misdirected energy.' Scottish writers will write in English 'for the simple reasons (1) that they will reach a larger public, and (2) that the English language is an immensely superior medium of expression.'

> Scots is no longer psychologically representative of or adequate to the modern Scottish temperament (can a hen re-enter the shell it burst in its chicken-hood?); and, gravest of all in certain respects, the fact that Scots has been irremediably prostituted to sentimental and comic ends.
>
> The reinstatement of Scots as a literary language would only be possible if the tendency towards urban centralisation could be reversed and a new peasantry brought into being, and even then generations would have to pass before the re-adopted language could absorb the life of that hypothetical nation so completely as to offer a medium in which a full-size writer could display himself effectively.

After going on to quote from Gregory Smith on Burns and other users of Scots, MacDiarmid argues that what unites Scottish writers is a certain 'family likeness', rather than the use of Scots vernacular language; ' "braid Scots" is, and will remain, the special preserve of the *tour de force* and the *jeu d'esprit* – a backwater of the true river of Scottish national expression'.[7]

Contributors to the ensuing *Scotsman* correspondence included Sir George Douglas, 'W. B.' and William Will, Honorary Secretary of the Vernacular Circle of the Burns Club of London. Will contended that 'The character of a people is expressed by its language', and vigorously supported reviving the use of Scots.[8] Debates over the literary use of the Scots vernacular continued. A September 1921 advertisement for *A Book of Scots* aimed at schoolchildren invokes 'the movement in furtherance of the cultivation of the vernacular' supported by such luminaries as 'Professor Craigie, of Oxford; Col. John Buchan, Mrs Violet Jacob, Miss Symon . . . Professor Grierson' and others.[9] Many of those arguing over the ideas of the London Burns Club's Vernacular Circle would be among MacDiarmid's contacts and supporters, but when Dr J. M. Bulloch's Vernacular Circle lecture on 'The Delight of the Doric in the Diminutive' was reported in the Scottish press Grieve went on the offensive. Where Bulloch praised poets like Mary Symon and relished a milieu where 'there were probably hundreds of mothers at that moment putting the "little wee bit loonikies and the little wee bit lassikies to their beddies" ', Grieve fired off letters attempting to counter this sort of infantilisation, arguing it did not represent Burns's best legacy:

> Some of the 'perfervids' attached to the London Vernacular Circle (not themselves particularly distinguished as creative artists) are making claims for the Doric which even writers such as Mrs Violet Jacob, John Buchan,

and Profesor Alexander Gray – who have added to its glories – repudiate. The latter recognise its insuperable spiritual limitations, as Burns did, and as future writers must increasingly do.[10]

That Grieve was preoccupied by the arguments generated by the London Burns Club's Vernacular Circle is confirmed by his lecture on 'Contemporary Scottish Poetry' to the Montrose Y.M.C.A. Literary and Debating Society in mid-December 1921. Reported in the *Montrose Review* (for which Grieve worked as a local journalist), this speech contends that,

> Literary circles in Scotland are torn in two to-day by a great controversy which, recurring intermittently during the past 50 to 100 years is growing more vexatious and bitter with time. It is, roughly speaking, the struggle as to whether Scottish literature and the Scottish dialect – 'braid Scots' – are synonymous terms, or whether the doric has now reached that stage of general disuse which prevents it from being, or again becoming in the future, the appropriate and adequate vehicle for the expression of the living spirit and experiences of the Scottish nation.

Going on to refer to the 'London Burnsians' and their attempts to foster a 'revival of "Braid Scots" as a written and spoken language', Grieve makes clear that

> my main grievance was that the London Burns Club had formulated an extensive scheme for resuscitating an admittedly dying language as a literary medium – but that in doing so they were altogether neglecting to provide for the sustenance of that part of living Scottish literature which is expressed in the English language common not only to England and Scotland, but to all the English-speaking world of America and the Colonies.

Yet even as he inveighs against writing in Scots, Grieve concludes his December 1921 talk by pondering on ways in which not only the language but also the spirit of Burns might be applied to contemporary literature:

> And yet I admit that even yet the Doric has its place. For literature is still being produced in the Doric. Even the merely linguistic influence of the great genius of Burns is unexhausted; but infinitely greater than that line of his which puzzles schoolboys in the 'Mouse' – 'A daimen-icker in a thrave' – is the spirit of his declaration, made not in the Doric, but in English, and yet with the true Scottish note in it:– 'A man's a man for a' that.' In literature as in life 'the letter killeth but the spirit giveth life.'[11]

A few days later, Grieve continued his public flyting: 'Surely the Burns cult is a phenomenon of which only a literary pathologist can be proud – an unique abnormality of mob-consciousness pickled in whisky. Burns only occupies the role of an eponym giving a name to a cult in spirit entirely different from anything traceable to him.'[12] As the argument continued into

1922, Grieve, rejoicing in 'my guerrilla warfare with the Vernacular Circle of the London Burns Club', sought to separate the spirit of Burns from that of Burns clubs, and insisted that the legacy of Burns could be parted from the Scots tongue.[13] As reported in *The Scotsman* and elsewhere, however, the Vernacular Circle argued determinedly for increasing use of the Scots vernacular.[14] Grieve put together an 'enormous mass of newspaper and other cuttings' about the associated controversy, but it does not seem to have been until September 1922 that he met the Vernacular Circle's leaders.[15]

He continued to plot a 'Scottish literary revival', but maintained that 'the first essential is to get rid of our provinciality of outlook'; he saw this need as quite different from the aims of 'the ardent minority bent upon the revival of the Doric'.[16] Yet Grieve went as the delegate of the Montrose Burns Club to the annual conference of the Burns Federation held in Birmingham at the start of September 1922. In August he had been full of aspirations for Scottish writing – 'Let Scotland go forward boldly as Belgium did, as Ireland has done, to the creation of its natural national literature.'[17] At the Burns Federation conference in Birmingham he found himself addressing an international audience of over two hundred delegates. Having been praised in the toast to 'Scottish Literature' for his work on *Northern Numbers* and his new periodical *The Scottish Chapbook*, Grieve gave a formal reply to this toast, telling the delegates that,

> Unifying love for the genius of Burns had brought them there, but the great national and international dreams which inspired his muse had not yet been realised, and Burns lived in vain as far as they were concerned if each of them was not doing his utmost for Bonnie Scotland's sake, and for the hastening of the time:
>
> > "When man to man the warl' owre
> > Shall brithers be an' a' that."
>
> Scottish literature in particular Burns charged with an imperative obligation to concentrate in the love of liberty and the love of love on the solution of the great social problems of humanity – and Scottish literature to-day was striving and must continue to strive to exercise what the genius of Burns recognised as its paramount function, albeit even Burns did not conceive the difficulties and complications which had since arisen.

Clearly Councillor Grieve of Montrose, a poet active in local politics, in the international League of Nations movement, and in campaigning for Scottish Home Rule, was attempting here to position himself as the true inheritor of Burns's legacy. Grieve's radicalism was to be seen as continuing Burns's dream of universal brotherhood, but attuned to the contemporary situation. If only Burnsians, and not least those of the Vernacular Circle, could perceive things this way: 'Those who forgetful of the vast changes which had come to pass since Burns's day and of the ever-increasing complexity of our industrial civilization, accused contemporary Scottish literature of being un-Scottish and un-Burnsian, were throwing away the substance alike of life and letters and grasping a shadow.' Applause greeted Grieve's final declaration of his own belief in 'the future of Scottish literature' and 'the continuance of Scottish nationality.'[18]

The following day when Dr Duncan McNaught was re-elected President of the Burns Federation, Grieve's work for contemporary Scottish literature was again praised. Among the Burnsians in Birmingham, he had found a sympathetic audience, even as he censured some of their attitudes. He also heard an international gathering relishing readings and recitations of poetry in Scots at the same time as applauding his own arguments. Soon, back in Montrose, he was boasting of his 'glorious and most useful time' among the Burnsians. He had been invited to address the Vernacular Circle of the London Burns Club. On 20 September he wrote to George Ogilvie,

> I have determined to transform the Burns movement at home and abroad: and am conducting an extensive and very subtle press campaign to that end . . . I am open to wager that over 30 columns of 'Burns Movement Re-Orientation' stuff appears in the press within the next six months. I was the 'stormy petrel' at the Brum Conference but the September *Chapbook* will give you an indication of what I am driving at in this connection.[19]

Though up to this point MacDiarmid's talents as journalist, propagandist, political activist and editor had outshone his gifts as a poet, there was surely another aspect of his visit to Birmingham which profoundly altered his poetry. For around the time he wrote the letter just quoted, and very shortly after he returned elated from the Burns Federation conference, he produced his first two poetic experiments using 'Braid Scots'. These were published on 30 September 1922 in *The Dunfermline Press*, one of the newspaper columns in which Grieve had previously attacked the aims of the London Burnsians' Vernacular Circle.

Acknowledging that 'I have strong views in regard to the literary uses of the Vernacular which I have on more than one occasion expressed at length in this column and elsewhere in the Scottish Press', Grieve nonetheless quoted extensively from the work of W. A. Craigie and presented two poems in which a 'friend' had busied himself in 'rescuing from oblivion and restoring to literary use forgotten words that have a descriptive potency otherwise unobtainable'.[20] The two poems were 'The Water Gaw' [sic] and 'The Blaward and the Skelly'. When the former was reprinted very soon afterwards in the October 1922 *Scottish Chapbook*, the article 'Introducing Hugh M'Diarmid' attributed the poem to a poet of that name, and explained in its opening sentence that, 'One of the objects of *The Scottish Chapbook* is to supplement the campaign of the Vernacular Circle of the London Burns Club for the revival of the Doric.' Though making clear that he does not support 'the campaign for the revival of the Doric where the essential

Scottish diversity-in-unity is forgotten, nor where the tendencies involved are anti-cultural', the author of this article praises the virtues of the new poem in Scots by 'Hugh M'Diarmid', concluding that his is 'an achievement which I hope Vernacular enthusiasts will not be the last to recognise'.[21]

All this was part of Grieve's intense courtship of elements in the Burns Federation which he felt might be sympathetic, particularly its Vernacular Circle. In another October 1922 piece he praises the Vernacular Circle's 'enthusiastic and indefatigable secretary Mr Wm Will', explaining that his own opposition to the Circle's campaign for 'Braid Scots' was not absolute but based on his worry about populism, since 'only a very small proportion of the population . . . is accessible to literary influences' and there is no point in simply appealing to the uneducated 'general public' in matters of literary taste.[22] For all his reservations, Grieve's 'conversion' to writing poetry in Scots was the result of his immersion in the arguments of the Burnsians. The following year his sonnet 'To Duncan McNaught, LL.D., J. P., President of the Burns Federation' urged readers to honour the man who had set in motion a way to realise the noblest dreams of Burns. With its exclamatory 'Burns International!', the poem situates Burns as the precursor of a successor who will fulfil a great political vision. This sonnet may laud McNaught and hope his successor will 'build' on Burns's 'foundation'; it also hints in verse at Grieve's attempt to 'transform the Burns Movement'.[23] In one crucial, linguistic sense that Movement had already helped transform Grieve.

If it was in a significant sense Grieve's prolonged encounter with the Burns Movement which gave rise in September 1922 to the Scots poetry of Hugh MacDiarmid, then his May 1923 address to the Vernacular Circle of the London Burns Club intensified his consideration of Burns and 'broad Scots'. In London he pronounced 'Will and Bulloch . . . the cerebrum and cerebellum of the Vernacular movement'; addressing the assembled advocates of the Scots tongue, 'On the principle of "Save us from our friends"', Grieve asked 'the Vernacular Circle of the London Burns Club to accept me as a most desirable enemy – which they did!'[24] He provoked controversy, sarcasm and denunciation when he presented his 'heretical discussion of the possibilities of braid Scots from the point of view of an admirer of D. H. Lawrence, James Joyce, and the late Marcel Proust'. Grieve admitted he 'got it fast and thick' as his auditors rounded on him and stood up for the values of 'reactionary provincialism in the heart of London'.[25] His account of his talk strongly suggests it articulated his new 'Theory of Scots Letters' which linked the Scots vernacular to Joyce, Lawrence, Proust and other avant-garde writers.[26]

Just how Burns fitted into all this is most evident in an article Grieve published in *The Scottish Nation* within days of addressing the London Burnsians. In this essay on 'Burns and Baudelaire' he maintained, 'Burnsians as a body are for the most part politically and socially opposed to all that

Burns stood for.' More than that, 'To the quest for increased facilities of human self-expression – to the evolution of the art of poetry – Burns contributes nothing.' While praising 'Burns the satirist' and the bawdy Burns as 'a forerunner of James Joyce', Grieve agreed with 'Dr M'Naught' that the Burns who became a government official was 'a shorn Samson'. Grieve wished Burns had been 'a real rebel'. 'The pity about Burns is that he never got beyond good and evil.'[27]

Such provocative campaigning for a new, Nietzschian Burns progressed alongside the Vernacular Circle's efforts. The year 1924 brought two books from major publishers furthering the revival of Scots. Prefacing *The Scottish Tongue* which collected lectures to the Vernacular Circle by Craigie, Buchan, Bulloch and Professor Peter Giles, William Will praised Scots as 'the language in which the mentality of the Lowland Scot can best be expressed'. Grieve's, though, was one of the lectures for which 'it had not been possible to find room' in the book.[28] Still, that same year, John Buchan's *The Northern Muse: An Anthology of Scots Vernacular Poetry* set 'The Watergaw' alongside Burns and Dunbar, while some phrases in that book's introduction suggest Buchan has been reading MacDiarmid's prose theorising about Scots. He mentions Gregory Smith, but celebrates Burns's Scots as a consciously assembled literary construction, distinctly removed from common speech. Buchan's Burns might almost have written 'The Watergaw'.

Grieve's imagining of a rebel, Nietzschian Burns is absolutely at one with the MacDiarmid who remixed those Burnsian elements of sex, Scots and religion in *Sangschaw*, *Penny Wheep* and *A Drunk Man Looks at the Thistle*. If many of the London Burnsians of the Vernacular Circle regarded Grieve as a 'pervert', he still hoped to sway their leaders and the intellectuals associated with them. In the case of Buchan, he seemed to have succeeded. Grieve's engagement with Burns and Burnsians helped produce his distinctive Scots acoustic – one that is at once Modernist and yet sounds at times like that of a folk poet. His most obviously Burnsian early experiment, 'The Blaward and the Skelly' (which Alan Bold later described with perceptive overstatement as 'virtually a redaction of the first song Burns ever wrote') was dropped when he assembled his first collection.[29] Included were not just the more Nietzschian lyrics such as 'The Sauchs in the Reuch Heuch Hauch' and 'Crowdieknowe' but also the nursery-rhyme-like 'O Jesu Parvule' and the maternal 'The Bonnie Broukit Bairn' – which might be more likely to appeal to lovers of the diminutive in Scots.

MacDiarmid's first book was surely designed to shock some Burnsians but also to appeal to the more adventurous among them. *Sangschaw* (1925) in its title appealed to the Burns Clubs and their song competitions; the volume's sympathetic preface by Buchan presented MacDiarmid as assembling his Scots 'as Burns did'; the book's longest poem, 'Ballad of the Five Senses', a Scots vision of a new beginning, is dedicated 'To Sir Robert

Bruce, President of the Burns Federation, in appreciation of his efforts
to foster a Scottish Literary Revival.' Under Bruce's presidency, the
Burns Federation had recently formed a Vernacular Circle in Scotland.
MacDiarmid's attempts to position himself as the true successor to Burns
are also evident in his choice of the title for his next book, *Penny Wheep*,
taken from Burns's poem, 'The Holy Fair'. Though it may be adapted from
a review in the *Glasgow Evening Times*, the blurb on the front dust jacket of
Penny Wheep, with its mention of 'ploughmen' and of 'the last 130 years'
(the time between the death of Burns and the 1926 publication of *Penny
Wheep*), as well as its hint that the author 'has revivified the body of Scots
poetry, and put the spark of hope into its almost moribund heart' – all help
position MacDiarmid as the saviour of the vernacular and as the true heir of
Robert Burns.

Penny Wheep contains too 'Garmscoile', a manifesto poem earlier entitled
'Braid Scots', which hymns the potential of the Scots language in ways that
parallel the enthusiasms of Grieve's prose 'Theory of Scots Letters'. Yet
'Gairmscoile' nowhere mentions Burns, while 'A Theory of Scots Letters'
invokes Burns and the London Burns Club only to express a wish to move
beyond them. In the last poem of *Penny Wheep*, 'Your Immortal Memory,
Burns!', MacDiarmid satirises those who know no poetry other than that
of Burns and who throng to functions where 'to thee, O Burns, / The
punctual stomach of thy people turns.' Here Burns is a 'Poet Intestinal'
of 'belchings and regurgitations' and, as such, surely an irrelevance to the
future of Scottish literature.[30]

This is substantially the Burns of the Supperers of *A Drunk Man Looks
at the Thistle*, a poem billed as 'in preparation' when *Penny Wheep* was published.[31] The opening section of *A Drunk Man* famously blasts the 'Croose
London Scotties wi'' their braw shirt fronts' at a Burns Supper, one of many
all round the world which make Burns a 'dumpin'-grun'' for 'sloppy rubbish'. Burns is envisaged as wishing to avoid almost all Burns Clubs, though,
addressed by the poet as 'Rabbie', he is told that 'the warld hath need, /
And Scotland mair sae, o' the likes o' thee!' Later in the poem Burns is 'Puir
Burns'; his countrymen are upbraided for their abandonment of the poet
William Dunbar whose rich medieval Scots language MacDiarmid sometimes saw as an alternative model.[32] The several other mentions of Burns
in *A Drunk Man* are largely tokenistic. What MacDiarmid is doing is less
invoking Burns than attempting to supplant him. The most famous drunk
man in Scottish literature is 'Tam o' Shanter', mock-hero of a poem in
which actual sights and drunken imaginings are so blended that it becomes
hard to know which are which: with subtle humour Burns plays out a duel
between the sexes. In its very different way MacDiarmid's poem revisits
this psychological space. Its speaker claims, 'I am like Burns' and 'I'm no
like Burns': both statements (for all they ostensibly concern the bard's sex
life) are true in a general sense.[33] MacDiarmid is following Burns's example

of exploring male Scottish psychology through the example of a drunk man, yet departing from it for far more extensive modernist flights. Drawing on Russian and other exemplars, these internationalise the poem's Scots view-point at the same time as complicating and deepening it. That MacDiarmid was still attempting to have his own work seen as the inheritor of Burns's legacy is confirmed by his contemporary selection of Burns's poetry for the Augustan Books of Modern Poetry series published in London in 1926 by Ernest Benn.

Prefacing this thirty-two-page booklet Grieve implies most poetry lovers now read little Burns. Yet he emphasises that 'Much of the best, and least-known, of Burns depends for appreciation on a thorough knowledge of Scots. This is its "growing end" – witness its part to-day in stimulating the most vital Scots poetry for over a century.' Just in case this nudge towards the poetry of Hugh MacDiarmid is missed, he emphasises that 'my ideas generally coincide with his [Burns's], especially where these are at odds with conventional opinion'.[34]

Grieve's take on Burns is certainly unconventional. He assumes that 'most of his love-songs have a deadly sameness'. For him the best of Burns would occupy only about sixty pages, around double the size of this selec-tion. Despite his stress elsewhere on the Burns of universal brotherhood, Grieve omits the song 'For a' that and a' that'; nor does he include such celebrated political poems as the song exhorting 'Scots, wha hae wi Wallace bled' or that denouncing 'Such a parcel of rogues in a nation'. Instead, he includes lesser, less familiar songs like 'O Merry Hae I Been Teethin' a Heckle' and 'The Lovely Lass o' Inverness'. Grieve's selection incorporates 'A Bard's Epitaph' and 'Awa' Whigs, Awa', but not, though he had declared in 1923 that 'The principal Burns to me is the Burns of the satires', 'Holy Willie's Prayer'.[35] It gives most space to 'Tam o' Shanter'. Yet in other ways the selection seems wilfully eccentric, suggesting a poet determined to present a kind of defaced Burns.

This need both to honour and to deface Burns characterises the cam-paigning Grieve of the 1920s who invented Hugh MacDiarmid. It leads soon enough to his turning once more against the Burns movement, the activites of whose Vernacular Circle in London were so instrumental in his turning to Scots in the first place. Part of this shows Grieve's characteristic need to bite the hand that fed him. Yet it also represents his realisation that most members of Burns Clubs had little interest in poetry in gen-eral, let alone modern poetry. Certainly they did not buy many of Hugh MacDiarmid's books; by the end of 1926 each of his three volumes of Scots poetry had sold only about a hundred copies.[36] There was a deep incompat-ibility between his avant-garde Modernist aesthetic and the Burns Clubs' general entrenched traditionalism. Out of his engagement with Burnsians and Burns the Scots poetry of MacDiarmid had been born. More than that, in a rough wooing Grieve had sought to win the Burns Movement as backers, as later he sought to align himself with the Scottish National Party, the Communist Party and with other causes where he might both offer and find support. Grieve's engagement with Burns and Burnsians can be tracked through his 1926 *Contemporary Scottish Studies* essays and beyond. Yet in his later work it seems to have been less productive for his poetry. In *Scottish Scene* (1934) he is still inveighing against

> Auld Lichts, Wee Frees, Burnsians, London Scots!
> Let them awa' like shadows at noon to their haunts![37]

By 1959 MacDiarmid could write in *Burns Today and Tomorrow* that he had 'proposed the chief toast at several Burns Suppers annually for the past thirty or forty years'. Yet his complaint remained that 'the Scots poetry that has been written in the last forty years by the so-called "new Lallans poets" has been cold-shouldered by the majority of Burnsians, who have shown a disposition lamentably different from that of Burns himself'.[38] MacDiarmid's attempt to reconnect the Burns Movement with modern poetry (not least his own) had failed. Yet without his engagement with that Movement, and especially with the arguments of the Vernacular Circle of the London Burns Club, the Scots poetry for which he is most celebrated might never have been written in the first place.

Before MacDiarmid's day, leading Burns Clubs had toasted contemporary poetry and Scottish literature, making serious efforts to engage with significant living poets. As the twentieth century developed, MacDiarmid's growing hostility helped set the tone for a stand-off between the Burns Movement and contemporary Scottish poets and intellectuals. Edwin Muir, MacDiarmid's early friend and encourager (though later execrated for his ostensible betrayal of poetry in Scots), enjoyed stating that he had never attended a Burns Supper. Supperers rarely toasted living poets or sought much serious engagement with Scottish literature. Though individual tributes to Burns were paid by Edwin Morgan (in *The Whittrick* and elsewhere), by Norman MacCaig (through his 1959 anthology *Honour'd Shade*), and by Iain Crichton Smith (most fully in his *The Human Face* (1996)), none of these was sponsored or supported by the Burns Movement.

Writing about Robert Fergusson, Burns articulated one of the greatest pleas for society to understand and support the modern poet,

> Curse on ungrateful man, that can be pleas'd,
> And yet can starve the author of the pleasure! (K 143, I, 323, 1–2)

Today few poets starve in Scotland; yet their support does not come from the international Burns Federation. It is mistaken of Scottish poets and intellectuals to view Burns Suppers and Clubs as untrue to the spirit of Burns. In writing about him elsewhere, I have tried to show such traditions are in several ways attuned to the Freemason poet whose work so often seems designed to collect a fraternal audience around it – 'And there's a hand, my trusty fiere! / And gie's a hand o' thine!' (K 240, I, 444, 21–2). From the 1997 essay collection *Robert Burns and Cultural Authority* to the 2009 anthology *New Poems, Chiefly in the Scottish Dialect*, I have worked with other contemporary Scottish and non-Scottish writers, female and male, to show that there remains a vital interaction between Burns and today's Scottish literature. To engage with Burns now may mean to react to his work in unexpected or expected ways – whether to his love poems or to his biblical paraphrase – and must not degenerate into pastiche or antiquarianism. Contemporary Scottish poetry has extended more than one hand towards the Burns Movement; I hope the Burns Movement will respond.

New opportunities, most obviously the National Trust for Scotland's Robert Burns Birthplace Museum complex at Alloway, should be made the most of. Nothing would be more appropriate to the legacy of Burns than to make his birthplace (on the model of Wordsworth's Dove Cottage) a venue for readings by the best Scottish and international poets, rather than simply a venue for school trips or gigs by thirteenth-rate 'makars'. I would like to think that, in the spirit *both* of MacDiarmid *and* of the Vernacular Circle of the London Burns Club, the Burns Federation might sponsor such readings, realising that this is the right moment for a re-engagement between contemporary poetry and Burns Suppers. There is no better time than now for Burns to be set again in one of the places he most belongs – among the poets.

Notes

1. Robert Brown, *Paisley Burns Clubs* (Paisley: Alexander Gardner, 1893), pp. 195–218.
2. Alan Riach, 'MacDiarmid's Burns', in Robert Crawford (ed.), *Robert Burns and Cultural Authority* (Edinburgh: Edinburgh University Press, 1997), pp. 198–215; Robert Crawford, 'MacDiarmid in Montrose', in Alex Davis and Lee M. Jenkins (eds), *Locations of Literary Modernism* (Cambridge: Cambridge University Press, 2000), pp. 33–56.
3. Hugh MacDiarmid, *Lucky Poet* (London: Jonathan Cape, 1972), pp. 191, 16.
4. Hugh MacDiarmid, *The Letters*, ed. Alan Bold (London: Hamish Hamilton, 1984), p. 21 (hereafter *Letters*); [C. M. Grieve], 'Burns Conference at Birmingham', *Montrose Review*, 8 September 1922, p. 6.
5. G. Gregory Smith, *Scottish Literature: Character and Influence* (London: Macmillan, 1919), pp. 133–4, 135, 138–9.
6. 'Burns Club of London', *The Scotsman*, 22 August 1921, p. 6.
7. C. M. Grieve, 'Encouragement of Scottish Literature', *The Scotsman*, 26 August 1921, p. 7.
8. William Will, 'Sir George Douglas and the Vernacular Circle', *The Scotsman*, 2 September 1921, p. 6.
9. 'A New Book of Scots', advertisement, *The Scotsman*, 19 September 1921, p. 2.
10. 'Scottish Diminutives', *The Scotsman*, 13 December 1921, p. 6; *Letters*, p. 751 (to the *Aberdeen Free Press*, 15 December 1921).

11. [C. M. Grieve], 'Is "Braid Scots" Dead?', *Montrose Review*, 16 December 1921, p. 6.

12. *Letters*, p. 753 (to the *Aberdeen Free Press*, 21 December 1921).

13. *Letters*, p. 69 (to George Ogilvie, 29 December 1921).

14. 'Scots Vernacular', *The Scotsman*, 14 February 1922, p. 8; 'Vernacular of Lowland Scotland', *The Scotsman*, 2 March 1922, p. 6; 'Vernacular of the Lowlands', *The Scotsman*, 11 April 1922, p. 8.

15. *Letters*, p. 755 (to the *Aberdeen Free Press*, 27 January 1922).

16. Hugh MacDiarmid, *The Raucle Tongue: Hitherto Uncollected Prose, Vol. 1*, ed. Angus Calder, Glen Murray and Alan Riach (Manchester: Carcanet, 1996), pp. 29, 30 (hereafter *RT*).

17. Ibid., p. 30.

18. [C. M. Grieve], 'Burns Conference at Birmingham', *Montrose Review*, 8 September 1922, p. 6.

19. *Letters*, pp. 76–7.

20. *RT*, pp. 31, 32.

21. Hugh MacDiarmid, *Selected Prose*, ed. Alan Riach (Manchester: Carcanet, 1992), pp. 9, 10, 12 (hereafter *SP*).

22. *RT*, pp. 33, 34, 35.

23. Hugh MacDiarmid, *Complete Poems 1920–1976*, ed. Michael Grieve and W. R. Aitken, 2 vols (London: Martin Brian & O'Keeffe, 1978), vol. II, p. 1224 (hereafter *CP*).

24. *RT*, pp. 46, 45.

25. Ibid., pp. 47, 48.

26. *SP*, pp. 20, 22, 23.

27. *RT*, pp. 69, 70, 71.

28. [William Will (ed.)], *The Scottish Tongue: A Series of Lectures on the Vernacular Language of Lowland Scotland* (London: Cassel, 1924), pp. x–xi.

29. Alan Bold, *MacDiarmid* (London: John Murray, 1988), p. 137.

30. *CP*, vol. I, pp. 77, 79.

31. Hugh M'Diarmid, *Penny Wheep* (Edinburgh and London: William Blackwood, 1926), dust jacket, pp. 75–8, advertisement opposite title-page.

32. *CP*, vol. I, pp. 84, 85, 106.

33. Ibid., p. 113.

34. C. M. Grieve (ed.), *Robert Burns* (London: Ernest Benn, [1926]), p. iii.

35. *RT*, pp. 41.

36. *Letters*, p. 346, n. 1.

37. *CP*, vol. I, p. 382.

38. Hugh MacDiarmid, *Albyn: Shorter Books and Monographs*, ed. Alan Riach (Manchester: Carcanet, 1996), pp. 205, 208.

CHAPTER 15

Ireland's National Bard

Bernard O'Donoghue

The rural Ireland I grew up in the 1950s was a remarkably bookish place. You were often advised to 'mind the books' and told 'learning is lightly carried'. A common dictum from people of earlier generations – the people who went through the primary National School system in the early part of the twentieth century – was 'though I did not go much to school myself, I met the scholars coming home'. There was a familiar curriculum in the 'primer' (pronounced 'primmer') in English (as there was for Irish too): Irish legends, like Oisin and the Fianna, tales from Shakespeare, and a substantial body of poetry learned by heart: Stevenson's 'Requiem'; Longfellow's 'My Lost Youth' and 'The Village Blacksmith'; Tennyson's 'Crossing the Bar'; Wordsworth's 'Daffodils' and so on.

Though you often heard these quoted with pride as a feat of memory, they remained page poems. There was another category of poetry which was encountered as part of the oral tradition, often first as songs heard by children from parents and grandparents. Without question Robert Burns was drawn on more commonly than anyone else in these cases: 'Ca' the yowes' (usually referred to as 'My Bonny Dearie'); 'Ye Banks and Braes o' bonie Doon'; 'Comin' through the Rye'; 'Charlie he's my darling' and countless others. It was not just Burns's songs either: everyone knew 'To a Mouse': 'The best laid schemes o' mice an' men / Gang aft agley' (quoted accurately without fail, as I remember). There were lines and phrases that everyone quoted, often without knowing they were Burns: 'The man of independent mind, / He looks and laughs at a' that'; 'While Willie's far frae Logan braes'; 'Such a parcel of rogues in a nation'; 'O wad some Pow'r the giftie gie us / To see ourselves as others see us!'; 'Flow gently, Sweet Afton'. In Irish dancehalls there was a practice of awarding what were called 'spot prizes', in which the band offered a prize to people who could come forward bearing various apparently unlikely items: a picture of a sailor (on a Player's cigarette packet, for the quick-witted or the habituated), or a picture of Robbie Burns – on a packet of 'Sweet Afton'.

There was no native Irish poet/songwriter who remotely rivalled Burns for popularity in that world, or who had such a presence in it. In the course of an interview at the STanza Festival (2010), Dennis O'Driscoll asked Seamus Heaney why 'Robert Burns's songs and poems have fared so much better as literature than Thomas Moore's'. Heaney said that Burns 'seemed a familiar, a family member speaker'. With Burns, Heaney said, 'you were coming home to yourself . . . Moore's writings are very conventional. His songs are beautiful with the airs; but there's nothing like "Ae fond kiss"; nothing that's so close to folk speech. He dates more.'[1] Moore was certainly popular: but 'Believe me, if all those endearing young charms', 'The Meeting of the Waters' and many other great songs, well known as they were, remained attached to a kind of drawing-room world, often to piano accompaniment. Their words were not woven into the everyday as Burns's were throughout the Irish countryside in the mid-twentieth century. And this was by no means confined to Heaney's north where of course the relationship to Scotland is particularly rich and intricate (part of what Heaney is saying). The same was true for County Cork in the 1950s.

I will come back to consider Burns in more detail. But it should be noted first that Scotland was a major element in Irish popular culture generally in that era. In the 1940s and 1950s (when radio was still relatively new) Radio Luxembourg had a place in cultural life that was almost part of the oral tradition in Ireland: and one of the great events of the week was *Scottish Requests* on Luxembourg at 8.00 p.m. on Friday nights. (*Irish Requests*, with Bridie Gallagher, Michael O'Duffy and the rest, was a later offshoot, on Thursdays at 9.30 p.m. – a less celebratory, less weekending hour, and generally a bit of a by-product of the Scottish predecessor, though a highly successful one.) Largely because of 'Scottish Requests', amongst the best-known singers in rural Ireland in that era were Scots: Robert Wilson and Kenneth McKellar for example.[2] The best-known bands were Scottish: Jimmy Shand ('The Bluebell Polka' and 'Whistling Rufus' were the staple of broadcast music at Cork-Kerry football matches in Killarney); and Jim Cameron whose jazzy, saxophone-driven version of 'Scotland the Brave' was the signature tune of the 'Mitchelstown programme' (which advertised the 'processed' cheese which was the only variety widely available in Ireland at the time). The most popular daytime radio programmes were these so-called 'sponsored' programmes, advertising various products: Donnelly's skinless sausages ('the talk of the nation', the jingle said); Urney's chocolate; Gâteaux's cakes; Walton's Music shop whose 'last word is: If you feel like singing, do sing an Irish song.'

Walton's cri de coeur was necessary because the tendency was often *not* to sing an Irish song. There were two dominant alternatives: the American and English chart songs as played on the BBC's *Housewives' Choice* and on Radio Éireann's *Hospital's Requests*; or Scotland. It is still the case that at the end of the night in Irish country pubs one of the commonest songs is 'The Northern Lights of Old Aberdeen', sung in a heart-wrung way by people who have never been anywhere near Aberdeen. The songs children learned at school were either in Irish or the Burns standards. In the 1950s Irish singers recorded Scottish songs without any suggestion that they were not part of their own ethnic heritage: Brendan O'Dowda, for example, singing the beautiful 'Lough Tay Boat Song' which he said he found at source. This moment of cultural history bears recalling because it immediately precedes the explosive popularity of Irish songs led by The Clancy Brothers and The Dubliners. That development was strongly reinforced by the folk era in America of course: Pete and Peggy Seeger, Woody Guthrie, Bob Dylan and the rest. In Scotland (and Manchester) the principal figure was Ewan MacColl whose repertoire included Burns, the Ballads and his own songs. All of these developments brought the songs and poems out of the folk tradition in some ways: the difference maybe was that thereafter people always knew what they were singing, rather than just inheriting it by memory.

This matter of the relationship of the 1960s musicians to the folk tradition raises too, of course, the place of Burns within that whole popular tradition, both geographically and textually. As everyone knows, his relation to the world of the traditional ballads is a complex one, like Yeats's to 'Down by the Salley Gardens' or Padraig Colum's to 'She moved through the Fair'. He collected and reworked a great number of traditional Scottish songs. Like his relationship to the musical tradition of Scotland and the Shetlands generally, his connection to subsequent Irish versions is often indirect. The echo of Burns in Irish music is immensely evocative but misty – perhaps all the more evocative for that. I will take just one famous and slightly involved example: O'Hagan includes 'Lady Mary Ann' in his relatively small selections from the poems, taking the text of the poem, I assume, from Kinsley's authoritative Oxford edition.[3] The poem is clearly a variant of the song widely known in Ireland and England as 'The Bonny Boy' (indeed as commonly played on the Walton's programme, and so presumably 'an Irish song'). There isn't room here to develop the comparison of the various versions in detail, though there is a striking general difference between Burns's poem and the Scottish tradition, on the one hand, and the tragic Irish (and English) versions, on the other. Burns ends in hope:

> But far better days I trust will come again,
> For my bonie laddie's young but he's growin yet. (K 374, II, 642, 19–20)

The Irish/English version – more faithful to the folk-version's tragic origins – ends 'Cruel death put an end to his growing', leaving his young widow to 'weave him a shroud of the ornamental brown'. As with many medieval ballads, lyrics and even romances, we are not entirely sure at what point a particular recension becomes a different work; but the fundamental similarities are unmistakeable. Of course several other Burns songs link to the ballad tradition in a similar way. 'Lord Ronald' ('Oh where hae ye been, Lord Ronald, my son?': K 352, II, 612, 1–2) extends backwards to the Middle Ages but is widely attested in Ireland, in versions whose music is analysed as classic material in the Irish *sean nós* singing tradition. 'Lord Gregory' ('Lord Gregory ope thy door': K 399, II, 678, 4) has an

Irish version that is localised in Cappoquin, Co. Waterford, named in the text.

It might seem that this is perhaps not so much a point about Burns in particular as about the ever-widening extension of the heritage of the ballad in English and Scots from the Middle Ages onwards. But it is more than this: Irish traditional music, notably in the names of dance tunes, is full of such half-parallels and echoes with Burns. Among the best known tunes are the reels 'My love is but a lassie yet' (which in Ireland never has the Burns words: K 293, II, 516)[4] and 'The Tarbolton'. The latter is a particularly interesting case because there is no suggestion of a connection with the Burns-related placename, though that is surely the origin of the Irish tune's name. The widely known Irish dance-tune 'The Drunken Gauger' (Exciseman) suggests comparison with Burns's profession, unloved both by him and by everyone else, and with his cheerful song 'The Jolly Gauger' (K 612, II, 902). 'Bonnie Dundee' and 'Johnie Cope' are likewise universally known dance tunes whose connexion with their origins in Burns and Scotland has been lost.

The central question raised insistently by O'Hagan in his introduction is: 'why is Burns so easy to market to the world?' He concludes – not entirely enthusiastically – that the poet 'has been harnessed now, like no one else, to represent the romantic spirit of the common man, and there are common men the world over who are keen to hear him'.[5] Is Burns then of equal appeal to 'the world over', as he was to Soviet Russia for example? Is he 'not only for [O'Hagan] or for Scotland, but for the world?'[6] To return to my central theme here, is there then nothing very particular about his bardic presence in Ireland in the mid-twentieth century? I think there was, simply in the pervasiveness of Burns echoes and quotations. The *particular* texts of Burns were seen as a resource that could be drawn on by Irish writers, with a status that was something like a secular Bible. O'Hagan notes Sean O'Casey's derivation of his title *The Silver Tassie* from the song 'My bony Mary'. At an earlier point in the tradition, the Irish song 'The Curragh of Kildare' has had its somewhat uninspired chorus deleted by Burns for his beautiful *reverdie* 'The Winter it is past' (K 218, II, 409).[7] Mick Hanly composed a new song called 'My Love is like a Red, Red Rose' which takes not only its title but its metrical structure and some of its lines from Burns. And it doesn't need remarking that Burns is a staple element in the repertoire of several Irish singers and groups: songs like 'Leezie Lindsay', 'McPherson's Farewell', 'John Barleycorn' and the rest. Some Burns songs have had a new incarnation in the context of modern socialist politics, in Ireland as well as Scotland: 'Such a Parcel of Rogues' and 'Ye Jacobites by Name' have gained a new familiarity. And it is arguable that some great twentieth-century songs, such as Hamish Henderson's 'Farewell to Sicily', could not have been written without Burns. He was the creator of their genre.

Such a genre of course reminds us that there is no doubt that the popularity of Burns in Ireland dates back to the Jacobite period. Again, there is a wider Scottish context here in which the Stuart and Napoleonic worlds are complicatedly intertwined.[8] In songs like 'The Bonny Light Horseman' the Bonnie Prince Charlie laments metamorphose seamlessly into the Napoleonic. Many of the most celebrated poems of the 'popular' Irish-language poet Eoghan Rua Ó Súilleabháin (1748–1784: thus an earlier contemporary of Burns and a similar *poète maudit* with a similar place in popular lore and imagination) were Jacobite songs in Irish. Indeed if we are to look for an Irish national bard to offer as an alternative to Burns, Ó Súilleabháin – the prototype for the poet in Thomas Flanagan's novel *The Year of the French* in 1979 – is as likely as anyone. But by the twentieth century that is a different story. A nomination for a poet whose language approximates to the everyday language of the people – more so than Thomas Moore or Yeats – has to be a writer in the modern English vernacular of Ireland.

Many elements of Burns's Scots vernacular are not readily intelligible in the south of Ireland though. As Heaney's wonderful 'A Birl for Burns', prefixed to O'Hagan's book, illustrates so eloquently, there is a surer linguistic affinity with Ulster Scots.[9] But Burns is the patron-figure of the English-derived vernacular of the Celtic nations. Hugh MacDiarmid recalls how the Scottish Renaissance Movement in the 1920s, in its attempt 'to get Scottish poetry out of the doldrums into which it had fallen after the death of Burns, adopted as its rallying cry 'Not Burns – Dunbar!'[10] But, understandable and successful as that movement was, its slogan is missing the point of Burns. Surely he, more than anyone, is the opposite of the 'apparently bottomless abyss of doggerel, moralistic rubbish, mawkish sentimentality and witless jocosity' into which, according to MacDiarmid, the once great Scottish tradition had fallen. Burns's unparalleled combination of the spare universality of the ballad's themes with a distinctive personal voice is exactly the cure for a' that. It is the recognition of those qualities of lucidity, vividness and general truth that finds an echo in every breast – as was claimed for Byron. They were certainly the qualities that made Burns's lines and songs the most prominent and loved vernacular literature in the Irish countryside I grew up in.

Notes

1. Dennis O'Driscoll, 'Talking Scots with Seamus Heaney', *The Dark Horse* 26 (Winter/Spring 2011), pp. 8–12, 9.
2. They are both mentioned in Andrew O'Hagan's delightful anniversary tribute *A Night Out with Robert Burns: The Greatest Poems* (Edinburgh: Canongate, 2008) as interpreters of 'A Red Red Rose': McKellar sings it 'with the sonority of the truly smitten'; Wilson 'packs it with regret' (24). My teenage sister Margaret was truly smitten with both of them. When Wilson briefly went mysteriously missing in County Waterford in the late 1950s, her worry about him disrupted her preparations for the Inter Cert examination.

3. O'Hagan, *Night Out*, pp. 28–9; K 374, II, 642. The prototype of the song is a great deal older, dating back at least to the early seventeenth century.

4. O'Hagan, *Night Out*, p. 14.

5. Ibid., p. xix.

6. Ibid., p. xxvii.

7. For a view that Burns's doctoring was a disimprovement, see Patrick Crotty, 'Introduction', in Patrick Crotty (ed.), *The Penguin Book of Irish Poetry* (London: Penguin, 2010), pp. xliii–lxxxviii, lxxv. Crotty's text 'My Love is Like the Sun' (pp. 419–20) is unquestionably the finest version of the poem.

8. The classic discussion of these affinities is E. W. McFarland, *Ireland and Scotland in the Age of Revolution: Planting the Green Bough* (Edinburgh: Edinburgh University Press, 1994). The best recent examination of the political significance of Burns is Liam McIlvanney's elegant *Burns the Radical: Poetry and Politics in Late Eighteenth-Century Scotland* (East Linton: Tuckwell Press, 2002).

9. O'Hagan, *Night Out*, pp. viii–ix.

10. Hugh MacDiarmid, 'Introduction', in Robert Henryson, *Henryson*, Poet to Poet (Harmondsworth: Penguin, 1973), pp. 7–16, 7. With reassuring perversity of course, MacDiarmid is going on to argue 'Not Dunbar – Henryson!'

CHAPTER 16

The Collapse of Distance: Heaney's Burns and the 1990s

Fiona Stafford

When Seamus Heaney was invited to lecture at the Burns Bicentenary celebrations in St Andrews in 1996, he struck a characteristically personal note, recalling the startling experience of reading Burns for the first time at school: 'The way Burns sounded, his choice of words, his rhymes and metaphors, all collapsed the distance I expected to feel between myself and the schoolbook poetry I encountered first at Anahorish Elementary School.'[1] As a boy, he had assumed that the printed page of the text book must inevitably silence playground chatter, transporting the entire class 'to a land of formal words where we would have to be constantly on our best verbal behaviour'. The discovery of Burns's Mouse, nestling between Shelley's Skylark and Blake's Tyger was unexpected, to say the least – 'the word "wee" put its stressed foot down and in one pre-emptive vocative strike took over the emotional and cultural ground, dispossessing the rights of standard English and offering asylum to all vernacular comers'.[2] It was certainly an inviting approach for an Irish poet to adopt when addressing a largely Scottish audience on the subject of their national bard, because it emphasised a common familiarity with language resistant to Standard English. Self-consciousness about the gulf between speech and school-book revealed an elocutionary sensitivity that might link twentieth-century Ulster with eighteenth-century Scotland. Since Heaney's host, Robert Crawford, was renowned for tracking an invidious cultural imperialism back to the time of Burns, it was a well-judged gesture of friendship, underlined by specific reference to Crawford's well-known *Devolving English Literature* (1992).

In 1996, as the impetus towards political devolution in Scotland gathered pace, such a clear nod to Scottish national feeling was only too appropriate. When Heaney's lecture appeared in print a year later in Crawford's *Robert Burns and Cultural Authority*, it seemed to endorse the editor's judgement that 'Burns's resolute deployment of the Scots vernacular is . . . the aspect of Burns's poetry which we most admire today.'[3] To see Heaney's essay, 'Burns's Art Speech', purely in the context of the St Andrews celebrations would, however, be to miss its wider significance for understanding Heaney's own work, Burns's place in late twentieth-century culture and even lyric poetry more broadly. Though first published in Crawford's Bicentenary volume, a revised version of the essay subsequently appeared in

Heaney's substantial prose collection, *Finders Keepers*, signalling its importance to Heaney as well as to Burns criticism. When republished in 2002,
'Burns's Art Speech' lost the reference to *Devolving English Literature*, lost
its crack about local rhymes and gained an epigraph from Joseph Brodsky,
through the deft redeployment of a quotation originally included in the
body of the essay. The very colloquial quality that Burns had elicited from
Heaney in St Andrews had, after all, been modified to fit the formality of
the printed page.

As Brodsky's words moved to prime position under the title, the essay
acquired the authority of established literary discourse:

> Poets' real biographies are like those of birds . . . their real data are in the way
> they sound. A poet's biography is in his vowels and sibilants, in his metres,
> rhymes and metaphors . . . With poets, the choice of words is invariably more
> telling than the story they tell . . . Joseph Brodsky, *Less Than One*.[4]

To introduce an essay with an epigraph of this kind was to indicate that
what followed had general as well as particular insights into poetry, drawn
from wide knowledge of different writers. Heaney had not lost interest in
the Scottishness of Burns, whose choice of 'vowels and sibilants . . . metres,
rhymes, metaphors' were largely determined by his native tongue; but the
quotation introduced a formal tone in contrast with the familiarity of Burns.
In *Finders Keepers*, the opening sentence below the epigraph reads 'From
the start, the way Burns sounded made me feel close to him' – a much more
emphatic expression of affinity than the somewhat apologetic tone of the
original: 'There is something about the poetry of Robert Burns and about
the figure of Burns himself that makes me uneasy about lecturing on him at
all.'[5] Heaney's discussion was now more clearly poised between the pano-
rama and the close-up, its poetic and personal detail gaining force from the
background of wider consideration.

The reference to Brodsky, who died on 28 January 1996, three days
after Burns Night, was, as this essay will demonstrate, an affectionate tribute to a much-lamented friend; but it reminded Heaney's readers that his
critical authority drew on acquaintance with poets of international standing
and numerous literary traditions, whatever his lingering affection for Scots
vocabulary. The confident assertion that 'Burns is a world poet because of
his genius, not because of his Scottishness' is possible because of the careful
references to both a personal, almost intuitive, understanding of Burns's
language and a gradually acquired knowledge of different poetic traditions.[6]
Heaney might claim an affinity with his Scottish predecessor, being similarly situated 'at the old crossroads where the local and the learned meet',
but since the insight emerged through conversation with a Russian dis-
sident poet it was a truth discovered rather than inherited.[7] The grand
statement about Burns as a world poet comes immediately after the more
cautionary observation that 'poems and poets do not become available to

their audience on the simple basis of ethnic or linguistic kinship'.[8] In other words, no amount of shared vocabulary would make Burns a congenial figure without his other fine qualities – the technical skill, humour, sympathy, honesty and depth of his poems, which combine to move readers everywhere, irrespective of their own modes of speech.

The care with which Heaney engaged with Burns reveals the potential difficulties of seeking connections between modern Irish poetry and Scottish tradition. It suggests a need to establish special credentials before any critical opinion might be offered – to divert attention from the obvious differences in time, place and religion and thereby establish common ground for literary understanding. The authority of wide literary knowledge is one source of credibility, lifelong familiarity with distinctive regional speech is another. If the personal note rang out clearly, it played against a recurrent theme, which muted self-indulgence to make the personal resonate with larger meaning, for Northern Irish homeliness was closely allied to less comfortable history – Burns's 'wee' was also a 'we'. Heaney explained his early familiarity with the word by recalling the traces of Elizabethan English and Lowland Scots that coloured the speech of Anahorish with Ayrshire resonances. To recognise shared pronunciation was also to acknowledge a connection that has often seemed much harder to articulate, especially for a Catholic poet from Derry. While John Hewitt had felt able to write about the Burns tradition in relation to the Rhyming Weavers of Ulster in the 1970s, the enduring presence of a Protestant poet was not necessarily a subject to appeal to Northern Irish Catholics during the Troubles.[9] In 1996, however, two years after the IRA Ceasefire, it was apparently possible to pay tribute to the rich linguistic legacy of Ireland's painful past and to point to cultural links rather than divisions.

Heaney's attitude at the Burns Bicentenary was markedly different from his adaptation of Burns's signature stanza in 1983, when Andrew Motion and Blake Morrison included his work in *The Penguin Book of Contemporary British Poetry*. In *An Open Letter*, Heaney's indignant 'My passport's green' recalled the self-assertive persona of Burns's verse epistles to John Lapraik and, in so doing, cast Burns as the voice of regional resistance to Standard English and metropolitan high-handedness.[10] By 1996, however, fresh from the international celebration of his Nobel Prize, Heaney's emphasis was on poetry's marvellous capacity to cross distances and make connections between those separated by geography, nationality, religion or time. The Nobel lecture, 'Crediting Poetry', began with recollections of the family wireless, with its exciting foreign languages and distant place names, opening imaginative horizons and extending sympathies beyond the confines of home.[11] The wireless was both an affectionate image of childhood and of words overcoming distance – a preoccupation which informed the lecture on Burns the following year.

Though not universally welcomed in Belfast, Heaney's Nobel award coincided with a general movement towards greater toleration of cultural difference within the North of Ireland.[12] His own hope, clearly articulated in 'Crediting Poetry', for 'a world where respect for the validity of every tradition will issue in the creation and maintenance of a salubrious political space' was fostered by the mood of the mid-1990s and found further expression at the Burns Bicentenary.[13] Heaney's willingness to acknowledge the familiarity of Burns's language accorded well with the contemporary revival of Ulster Scots. As Liam McIlvanney has pointed out, the Ulster-Scots Language Society was founded in 1992 and the Good Friday Agreement, signed six years later, included a clause recognising the cultural richness of Ireland. Heaney's acceptance of the common linguistic inheritance of Ulster and Ayrshire was thus in keeping with the contemporary movement towards recognising 'the importance of respect, understanding and tolerance in relation to linguistic diversity, including in Northern Ireland, the Irish language, Ulster Scots and the languages of the various ethnic communities'.[14]

The desire, evident in 'Crediting Poetry', for 'a less binary and altogether less binding vocabulary', also informed Heaney's translation of *Beowulf*, another work of the 1990s, which included a passionate account of his liberation from linguistic conditioning.[15] Again he returned to his education, recalling an undergraduate lecture where John Braidwood had explained that 'whiskey is the same word as the Irish and Scots Gaelic word *uisce* meaning water, and that the River Usk in Britain is therefore to some extent the River Uisce (or Whiskey)'.[16] The effect of this revelation was apparently just as startling as his early encounter with Burns, for 'The Irish/English duality, the Celtic/Saxon antithesis were momentarily collapsed and in the resulting etymological eddy a gleam of recognition flashed through the synapses.'[17] The collapse of distance is very similar to that celebrated in 'Burns's Art Speech', but here it related explicitly to the rigidity of cultural divisions within Ireland and the heady excitement of discovering a way to creative freedom. The confluence of 'the Usk, the uisce and the whiskey' was 'a place where the spirit might find a loophole, an escape route . . . into some unpartitioned linguistic country'.[18]

Heaney's fascination with the word 'whiskey' as the key to unlocking prisons of entrenched opinion in Ireland made him similarly receptive to Burns's bold mixture of different linguistic traditions – 'Burns, we gratefully realise, opened his door to a great variety of linguistic callers.'[19] Far from being limited to the language of his neighbours, Heaney recognised Burns's readiness to adopt phrases from Beattie, Thomson, Milton or Pope. Burns knew very well that 'FREEDOM and WHISKY gang thegither' (K 81, I, 191, 185), a partnership that gathers additional force when seen in the light of Heaney's enthusiasm for etymological liberation. Despite glimpses of a new linguistic freedom, however, the Burns essay still reveals an acute awareness of the old divisions of Heaney's homeland, including not only warm acknowledgement of Ulster Scots but also extensive reference to the poetry of Gaelic Ireland. For no sooner has the colloquial closeness of 'To a Mouse' been celebrated than a connection to MacGiolla Ghunna's 'The Yellow Bittern' is suggested, while Burns's 'The Vision' is presented as an *aisling*. The balance is every bit as delicate as that between the local and the learned and signals a similar desire for inclusiveness. Heaney was only too aware of the potentially alienating effects of certain kinds of closeness or 'kinship' and hence the instinct to stand back, to take stock, to consider other points of view. At the same time, his receptiveness to the emotional charge of lyric poetry meant that some collapsing of distance seemed crucial to artistic achievement.

As the Burns essay unfolds, initial gratitude for familiar vocabulary is overtaken by the revelation of different kinds of intimacy. The early surprise of recognising home in a schoolbook leads to an even more startling experience of collapsing distance when the mature poet re-encounters Burns. For while Heaney emphasises the common inheritance of Ulster Scots in the vocabulary of Irish and Scottish poets, the 'collapse of distance' described in his essay is more emotional than political. The correspondence perceived between Burns and MacGiolla Ghunna lies not so much in the capacity to pronounce 'och' as in 'a similar sense of vulnerability and sympathy'.[20] To read 'Burns's Art Speech' means grappling with the profoundly human quality of Heaney's attitude to literature and therefore with the feelings embodied in lyric poetry.

Questions over whether lyric verse can touch readers of very different creeds and classes are recurrent in Heaney's critical meditations. If poets' biographies lie in their choice of words and rhythms, however, their own language may alienate some readers, irrespective of what their poetry might attempt to convey. Ever since *Poems, Chiefly in the Scottish Dialect* first appeared in 1786, critical responses have been coloured by a suspicion that no one outwith Scotland could fully understand Burns. The issue that informs 'Burns's Art Speech' is central to Heaney's wider sense of a poet's social, moral and artistic responsibilities and the related internal conflicts. His critical reading moves accordingly between intense identification and judicious reflection, between crediting the emotional force of poetry and attending to its complexity – between closeness and distance.

For Heaney, Burns's skilful deployment of the spoken word is meaningful not just as an assertion of the value of non-standard language but rather as evidence of an 'emotional fidelity' and refusal to condescend. It is the unexpected 'outrush of fellow-feeling', a discovery of equality in the unlikeliest place, that demolishes the distances between poet, object and audience. Burns's emotional truth prompts a correspondingly honest self-exposure in Heaney, which demonstrates, in turn, the power of lyric poetry to move readers, deepen sympathy and encourage self-knowledge.

It rapidly becomes obvious that the anecdote about familiar colloquialisms was a prelude to explaining the poem's real meaning to the adult poet:

> The plough of the living voice gets set deeper and deeper in the psychic ground, dives more and more purposefully into the subsoil of the intuitions until finally it breaks open a nest inside the poet's own head and leaves him exposed to his own profoundest forebodings.[21]

The image of ploughing has special resonance for both Burns and Heaney, but all readers can share the experience of finding their secret psychic nests broken open by a poem. If such emotional fidelity induces momentary panic, it is checked by the profound sense of fellow-feeling and admiration for the words that could work such an epiphany. This is the real collapse of distance celebrated in Heaney's essay on Burns.

Heaney offers a kind of criticism that leaps over state boundaries and academic periodisation to reveal new things about both the poet observed and the poet-observer. As Don Paterson has pointed out, Burns is so complicated and multi-dimensional that all readers can respond to his work 'according to their own personal, critical or neurotic agenda'.[22] Though Heaney's reading could hardly be described as 'neurotic', it is unashamedly personal and very much part of his own critical project. He has written eloquently about the capacity of poems to provide various kinds of 'redress' and Burns elicits a gratitude akin to that accorded to the other great poets in Heaney's personal Pantheon.[23] Though separated by two centuries, by education, by religion, by the Irish Sea and by the culture that has grown up around each, Heaney insists that the distances can still collapse to reveal an essential sympathy. But whether his image of Burns is really a projection of his own compulsions is a matter for further consideration. Does the value of 'Burns's Art Speech' lie in its revelations about Burns, about lyric poetry, or about Heaney?

If we compare Heaney's essay with some of the other chapters in Crawford's Bicentenary volume, it soon becomes clear that not all the contributors were as quick to find distances collapsing. As was to be expected in 1996, Burns was attracting special attention in Scotland, but, far from uniting opinion, his work seemed to reveal all kinds of internal division. Unlike the two-hundred and fiftieth celebrations of 2009, when Burns's birth provided the focus for a national Year of Homecoming, Scottish cultural self-confidence was rather less secure. Though still incontrovertibly the national Bard, whose great anthem of democracy, 'A Man's a man for a' that', would be the obvious choice for opening the new Scottish Parliament in 1999, Burns's work provoked complicated responses from those who might be assumed to be his chief representatives in the late twentieth century. Crawford's own essay for the Bicentenary volume begins with emphasis on the Scots language, but then develops into an analysis of the masculine sociability celebrated in the poems of Fergusson and Burns. The heartwarming camaraderie of 'To a Haggis' and its inspiration, Fergusson's 'To the Principal and Professors of the University of St Andrews, on their superb treat to Dr Samuel Johnson', is shown to be founded on exclusion – not just of the foreign but also the female. As Crawford points out, both Fergusson and Burns 'nourished and were nourished by' the exclusively male clubs of eighteenth-century Scotland.[24] For the poet whose collection, *Masculinity*, appeared in the same year as the Burns Bicentenary, the culture of the drinking club was not merely a subject for historical analysis. Far from emphasising his personal closeness to Burns, Crawford, though not immune to the comic vitality of eighteenth-century masculine culture, perceived a world polarised by gender and thus representing a distance to be reinforced rather than collapsed.

For Crawford, as for many of the Scottish poets who reflected on their great bard's birthday in 1996, Burns was both a national success and a national embarrassment. Pride in a poet who was known across the world, who stood for the use of Scots as a literary language, and whose technical virtuosity was matched by an astonishing range of tones and registers was uncomfortably mixed with concerns about the images his popularity had generated. Crawford's desire to situate masculine clubs firmly in the eighteenth century reflected his uneasiness about the culture that continued to flourish in Burns clubs across the globe, where haggis and whisky made for a particular kind of male communion. His volume includes A. L. Kennedy's vivid account of her own encounter with a remarkable image of Tam o' Shanter pursued by a scantily clad, but 'monumentally well endowed', witch on the wall of a Burns Club in the Heart of England.[25] The arresting anecdote leads on to a discussion of Burns's sex life and the surrounding myths, which have contributed to a modern, popular idea of 'the writer' as a 'boozing, fornicating, self-destructive' figure.[26] Kennedy argues that, as a woman writer, she is denied both the model and the forgiving fascination that extends to her male counterparts: 'Our archetypes are held to be 110 per cent male, and the malest of them all is Burns'.[27] The essay is entertaining enough but, like Crawford's contribution, it reveals an aspect of Burns – or at least of his legacy – that has not been as inclusive as the more sympathetic responses to his work might suggest.

In 1996, Burns's massive popularity, though evidence of his undiminished importance to so many Scots, seemed to prompt disquiet rather than satisfaction from many modern poets. Paterson noted that the Bicentenary was greeted by 'almost swaggering indifference from the Southron literati', but laid the blame on Scottish rather than English doorsteps, observing that 'the greatest service the Scots could perform would be to rescue Burns from his own bardolatry'.[28] In Paterson's eyes, it was not Burns's language that deterred non-Scots from taking his work seriously, for he was as conscious as Heaney of Burns's linguistic range and more willing to admit that 'even Scots readers will struggle, in places, without a glossary'.[29] For Paterson, the obstacles to reaching Burns were not those imposed by language, time or place but rather by the well-intentioned adulation of biographers and Burns Clubs. As long as Burns remained 'within his sealed shortie tin', he was not so much at a distance that needed collapsing as in a prison waiting to be liberated.[30]

George Mackay Brown, who wrote several poems for Burns in the 1990s, seemed especially troubled by the mixed legacy. His complicated sympathies emerged in poems such as 'A January Day: Burns', with its admiration for the poet and dismay at his audiences:

> I thought of the immortal
> January maker, created (it seems)
> To hammer out winter's worst
> For hansel of delight for a few dour folk.[31]

In his 1996 poem for Burns Day, Mackay Brown imagined the Lords of Hell keeping their eye on 'a young farmer / With a liking for fiddles and girls' but, having failed to defeat him through the normal methods, turning to desperate measures:

> We will try diminishment now
> With couthy quotes, skirlings, haggis suppers.[32]

Perhaps his most substantial Burns poem, 'January, the Twenty-fifth', written in 1990, shows that Mackay Brown was as alert as Paterson to the multifaceted attraction of Burns, but the point was made through simple words, apparently overheard in the local pub:

> The old men said the name Robbie Burns
> As if he'd farmed
> Very recently, in Cairston or Stenness or Hoy.[33]

The tone is as affectionate as Heaney's at the Bicentenary and similarly captures the appeal of Burns to the bloke at the bar – to the heirs of Tam and Souter Johnnie. Though sympathetically portrayed, however, the men's shared admiration for Burns's dual successes – '*What a man, what a man!* they said . . . *What a man for the drink! / What a man for the lasses!*' – are reminiscent of the uneasiness acknowledged by Crawford and Kennedy. The Orcadian Burns was just as exclusively male as the figure encountered by Kennedy in the heart of England, it seems.

Mackay Brown knew that the brotherhood created by poetry could also be exclusive and so his poem, unsentimental in its exposure of a camaraderie based on rejection, shows a nameless tinker being laughed out of the warm bar. It is hardly the image of a poet who offers asylum to all. Mackay Brown demonstrates nonetheless, how poetry can still provide solace to the scapegoat, as the tinker, forced to retreat in shame, emerges from the poem as the voice of wisdom, unconsciously able to express a truth withheld from those who think they know. The question that has provoked such hilarity among the regulars is simple enough: 'Is Burns still alive?' But the real answer is understood by the poet-narrator, whose closing advice to 'Stand a moment / There, on the brae: under the white star' is taken directly from songs composed two centuries earlier and still being sung.

Burns's popular appeal is deftly caught, nevertheless, in a poem that pays him tribute in refusing to gloss local place names or make concessions to remote readers. Mackay Brown was just as much a poet of the parish as Burns – a quality celebrated by Patrick Kavanagh in an essay cited approvingly by Heaney in 'Burns's Art Speech'.[34] Mackay Brown also associated Burns with childhood, though, unlike Heaney's warm recollections, the temperature of Mackay Brown's poem cools as the scene shifts from the pub to the classroom where the Hamnavoe children groan inwardly at being instructed to learn 'To a Mouse' by heart. There is no delightful collapse of distance here, as Burns's poem is imposed on baffled schoolchildren. Mackay Brown looked back on his formal education with horror, believing that the formative years were better spent swimming, sailing or hill-climbing than 'cutting up' texts and thereby instilling a widespread 'charnel-house revulsion' of literature.[35] In his poem, Burns seems another brick in the wall of the Stromness Academy and the lasting memory of mental hard labour reveals his indignation over the failure of the Scottish education system to nurture any love of literature in young minds.

The language employed to convey the schoolboys' struggle, however, echoes both Burns and Heaney:

> Words like thistles and thorns
> They ploughed through the winter language
> And pity ran for cover
> This way and this, and entered
> A few small cold wondering hearts.

The lines may recreate the reluctance of the classroom but they also reveal the consolations of poetry, through echoes of 'To a Mouse' and the Glanmore Sonnets. Painful memories of school are infused with a more positive, retrospective understanding of poetry, to reveal that learning 'by heart' was, after all, an education of the heart, achieved by ploughing through hard words. Mackay Brown's poem demonstrates that at least one of the young souls had a fair seed time, even if he hadn't realised it at the time.

Though isolated from the cultural mainland in Orkney, Mackay Brown shows, through echoes of Heaney, that contemporary poems can still reach out to other poets, offering powerful defences against the Lords of Hell. Despite the acknowledgement of some less appealing dimensions of Burns's place in Scottish culture, Mackay Brown presents him as a living presence, capable of crossing distances, uniting generations, inspiring warm emotions, rescuing the lonely – and provoking fresh composition. For his own readiness to respond in verse rather than prose is in itself a testament to Burns's long creative life. Rather than employ Standard Habbie, he recalls Burns not only through images of an Orkney January but also through snatches of song and the mixture of longer and shorter line stanzas that seem to gesture towards the familiar poems. Douglas Dunn has suggested that the Burns stanza cannot be employed effectively by contemporary Scots because, to be true to Burns's spirit, poetry must be 'progressive . . . experimental and courageous'.[36] While he accepted that poets from other nations, including Heaney, could adapt the stanza skilfully, he was adamant that modern Scottish poetry demanded that newer forms are needed. Paterson agreed, though it was the Habbie's accommodation of 'both humorous and grave registers within the same poem' that struck him as rendering it unusable by contemporary poets.[37] In either case, self-consciousness over the national bard would have made it difficult for a Scottish poet in the 1990s to compose a poem like Heaney's 'A Birl for Burns'. Nevertheless, Mackay Brown's repeated, troubled tributes during the dark winters of the 1990s show that some contemporary poets at least were prepared to address their complicated responses in verse, if not in Burns's own stanza, 'tight and trig'.[38]

Though Dunn has largely eschewed Standard Habbie (except for a poem in *St Kilda's Parliament*), he is nevertheless clear about the reasons for Burns's cultural longevity, independently of the annual January rituals and recitations. Less troubled by the Burns cult than many of his colleagues, Dunn's essay in the Bicentenary volume emphasised that the poet's survival resulted from his technical virtuosity. Dunn explored Burns's 'entire system of resonance, his acoustic and voice', including his rapid mastery of Standard Habbie and accomplished use of the challenging Scottish forms of *Christis Kirk* and *The Cherry and the Slae*.[39] The concern, throughout, was not with technical exposition alone, however, but with the psychological dimensions of Burns's choices. In 'Holy Fair', for example, the 'technical sorcery of the verse is a counterpart to the gaiety and animation of the scenes which it brings to life'.[40] The varied appeal of Burns is abundantly evident in Dunn's attention to both the lively comic verse and the special 'sorrow' of a man forced to defend his own world from the prejudices of outsiders. Though unperturbed by Burns's modern followers, Dunn still demonstrated powerful sympathy for a fellow artist, thwarted and dismayed by his audience.

Like Heaney, Dunn also turned to Brodsky in order to make sense of Burns's practice: ' "Sorrow controlled by meter" may do for you as a provisional definition of humility, if not of the entire art of poetry.'[41] Dunn quotes from Brodsky's essay on Auden which suggested that poetic metres not only express but also offer a means to control powerful feeling. Brodsky, too, had spoken with the authority of a practising poet, observing that 'one doesn't choose one's meter; it's the other way around, for meters have been around longer than any poet'.[42] This is, paradoxically, why rhymes and metres reveal so much about the poet and why Dunn emphasised the special rhythms of Burns's traditional Scottish metres. The poet's biography is evident in his metrical choice not just because he uses what is available locally but also, as Dunn and Brodsky both recognised, because rhymes and rhythms have special psychic resonance. Heaney was equally conscious of Burns's 'deeper poetic self', finding, when he revisited the poetry for the Bicentenary, 'something much bigger and older and more ballad-fastened', whose cadence matched the 'contours of immemorial utterances made to the same effect'.[43] As he had put it more succinctly a few weeks before in 'Audenesque', his own elegy for Brodsky, 'Grief and metre order us.'[44]

Thoughts of Brodsky dominated the winter months of 1996, between the anniversary of Burns's birth and the Bicentenary gathering in St Andrews. When Heaney commemorated Brodsky, the poem published on 9 February in the *Times Literary Supplement* was 'Audenesque' not only in its evocation of 'In Memoriam W. B. Yeats' but also in its recollection of Brodsky's aesthetic ideas: 'Joseph, yes, you know the beat / Wystan Auden's metric feet / Marched to it, unstressed and stressed'. It is unsurprising then, that the lecture on Burns, delivered in April should have included a conversation with Brodsky on the question of rhymes – 'what was the best rhyme in English for love? Dove? Move? Shove?' 'No, no', said Joseph, 'the best rhyme is Auden's, – Diaghelev!'[45] In the lecture, the exchange sounded anecdotal – good crack appropriate for Burns – but it was also alluding less obviously to Brodsky's analysis of 'On September 1, 1939', which dwelled on Auden's use of rhyme and the daring pairing of 'love' with 'Diaghelev':

> What mad Nijinsky wrote
> About Diaghilev
> Is true of the normal heart;
> For the error bred in the bone
> Of each woman and each man
> Craves what it cannot have,
> Not universal love
> But to be loved alone.[46]

In Auden's poem, the two rhyme-words are separated by four others, one of which ends in a half-rhyme – 'have'. For Brodsky, this imposition of distance was crucial, since it precluded any easy equation of 'Diaghelev' and 'love', embodying in the frustrated rhyme its painful truth: 'Diaghelev cannot have love'. Since he also suggested that 'Diaghelev' stands for art, Brodsky was making a specific point about Auden's poem and a much larger point about lyric poetry in general, which of course has a bearing on understanding both Burns and Heaney.

Heaney's admiration for Burns's ability to collapse distances takes on a new dimension once the more pervasive presence of Brodsky becomes visible, since it extends his discussion beyond the specific case. In 'On September, 1939', Brodsky had developed thoughts on the essential principle of rhyme, suggesting that it enabled a sense of 'proximity between seemingly separate entities', making rhyme itself a kind of 'closeness'.[47] According to Brodsky, this was the key to poetry's general value for humanity, since 'closeness', whether between 'objects, ideas, concepts, causes and effects' was a kind of rhyme. Heaney's comment that the way 'Burns sounded made me feel close to him' takes on an even deeper resonance when read in proximity to Brodsky's argument and, by effectively demolishing the distance between poet, reader and text, it also collapses time.

To argue that rhymes are a means to similarities between things normally seen as separate is to suggest that traditional lyric poetry is largely driven by a desire to collapse distance. This is certainly true of the lyric chosen by Heaney to illustrate Burns's deep, poetic self and his instinct for 'immemorial utterances' – 'Ae fond kiss, and then we sever!' Brodsky's essay, though focusing intently on Auden's language, metre and rhyme, was also premised on the hope that readers would develop, through better understanding of the poet's craft, 'the same sentiment toward this poem as the one that prompted it into existence – one of love'.[48] If poetry is prompted by love, or by a craving for what it cannot have, then the collapse of distance must be its goal. The corollary, of course, is that overcoming distance would necessarily halt the driving intensity of art, charging the pursuit with dread as well as desire. And it is worth recalling Paterson, here, who regards Burns as 'at heart a love-poet' and observes that 'the exact synonym of "consummated" in Burns's psyche' is '"finished"'.[49] The principle of proximity requires a sense of distance to realise its own value, while the lyric moment is intensified by the recognition of loss, absence or transience. Whether a poem is attempting to bridge the gulf between lovers, between the mourner and deceased, the adult and childhood, the exile and nation or, simply, the poet and reader, its rhymes, words and metres work together to make the distance collapse.

Much modern lyric verse is born from a sense of longing, and the feeling, expressed by Dunn in relation to the Burns stanza, that traditional rhyme schemes are no longer quite right for the modern world only adds to the distance against which lyric is poised. Heaney's 'Audenesque' nevertheless wears its rhymes and allusiveness boldly, as if the shock of sudden bereavement must be countered by marshalling a great troop of strong poetic voices. Whether Auden's marching feet can cross the great gulf between the living and the dead, or merely serve to accentuate it, is part of the elegist's struggle with a form in which the consciousness of distance and desire for its collapse are most intense. The poem is more than an expression of personal grief or meditation on death, for Heaney paid tribute to his friend by writing him into a great tradition of earlier elegies and, in so doing, explored the same large questions he would consider at the Burns

Bicentenary: how and why are poets remembered? And what is their true legacy, private or public?

Although Heaney imitated Auden's form, he was answering the famous pronouncement that 'poetry makes nothing happen', by celebrating Brodsky's creative energy ('revving English like a car') and his high-profile resistance to the Soviet state (in the recurrent image of ice). The intricacy of the allusive patterning was also part of Heaney's affirmation of poetry as an active force, since the cryptic reminiscences demand the participation of others to achieve full meaning. Scattered readers and dead poets gather together in 'Audenesque' to reveal the power of poetry to live on, long after the death of the author. For if Heaney was explicitly evoking Auden's elegy for Yeats, he was also approaching it less obviously through a parallel memory of railway journeys and poets' conversations in Brodsky's own elegy for Auden, 'York: In Memoriam W.H. Auden'.[50] Brodsky's 'York' registers some disquiet about its subject, but the following, and final, poem in the sequence nevertheless ends with an image of lyric survival, 'the clearer the song is heard, the smaller the bird'.[51] The concluding note recalls the very passage from Brodsky's essay chosen by Heaney for the Burns essay – 'Poets' real biographies are like those of birds.' And so the song lives on, despite the inevitable decay of the individual singer, while the real life – and legacy – of the poet lies in his work. What consoled Brodsky in the face of Auden's death is just what Heaney found so comforting in Burns – an image of words triumphant over what might seem an untraversable distance.

Although Heaney recalled Brodsky's elegy in his own lament, the personal loss was still perhaps too raw for consolatory meditation on the residual clarity of a poet's words. He nevertheless followed both Brodsky's tribute to Auden and Auden's to Yeats, acknowledging in 'Audenesque', 'Repetition is the rule'. This was not so much the classic elegist's struggle to free the ego as a tribute to someone possessed of a deep understanding of the psychological dimension of rhyme and metre.[52] 'Audenesque' begins by lining up true rhymes in brisk couplets, but then breaks from the rule into half-rhymes, 'cold/world', 'frost/breast', 'break/unlock', 'strength/month'. Some seem chosen especially to amuse Brodsky, as in 'produced/Massachusetts', but the wit is taut with sorrow and the half-rhymes suggest more obviously the failure of desired proximity. The very awkwardness of the couplet, 'Like a deck where mind took-off / With a mind-flash and a laugh', nevertheless prompts consideration of alternatives to 'laugh' and, with recollections of Brodsky's 'Dove? Move? Shove? . . . Diaghelev', we might arrive at 'Love'. The word is avoided in the elegy, but it is there in the intertexts – in Brodsky's elegy and essay on Auden, in Burns and in 'Burns's Art Speech'. Even the striking reference to Brodsky's 'peremptory trust / In words alone' carries an echo of Heaney's elegy for Robert Lowell, 'promulgating art's deliberate, peremptory love'.[53] Heaney may have been facing the fact of Brodsky's death and the end of his 'peremptory trust', but his choice of language quietly counters the sense of absolute ending and reveals a shared faith in the survival of the song. At the end of 'Audenesque', it is George Herbert's 'Love' as much as Auden's inviting the mourner to sit and eat, and thus affirm Brodsky's belief that poems are prompted into being by love.

What 'Audenesque' makes happen is a return to the words of a dead man, modified perhaps, but essentially retaining life and energy. An ending cannot be an ending when a poem has worked so insistently to send readers backwards and forwards, round and round. Literary allusions provide a vital resistance to the idea of ending and so brace the elegy in its confrontation with death. Poems which take their impulse from grief, that most isolating emotion, are often those most given to gathering together other poems and poets, in a vital interplay of creation and recollection. Readers who accept the quick-eyed invitation find themselves listening very carefully to the rhymes, cadences, tone and individual words. For the very elements that constitute the poet's 'real biography' are also the means to recover creative life. The operations of language may not be immediately apparent and, if 'love' is so pervasive in 'Audenesque', may not even be articulated directly at all. And yet, once the connections between words are made, it does seem possible to unlock the ice, bring blood back into the cheeks.

The grieving poet may know that 'no vodka, cold or hot, / Aquavit or uisquebaugh' can revive his departed friend, but the very words chosen can work to lighten the despair. Brodsky's vodka may be a personal memory, but it earns its place in the poem through its acoustic rightness, alliterative and assonantal, its allusive power – again recalling Heaney's Lowell – and its metaphorical and metamorphic capacities. Vodka is a translation of 'water' but, like aquavit and uisquebaugh, it is the water of life not the ice of death. The apparent failure of spirit in 'Audenesque' is checked by Heaney's frequent contemporary affirmations of the heart-reviving power of language. 'Uisquebaugh' was the very word that offered his own spirit a 'loophole, an escape route', by revealing 'an elsewhere of potential that seemed at the same time somewhere being remembered'.[54] And so whisky frees language and unites poets, bringing together Heaney and Brodsky with Burns, whose very name encapsulates both fire and water. If Burns exclaimed that 'FREEDOM and WHISKY gang thegither', he also knew it as the remedy for 'grief an' care', though he could not have anticipated the many dimensions his words might eventually acquire.

Whisky, according to Heaney, is the great collapser of distance and, although he was writing specifically of etymological border crossings his insight has far-reaching implications. For if a single word can provide a loophole for the spirit, then reading may legitimately involve following such escape routes into other poems, thus opening new windows into the place of departure. All kind of words can act as connections between poems, through allusion, rhyme or image, and, as the reader's imagination is prompted into participation, the sense of proximity between the poem being read and those remembered comes alive. If whisky is a word, then words can also be whisky, reviving dormant memories and feelings, collapsing the distances that may seem to stretch around. Paterson's recognition that everyone reads Burns according to his or her own personal agenda may seem to render everyone's opinion invalid but it is, in fact, a very helpful insight. Heaney's response to Burns is deeply personal and *therefore* invaluable. Poets' biographies are evident in their 'choice of words', a fact embodied in Heaney's own use of Brodsky's comment as an epigraph for his essay. Exploring feelings of closeness to Burns meant recalling memories of a recently departed friend, whose presence made visible aspects of the Scottish poet that might otherwise have remained unrealised. Heaney's Burns is bound up with Heaney's Brodsky and both memories prompted difficult feelings for the living poet. The self-exposure confessed in relation to 'To a Mouse' is closely related to the revelations of 'Audenesque', for thoughts of the births and deaths of great poets can startle the 'tim'rous soul . . . into a bleak recognition of its destiny'.[55] At the same time, the words of dead poets still have the power to reach the living reader and their legacies, like those of birds, lie in the way they sound. Heaney's epigraph is also an epitaph – to Burns, Brodsky and, ultimately, to Heaney himself.

Notes

1. Seamus Heaney, 'Burns's art speech', in Robert Crawford (ed.), *Robert Burns and Cultural Authority* (Edinburgh: Edinburgh University Press, 1997), pp. 216–33, 217. All further references are to this version, unless otherwise indicated.
2. Ibid., p. 218.
3. Robert Crawford, 'Robert Fergusson's Robert Burns', in Crawford (ed.), *Burns and Cultural Authority*, pp. 1–22, 1.
4. Seamus Heaney, *Finders Keepers* (London: Faber, 2002), pp. 347–63, 347. The passage also appears in the earlier version of the essay, in Crawford (ed.), *Burns and Cultural Authority*, though not as an epigraph. It comes from Brodsky's essay on Derek Walcott, 'The sound of the tide', in Joseph Brodsky, *Less Than One* (Penguin: Harmondsworth, 1987), p. 164.
5. Heaney, 'Burns's art speech', p. 216.
6. Ibid., p. 225.
7. Ibid., p. 217.
8. Ibid., p. 225.
9. John Hewitt (ed.), *Rhyming Weavers of Antrim and Down* (Belfast: Blackstaff, 2004); Frank Ferguson and Andrew R. Holmes (eds), *Revising Robert Burns and Ulster: Literature, Religion and Politics, c1770–1920* (Dublin: Four Courts, 2009).
10. Seamus Heaney, *An Open Letter* (Derry: Field Day, 1983).
11. Seamus Heaney, 'Crediting poetry', in Seamus Heaney, *Opened Ground: Poems 1966–1996* (London: Faber, 1998), pp. 445–67, 449.
12. On the controversy over Heaney's Nobel award see Fran Brearton, *The Great War and Irish Poetry* (Oxford: Oxford University Press, 2000), pp. 219–25.

13. Heaney, 'Crediting poetry', p. 460.
14. Liam McIlvanney, 'The language, literature and politics of Ulster Scots', in Liam McIlvanney and Ray Ryan (eds), *Ireland and Scotland, Culture and Society, 1700–2000* (Dublin: Four Courts, 2005), pp. 203–26, 211.
15. Heaney, 'Crediting poetry', p. 461.
16. *Beowulf*, translated by Seamus Heaney (London: Faber, 1999), p. xxiv.
17. Ibid.
18. Ibid.
19. Heaney, 'Burns's art speech', pp. 227–8.
20. Ibid., p. 224.
21. Ibid., p. 219.
22. Don Paterson, 'Introduction', in Robert Burns, *Poems*, ed. Don Paterson (London: Faber, 2001), pp. vii–xvii, vii.
23. Seamus Heaney, *The Redress of Poetry* (London: Faber, 1995).
24. Crawford, 'Robert Fergusson's Robert Burns', p. 8.
25. A. L. Kennedy, 'Love composition: the solitary vice', in Crawford (ed.), *Burns and Cultural Authority*, pp. 23–39, 24.
26. Ibid., p. 38.
27. Ibid., p. 39.
28. Paterson, 'Introduction', p. xvii.
29. Ibid., pp. viii–ix.
30. Ibid.
31. George Mackay Brown, 'A January Day: Burns', in George Mackay Brown, *Northern Lights* (London: John Murray, 1999), p. 10.
32. George Mackay Brown, 'The Lords of Hell and the Word: A Poem for Burns Day', in George Mackay Brown, *The Collected Poems of George Mackay Brown*, ed. Archie Bevan and Brian Murray (London: John Murray, 2005), pp. 347–9.
33. Brown, *Northern Lights*, p. 11.
34. Heaney, 'Burns's art speech', p. 225; Patrick Kavanagh, *Collected Prose* (London: MacGibbon and Kee, 1967), pp. 281–3.
35. Maggie Ferguson, *George Mackay Brown: The Life* (London: John Murray, 2006), pp. 27–8.
36. Douglas Dunn, '"A Very Scottish Kind of Dash": Burns's native metric', in Crawford (ed.), *Burns and Cultural Authority*, pp. 58–85, 83.
37. Paterson, 'Introduction', p. xvi.
38. Seamus Heaney, 'A Birl for Burns', in Andrew O'Hagan (ed.), *A Night out with Robert Burns* (Edinburgh: Canongate, 2008), p. ix.
39. Dunn, 'Burns's native metric', p. 58.
40. Ibid., p. 65.
41. Ibid., p. 79, citing Brodsky, '"On September 1, 1939" by W. H. Auden', in Brodsky, *Less than One*, p. 351.
42. Brodsky, *Less than One*, p. 325.
43. Heaney, 'Burns's art speech', p. 229.
44. *Times Literary Supplement*, 9 February 1996; republished in Seamus Heaney, *Electric Light* (London: Faber, 2001), pp. 64–6.
45. Heaney, 'Burns's art speech', p. 217.
46. Brodsky, *Less than One*, pp. 345–6.

47. Ibid., p. 350.

48. Ibid., p. 305.

49. Paterson, 'Introduction', pp. xii–xiii.

50. Joseph Brodsky, *Collected Poems in English* (Manchester: Carcanet, 2001), pp. 137–9

51. Ibid., p. 139.

52. See Peter Sacks, *The English Elegy* (Baltimore: The Johns Hopkins University Press, 1985).

53. Seamus Heaney, 'Elegy for Robert Lowell', in Seamus Heaney, *Field Work* (London: Faber, 1979).

54. *Beowulf*, p. xxiv.

55. Heaney, 'Burns's art speech', p. 220.

The Old Second Division

Bernard O'Donoghue

Before the days of Flymos, to cut the sloping lawn
above the lake in the sixties state-of-the-art Business School
I held a rope supporting small Mr Howard
from Cowdenbeath (the old Scottish Second Division)
on a tight rein while he snipped the grass with shears.

He talked as he worked: for example about the time
when he was cycling along the Ring Road
at 3 a.m. one New Year's Day and suddenly felt
not so much drunk as very, very tired
so he laid his bike down and slept on the hard shoulder.

In the evening sometimes I went round
to his well-kept house in the suburbs
where he smoked Capstan, gave me a can
of McEwan's Export, and played me Beethoven
on the stereo he bought after his wife died.

Notes on Contributors

Rhona Brown is a lecturer in Scottish Literature at the University of Glasgow. She specialises in eighteenth-century Scottish literature, focusing particularly on the work of Robert Fergusson, Robert Burns, Allan Ramsay and their contemporaries. Her monograph, *Robert Fergusson and the Scottish Periodical Press* is shortly forthcoming, and she is currently continuing work on Fergusson, Scottish magazine culture and the work of James Beattie.

Gerard Carruthers is Professor in Scottish Literature since 1700 at the University of Glasgow. He is the author of *Robert Burns* (2006), editor of *The Edinburgh Companion to Robert Burns* (2009) and co-editor of *Fickle Man: Robert Burns in the 21st Century* (2009). He is General Editor of the new multi-volume Oxford University Press edition of the works of Burns.

Robert Crawford is Professor of Modern Scottish Literature at the University of St Andrews. His books of poetry include *Selected Poems* (2005) and *Full Volume* (2008). His recent publications relating to Burns include a biography, *The Bard* (2009), as well as *The Best Laid Schemes: Selected Poetry and Prose of Robert Burns* (co-edited with Christopher MacLachlan, 2009) and *New Poems, Chiefly in the Scottish Dialect* (2009), an edited anthology of new work by contemporary Scottish poets.

Patrick Crotty is Professor of Irish and Scottish Literature at the University of Aberdeen. His *Penguin Book of Irish Poetry* appeared in 2010. He is currently editing *The Complete Collected Poems of Hugh MacDiarmid*.

Douglas Dunn was Professor of English in the University of St Andrews 1991–2008. He has published collections of poetry and short stories, and edited several anthologies.

Stephen Gill is now retired from teaching, but was for many years a Tutorial Fellow of Lincoln College, Oxford. His edition of *The Salisbury Plain Poems* inaugurated the Cornell Wordsworth series in 1975 and he has written *William Wordsworth: A Life* (1989) and *Wordsworth and the Victorians* (1998). His latest book is *Wordsworth's Revisitings* (2011).

Mina Gorji is a lecturer at the English Faculty, University of Cambridge, and a Fellow of Pembroke College, where she teaches mostly eighteenth-century and Romantic literature. She has published a study of John Clare's poetry (*John Clare and the Place of Poetry*) and essays on, among other things, rudeness, allusion, literary awkwardness and weeds.

Michael Griffin lectures in eighteenth-century and Irish studies at the University of Limerick. He has published widely on eighteenth-century studies, utopian studies and Irish writing in English, in journals such as the *Review of English Studies*, the *Field Day Review*, *Utopian Studies*, *Eighteenth-Century Ireland* and *History Ireland*. His current research projects include editions of the poetry of Laurence Whyte and Thomas Dermody, and a study of the beginnings of print culture and Anglophone poetry in Munster in the eighteenth century.

Brean Hammond is Professor of Modern English Literature at the University of Nottingham. He has recently written a monograph on Swift for the Irish Academic Press and has edited the play *Double Falsehood* for the Arden Shakespeare series. Relevant to this collection, he has produced the entry on Lord Byron in the *Edinburgh Companion to Scottish Romanticism*, edited by Murray Pittock.

Freya Johnston is a University Lecturer and Tutorial Fellow in English at St Anne's College, Oxford. She is the author of *Samuel Johnson and the Art of Sinking, 1709–1791* (2005) and general co-editor, with Matthew Bevis, of *The Cambridge Edition of the Novels of Thomas Love Peacock* (2015).

Claire Lamont is Emeritus Professor of English Romantic Literature at Newcastle University, specialising in English and Scottish poets and prose writers of the late eighteenth and early nineteenth centuries. She has written particularly on Johnson and Boswell, Austen, Wordsworth and ballads, and is a general editor of The Edinburgh Edition of the Waverley Novels.

Andrew McNeillie's most recent collection of poems is *Losers Keepers* (2011). He is Professor of English at Exeter University, having previously been the literature editor at Oxford University Press, for whom he commissioned the new Oxford Edition of Robert Burns.

Bernard O'Donoghue was born in County Cork in 1945. Since 1965 he has lived in Oxford where he teaches Medieval English at Wadham College. He has published six books of poems, of which the most recent is *Farmers Cross* (2011).

Meiko O'Halloran is a lecturer in British literature of the eighteenth and nineteenth centuries at Newcastle University. Her publications include essays in two volumes of the *Stirling/South Carolina Collected Works of James Hogg*, *The Queen's Wake*, edited by Douglas Mack (2004); *Midsummer Night Dreams*, edited by Jill Rubenstein and completed by Gillian Hughes with Meiko O'Halloran (2008); and *James Hogg and the Literary Marketplace*, edited by Sharon Alker and Holly Faith Nelson (2009). She is currently completing a monograph on James Hogg.

Murray Pittock is Bradley Professor of English Literature at the University of Glasgow. He is Principal Investigator of the AHRC awards 'Inventing Tradition and Securing Memory: Robert Burns 1796–1909' and the 'Global Burns Network', and Co-Investigator of the AHRC project 'Editing Robert Burns for the 21st Century'.

David Sergeant is the Mary Ewart Junior Research Fellow at Somerville College, Oxford. He has written on Rudyard Kipling, Doris Lessing and Ted Hughes, and published a collection of poetry, *Talk like Galileo* (2010).

Fiona Stafford is Professor of English Language and Literature at the University of Oxford and a Fellow of Somerville College. Her books include *Starting Lines in Scottish, Irish and English Poetry, from Burns to Heaney* (2000) and *Local Attachments: The Province of Poetry* (2010).

Index